The Jacobin Club
of Marseilles,
1790–1794

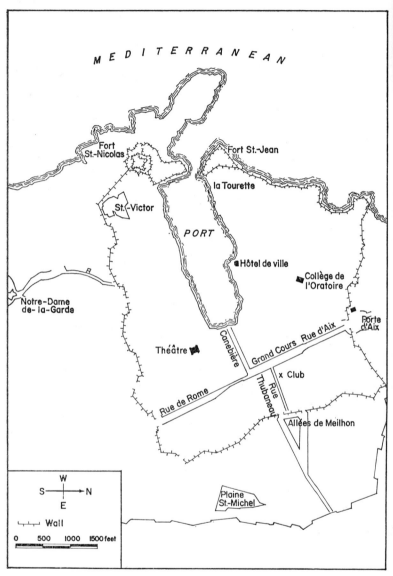

MARSEILLES

The Jacobin Club
of Marseilles,
1790–1794

Michael L. Kennedy

Cornell
University
Press

ITHACA
AND
LONDON

Cornell University Press gratefully acknowledges
a grant from the Andrew J. Mellon Foundation that
aided in bringing this book to publication.

First published 1973 by Cornell University Press.
Published in the United Kingdom by Cornell University Press Ltd.,
2–4 Brook Street, London W1Y 1AA.

Printed in the United States of America by Vail-Ballou Press, Inc.

*Librarians: Library of Congress cataloging information
appears on the last page of the book.*

To Adele

Contents

Maps

"Allons, enfants de la Patrie,
Le jour de gloire est arrivé."

Preface

The Rue Thubaneau is today a narrow, seamy, thoroughly disreputable little street adjoining an Arab quarter in central Marseilles. Night and day, a drab array of vagrants, addicts, and prostitutes loiters on its sidewalks and crowds its doorways and bars. Thick accumulations of soot have powdered the buildings a dull, uniform gray. Number 25 Rue Thubaneau does not seem, at first glance, dissimilar from the rest. A green neon light inside dimly beams "baths and showers." Few pedestrians notice the small, weather-stained plaque beside the doorway. It reads:

> Ici
> en 1792 fut chanté
> pour la première fois
> à Marseille
> Par François Mireur
> *L'hymne de*
> *Rouget de Lisle*
> La Marseillaise

No other marker warns the passer-by that this bathhouse served from 1790 to 1795 as the meeting-place of the Jacobin society of Marseilles. This proud Club of the Rue Thubaneau, "the most powerful and the most active society of the Midi," [1] is the subject of this book.

At the zenith of its power, 1791–1793, the Club of Marseilles was indeed the most potent and feared political authority in southeastern France. Its importance derived from its virtual hegemony over France's third largest city, the most influential in the Midi. In an age when poor harvests brought famine, the people of Provence looked to Marseilles for overseas grains. When poor communications made Paris a distant two weeks' journey, the Var, Basses-Alpes, and Bouches-du-Rhône sought political guidance and intellectual inspiration from the "capital of the Midi." During the Revolution Parisian officials often cried out against the "tyranny" of Marseilles over its neighbors.

From its base in Marseilles, the Club of the Rue Thubaneau intimidated local and regional administrators and defied national emissaries in the Midi. "Among all the agents, good and bad, official and unofficial," wrote a commissioner of the minister of the interior at Arles in November, 1791, "it alone governs and is inviolable." [2] Through its political pamphlets and newspapers it disseminated Jacobin propaganda to the most remote hamlets of Provence. Its commissioners, escorted by armed national guardsmen, tramped across a half-dozen departments of southeastern France, invading communes, establishing affiliated clubs, arresting suspects, and collecting "contributions." Its recruits, the celebrated battalion of August 10, helped overthrow the monarchy in 1792 and immortalized the hymn of Rouget de Lisle.

[1] C. Cauvin, "Etudes sur la Révolution dans les Basses-Alpes: Une incursion des Marseillais à Digne en 1793," *Annales des Basses-Alpes*, No. 83 (1901), 245.
[2] AN, F7 3659[2], Debourge to M. Etienne, Nov. 2, 1791.

The development of Jacobin societies remains one of the
most interesting and important aspects of the French Revolution. Hundreds of books and articles have appeared, analyzing
their political actions, doctrines, organization, and personnel.[3]
Most major popular societies of France, and many of the
smaller ones, have had their historians. Yet, despite its significant role during the Revolution, the Society of the Rue
Thubaneau has been neglected. No one has made a successful
effort to examine its organization or personnel. General his-
tories of Revolutionary Marseilles provide only fragmentary
political narratives. Alfred-Chabaud, a historian of the Mathiez
school and editor of the *Mémoires* of Barbaroux,[4] proposed a
history of the Club before World War II and spent many

[3] The classics are Alphonse Aulard, *La Société des Jacobins: Recueil
de documents pour l'histoire du club des Jacobins de Paris* (Paris,
1889–1897); Crane Brinton, *The Jacobins: An Essay in the New His-
tory* (New York, 1930); L. de Cardenal, *La Province pendant la
Révolution: Histoire des clubs Jacobins, 1789–1795* (Paris, 1929);
Gaston-Martin, *Les Jacobins* (Paris, 1945). On Provence compare
H. Labroue, "Le Club Jacobin de Toulon, 1790–1796," *Annales de la
Société d'études provençales*, IV (1907), 1–51; Félix Ponteil, "La So-
ciété populaire des antipolitiques et le sentiment patriotique à Aix-en-
Provence en 1792–1795," *Revue historique de la Révolution française*,
X (1916), 202–218, XXIII (1918), 30–47, 266–290, 454–474, 577–589,
XIV (1919), 40–45.

[4] Charles Barbaroux, a lawyer, was born in 1767 at Marseilles. He
acquired notoriety as a fiery supporter of the Revolutionary cause in
1789. In April, 1790, he helped found the Club and officiated as one of
its secretaries. He was elected as a representative of the Bouches-du-
Rhône to the Convention in September, 1792. In Paris he became an
outspoken Girondin and fled the capital after the days of May 29–
June 2, 1793. He was executed at Bordeaux on June 25, 1794. Barbaroux
is celebrated for his memoirs, written while he was a fugitive. The
footnotes and comments on Barbaroux contained in Alfred-Chabaud's
edition, *Mémoires de Barbaroux* (Paris, 1936), remain, in the present
writer's opinion, the best secondary source on the Society.

years compiling information. He was deported by the Germans, however, and died in a concentration camp before he could complete his work.

The neglect of the Club of the Rue Thubaneau is due primarily to the nearly total destruction of its archives. The documents of private organizations do not usually find their way into public collections. In the case of the Jacobins, former members often found it in their interest to destroy portions of the records. In Marseilles as in Paris, mysterious post-Revolutionary fires consumed the official papers of the clubs. The files of the popular societies in series L of the departmental archives of the Bouches-du-Rhône provide a vivid illustration of the dearth of documents on the Club. They house thirty-eight cartons of manuscripts on the comparatively small club of Antipolitiques of Aix-en-Provence but only six on the Society of Marseilles. To supplement the small amount of documentary material available, I undertook research in widely dispersed archives and libraries of France. The result of this research was the discovery of some previously untapped materials, which have been used in writing this book.

In general, the book follows the basic method of organization utilized by Crane Brinton and L. de Cardenal in their classic works on the Jacobins. Since no good history of Marseilles is available in English, Chapter 1 sketches the political, social, and economic character of Marseilles in 1789. Subsequent chapters are based largely upon original research and deal exclusively with the Club; they trace its origins, describe its political history, analyze its personnel, organization, and ideology, and discuss its manifold activities.

This book would not have been possible without the assistance of a host of archivists and librarians in Marseilles, Paris, and elsewhere in France. I also received valuable aid from a number of French scholars including G. Martinet at Marseilles and M. Vovelle at Aix-en-Provence. In addition, I wish to thank Beatrice Hyslop, Pierre Laurent, S. W. Halperin, James Casada, and Earl Wilcox, all of whom read and criticized this book at various stages of its development. Expressions of gratitude are likewise in order to former teachers such as Ralph Lynn, Gordon McNeil, and Hans A. Schmitt, who initiated my interest in French history. Special thanks are due to my wife, who typed the original manuscript and helped me at every stage of my work.

Portions of the material in Chapter 3 are reprinted by permission from my article "Some Journals of the Jacobin Club of Marseille, 1790–1794," in *French Historical Studies* (Fall, 1972).

MICHAEL L. KENNEDY

Winthrop College

Abbreviations

AD, B-du-Rh	Departmental Archives of the Bouches-du-Rhône
AD, Basses-Alpes	Departmental Archives of the Basses-Alpes
AD, Drôme	Departmental Archives of the Drôme
AD, Hérault	Departmental Archives of the Hérault
AD, Tarn	Departmental Archives of the Tarn
AD, Var	Departmental Archives of the Var
AM	Municipal Archives of Marseilles
AN	National Archives
BM	Municipal Library of Marseilles
BM, Aix	Municipal Library of Aix
BM, Poitiers	Municipal Library of Poitiers
BM, Toulon	Municipal Library of Toulon
BN	National Library of France (Bibliothèque nationale)
CC	Archives of the Chamber of Commerce of Marseilles
JdD	*Journal des départements méridionaux et des débats des amis de la constitution de Marseille.* (For copies of this paper see BM, 1716–1717; BN, Lc^{11} 635 (71). One hundred eighty-four issues (four pages, quarto) appeared between March 6, 1792, and May 7, 1793.)

The Jacobin Club
of Marseilles,
1790–1794

SOUTHEASTERN FRANCE

I

Marseilles in 1789

Marseilles is a bride of the sea, a city wedded to trade and commerce. For nearly twenty-five centuries, until the construction of a modern port in the nineteenth century, its economic heart was a small inlet of about seventy acres called the Lacydon. Arthur Young, the famous English agronomist who visited the city on his travels through France in 1790, dismissed this body of water as a "horsepond," [1] but it actually is a magnificent natural harbor. The Old Port, as this rocky cove is called today, is still the geographical center of Marseilles.

The cove and the amphitheater of small mountains which nearly surround it have served to separate the city from its neighbors. A seafaring people, the Marseillais looked outward to the Mediterranean. In 1789 only two decent roads crossed the mountains to the interior. Paris was thirteen days' travel by coach, six by the fastest courier. Moreover, many Marseillais spoke Provençal as their mother tongue. It was the city's introversion, historians have suggested, which caused it to welcome decentralization so fervently in 1789–1790, and to

[1] *Travels in France during the Years 1787, 1788, and 1789* (Cambridge, 1929), p. 229.

rebel against the centralizing tendencies of the Mountain in 1793.[2] In an epistle to the Committee of Public Safety on February 2, 1794, the representative-on-mission, Fréron, lamented: "The Marseillais naturally regard themselves as a separate people. The geographical setting, the mountains, the rivers which separate them from the rest of France, their particular language, all nourish a federalist outlook. . . . They see only Marseilles. Marseilles is their fatherland, France is nothing." [3]

Twenty-four centuries welded together by fact and legend into history accentuated the separatism of the Marseillais. Founded by Greeks of Phocaea around 600 B.C., Marseilles was born a "granddaughter of Athens." In antiquity she boasted of being the "civilizer of the Gauls," "sister" of Rome against Carthage, enemy of "the tyrant" Julius Caesar, and an important center of arts and letters. Much later, during the thirteenth century, Marseilles was for a time an independent republic. Between 1246 and 1257, Charles of Anjou added the city to Provence, and the Marseillais became, after a time, fiercely loyal to the rulers of this independent county. In 1481 Louis XI integrated Marseilles into the kingdom of France, but she retained semi-autonomy under the rule of a man or a party. During the religious wars she took the Catholic side and was one of the last French cities to recognize Henry IV. In the time of the Fronde she rebelled against the rule of Mazarin and Louis XIV. Only in 1660, when King Louis

[2] See Alfred-Chabaud, "Essai sur les classes bourgeoises dirigeants à Marseille en 1789," *Documents relatifs à la vie économique de la Révolution* (Besançon, 1942), p. 51; A. Crémieux, "Le Particularisme municipal à Marseille en 1789," *La Révolution française*, LII (1907), 193–215.

[3] E. Poupé, *Lettres de Barras et de Fréron* (Draguignan, 1910), pp. 154–161.

himself entered Marseilles through a break in the walls, was the recalcitrant city brought to heel.[4]

In 1660 a long period of political repression commenced. Louis XIV left regiments to police the city, condemned the separatist rebel leaders, and suppressed the independent municipal consulate. On his orders, engineers built two forts, St.-Nicolas and St.-Jean, on either side of the harbor entrance to guard the port and to overawe the people. In 1693 an intendant returned to Provence. From his seat in Aix he dominated the administration and finances of the city.

Despite these measures Marseilles maintained certain privileges until the Revolution. Provence was a *pays d'état;* Marseilles was technically a separate region, only required to send deputies as observers to the Estates of Provence. The citizens of Marseilles were free from the *taille* (property tax), *dîme* (tithe), *corvée* (statute labor), and all personal taxes, and the law spared them the necessity of lodging troops. Marseilles also retained a measure of self- government. By virtue of royal letters patent issued in 1766, she had a mayor chosen from the nobility, a first alderman selected from among the non-noble wholesale merchants (*négociants*), a second alderman who was a retail merchant (*marchand*) or bourgeois, and a thirty-six-member municipal council. These officials performed certain administrative functions and made some lesser municipal appointments.

These few liberties failed to satisfy the Marseillais. The cahiers drawn up by the various classes in 1789 cried out against the rule of the intendant and called for a return to the municipal regulations that had been in force before the loath-

[4] For a general political narrative of Marseilles' pre-Revolutionary history see Raoul Busquet, *Histoire de Marseille* (Paris, 1945).

some date of 1660, when political rights had been lost. It is appropriate to say that the spirit of the Fronde and of the thirteenth-century republic was still alive in 1789.[5]

If the period after 1660 marked a decline in political independence, it was also, on the whole, a time of great economic expansion. The edict of 1669 that made Marseilles a free port and the work of the agents of the Minister Colbert did much to augment commerce. By 1789 Marseilles accounted for one-fifth of all the overseas commerce of France; one authority contends that the city had already surpassed Bordeaux as the country's leading port. In 1785, 4,526 ships entered Marseilles; 945 vessels claimed the city as their home port. Out of a global commerce of 200 million livres, the Levant trade took up by far the largest share, but the "blue flag of Provence appeared in all the known seas." [6]

After a long period of stagnation, industrial expansion had also begun about 1670. Old industries such as leather and soapmaking expanded. Textiles also flourished. A mid-eighteenth-century economic recession interrupted industrial development, but expansion began again in the years just before the Revolution. Paul Masson divides the industries of Marseilles in 1789 into three principal groupings: chemical, clothing, and food processing. Within the first category, soapmaking, tanning, glassmaking, the manufacture of candles and starches, and the refining of sulphur occupied the first rank. In clothing the fabrication of cotton cloth, calico prints, silk hose, hats, shoes, and bonnets shared prominence. Alongside traditional food-processing industries like winemaking and

[5] Crémieux, pp. 193–215.

[6] Paul Masson, *Marseille depuis 1789: Etudes historiques;* I, *Le Commerce de Marseille de 1789 à 1814* (Paris, 1919), 11. Laurent Lautard, *Esquisses historiques: Marseille depuis 1789 jusqu'en 1815,* I (Marseille, 1844), 9.

baking, such new activities as the refining of sugar acquired a significant place.[7]

The reign of Louis XIV also altered the physical complexion of Marseilles. In 1660 Nicholas Arnoul, an agent of Colbert, initiated a remarkable expansion which enlarged the area of the city from 160 to 481 acres. By the time of the Revolution, houses filled the whole perimeter. The oldest and most densely populated section of the city was an area bounded by the Joliette basin, Fort St.-Jean, and the Grand Cours. Here, streets were narrow, gloomy, and steep, and buildings sometimes rose to a height of seven stories. In 1789 Marseilles boasted two splendid avenues, the Canebière and the Cours Belsunce. The latter formed part of a long, leafy artery which bisected the city and connected the Porte de Rome with the Porte d'Aix. Cafés and hotels bordered it. The Rue Thubaneau joined the Grand Cours just two blocks north of the Place St.-Louis.[8]

The land between the walls of the city and the mountains was called the *Terroir* (meaning "area of soil"). The Abbé Louche estimated that 5,000 houses stood in the Terroir in 1789, mostly clustered around springs and small streams. The Terroir served primarily as agricultural land, although rich merchants also owned country houses there. Three suburbs had spread beyond the walls. One occupied ground on the north side of the road to Aix; a second extended beyond the Porte de Rome, and a third beyond the portes des Capucines and Noailles.[9]

Eighteenth-century Marseilles was a filthy and unhealthy

[7] Paul Masson, *La Provence au XVIII siècle* (Paris, 1936), pp. 658–699.

[8] *Ibid.*, p. 765. See also Alfred-Chabaud, "Essai . . . ," p. 52.

[9] Jules Louche, "Marseille et ses habitants à la veille de la Révolution," *Revue de Marseille*, XXXVIII (1891), 240–261.

place. Refuse decomposed in the streets and nauseating odors filled the air. The city's history had been marked by a series of devastating plagues, the worst of which, in 1720–1721, caused the death of 40,000 people. Despite this disaster, the population of Marseilles had returned to its preplague level by 1730 and climbed throughout the remainder of the eighteenth century. The census of 1790 counted 106,585 people in the city and its Terroir; another taken in the summer of 1793 arrived at a figure of 111,410.[10] It seems safe to say, therefore, that there were approximately 110,000 people in Marseilles during the Revolution.

The ecclesiastical population in 1789 was about six hundred. Monseigneur de Belloy, bishop of Marseilles since 1755, administered the city and its Terroir, which were divided into five parishes. Marseilles also possessed the rich abbey of St.-Victor, the oldest abbey in France. The Church, regular and secular, maintained eight hospitals and staffed and directed the colleges of the city. As elsewhere in France, tension existed between the upper and lower clergy. The bishop and his close followers emigrated early in the Revolution.[11]

The nobility of Marseilles was of relatively minor importance. Only eighty families represented this order at the Estates-General in 1789, the overwhelming majority of them being nobles of the robe. Very little distinguished them from the wealthy merchants (*hauts commerçants*), i.e., the whole-

[10] Ch. Carrière, *et al.*, *Marseille: Ville morte* (Marseille, 1968). For the census of 1790 see Masson, *La Provence au XVIII siècle*, p. 764; for 1793 see AD, B-du-Rh, L 1982, Census of the population.

[11] M. Vovelle, "Prêtres abdicataires et déchristianization en Provence," *Actres du quatre-vingt-neuvième congrès national des sociétés savantes*, I (1964), 63–95; M. Santini, "Le Clergé et la vie religieuse à Marseille pendant la Révolution, 1789–1795" (unpublished thesis, University of Aix, 1964).

salers and shipowners (*armateurs*). Bonds of marriage united the two groups, and their cahiers had a great deal in common. The wealthy merchants carried on the maritime trade of Marseilles. Alfred-Chabaud has shown how this closely inter-related elite of great families dominated the life of the city. Economically, they provided work for the major part of the population. Culturally, they dominated the learned societies and sponsored magnificent social events. They also monopo-lized local politics prior to the Revolution. The instrument of their power was the Chamber of Commerce of Marseilles, established in 1599, a powerful organization that directed Mediterranean commerce and gave advice to local officials on other economic affairs.[12]

The ostentatious display of the wholesale merchants some-times inspired envy and dislike. They went to the bourse every day in gilded carriages, elaborately coiffured and wear-ing embroidered garments, silk opera hats, and ornate swords. In 1790 some of the greatest among them were Club members, but irreconcilable enmities soon developed. During the Terror thirty-one wholesale merchants died on the guillotine.[13]

Marseilles had a large amorphous middle class, difficult to catalogue. Some bourgeois and property owners (*proprié-taires*) equalled the wholesalers in wealth and influence. Brokers and merchant captains functioned as close allies of the wealthy merchants. The professions were popular and prestigious; lawyers often attached themselves to the Parle-ment at Aix, and doctors, actors, and artists were respected members of Marseilles' intellectual and social world. Petty

[12] Alfred-Chabaud, "Essai . . . ," pp. 64–90. See also Louis Bergasse, *Notice historique sur la Chambre de Commerce de Marseille, 1599–1912* (Marseille, 1913).
[13] AD, B-du-Rh, L 3122.

shopkeepers (variously called *marchands, boutiquiers,* and *magasiniers*) filled the lowest levels of the traditional bourgeoisie.

An urban working class proletariat, properly speaking, did not exist in Marseilles in 1789. Rather, the working classes consisted, by and large, of artisans belonging to corporations or guilds. In 1776, there were fifty incorporated and twenty-four unincorporated guilds. All of these trades submitted to royal ordinances which fixed conditions of work, defined privileges, and arbitrated conflicts.[14] Disputes often arose both between professions and intra-professionally between masters (whom we can scarcely separate from the middle classes) and journeymen. In 1791, for example, a group of journeymen bakers complained to the Club that their masters forced them to work on holidays and generally abused them.[15] Perhaps the most unfortunate people in Marseilles were the poor shepherds and cultivators of the Terroir. Their cahiers revealed bitter economic grievances.[16]

Collectively, the popular classes suffered under a fiscal regime that oppressed the poor and favored the rich. The Marseillais, as we have seen, paid no direct taxes. Instead, they were taxed indirectly through levies on goods such as bread, wine, and meat. The people profoundly resented these impositions and accused the tax-farmers of arbitrary and corrupt practices. Discontent worsened during the severe winter of 1788–1789, when the cost of bread rose abruptly. Meetings of "patriots" began to take place, and brochures denouncing economic conditions appeared in great numbers.

[14] Félix-L. Tavernier, "Une Exposition sur la vie de Marseille au temps de Louis XVI," *Marseille,* No. 35 (1958), 13–17.

[15] AM, I₂, General police (unclassified), carton 1791.

[16] Alfred-Chabaud, "Essai . . . ," pp. 62–64.

In this threatening atmosphere the elections for the Estates-General occurred, and the Revolution erupted in Marseilles.[17] During a meeting of the third estate of the seneschalsy of Marseilles a young ex-teacher, Etienne Chompré,[18] denounced the methods of Rebuffel, the tax-farmer-general. On March 23, 1789, a crowd assembled in the Plaine St.-Michel; orators berated the tax-farmers, the mayor, and the aldermen. The crowd sacked the houses of Rebuffel and the intendant, and the mayor and several other municipal officials fled the city. The next day a group of patriots formed a citizen's militia to maintain civil order. In the meantime, representatives of the clergy, the nobility, and the third estate united with the existing municipal council to form a Council of Three Orders, which acted to lower the price of bread, beef, and mutton. On May 11, 1789, a royal decree granted amnesty to those implicated in the riot of March 23, and disorders ceased temporarily.

Meanwhile the seneschalsy of Marseilles elected its depu-

---

[17] For general accounts of the events of March, 1789–April, 1790, see C. Lourde, *Histoire de la Révolution à Marseille et en Provence depuis 1789 jusqu'au Consulat* (Marseille, 1838–1839), vol. I; S. Vialla, *Marseille révolutionnaire, l'armée nation (1789–1793)* (Paris, 1910); Georges Guibal, *Mirabeau et la Provence* (Paris, 1901), vol. I; Barbaroux, *Mémoires*.

[18] Chompré was born in Paris in 1742 and died there in 1811. In 1767 he moved to Marseilles where he taught for a time at a girls' school. By 1789 he had become chancellor at the Roman consulate. On the orders of Bournissac (see below) he was imprisoned for a short time at Fort St.-Jean in December, 1789. After his release he became first a municipal officer, in February, 1790, then administrator of the Department, in 1791–1792, and finally chief clerk of the Revolutionary Tribunal of the Bouches-du-Rhône during the Terror. He was president of the Club in October–November, 1791, and October–November, 1792, and secretary in the summer of 1794, when he edited the *Tribune populaire*, the Society's journal.

ties to the future National Assembly. On the urging of representatives from the citizen's militia, the third estate chose Mirabeau and three wholesale merchants as its deputies. When the Great Tribune opted to represent Aix, where he had been elected, a fourth wholesaler took his place in Marseilles. This deputation proved ineffectual, however, and Marseilles had to rely repeatedly on Mirabeau as the defender of its interests.[19]

On May 20, 1789, the Comte de Caraman, lieutenant-general of Provence, entered the city. Caraman represented the counterrevolutionary faction in Marseilles and the Parlement and intendant at Aix. On his arrival he suppressed the Council of Three Orders, exiled six leaders of the patriot (revolutionary) party, and established a new civic guard of sixty companies. Of the captains named by the Municipality, twenty-eight came from the order of the nobility and thirty-two from the wealthy merchants. Patriotic pamphlets denounced the new "bourgeois guard" as a "blind instrument" of the aristocracy. Tension prevailed throughout the summer. The news of the capture of the Bastille forced Caraman to recall the Council of Three Orders. On July 23, some 6,000 citizens assembled, demanding trial of the intendant, recall of the patriotic exiles, and reform of the bourgeois guard. On July 27 and 28, about 4,000 Marseillais marched on Aix and freed 69 prisoners detained there by the Parlement. Finally, on August 19, 1789, the bourgeois guard fired on a crowd massed at the Esplanade de la Tourette. In retaliation a mob sacked the house of an alderman believed to be a counterrevolutionary. At that point Caraman intervened with the Swiss regiment of Ernest, made twenty-three arrests, and trained the cannons of Forts St.-Nicolas and St.-Jean on the city.

[19] Jules Viguier, "Marseille et ses représentants à la Constituante," *La Révolution française*, XL (1901), 193–201.

On August 21, 1789, the provost-marshal of Provence, Senchon de Bournissac, arrived in Marseilles. Acting on behalf of a coalition that included St.-Priest, royal minister of the interior, the intendant, the Parlement, and others, such as Rebuffel, who had profited from the old order, Bournissac instructed his agents to put up posters listing the names of patriots and identifying them as *chefs de brigands*. Citizens were arrested in their homes, and many were placed in irons at Fort St.-Jean and the Château d'If. Their trials, which lasted until February 23, 1790, were a mockery of justice, with the court meeting secretly behind the walls of Fort St.-Nicolas and the protection of the Swiss regiment of Ernest. The oppressed patriots requested the envoy of an extraordinary commissioner from Paris to oversee the workings of this inquisitorial tribunal; D'André, deputy of the nobility of Aix, arrived on this mission on September 15, 1789, but proved a faithful ally of the provost. Passions ran high throughout the fall and winter of 1789–1790. Finally, Mirabeau took the case of the Marseilles patriots to the National Assembly, and on December 8 its decree removed the direction of the trials from Bournissac's hands.

On January 28, 1790, the districts (sections) of Marseilles and the Terroir chose a new mayor and twenty-five municipal officers; the sections elected forty-two notables several days later. The election of Etienne Martin, called "the Just," [20] as mayor and the installation of the municipal officers on February 9, 1790, marked a complete victory for the patriots and

[20] Martin, a wholesale merchant, was born in Marseilles in 1745 and died there in 1834. He served as mayor until his election to the Legislative Assembly in September, 1791. He was president of the Club three times in 1790–1791, although he rarely attended. After a dispute in December, 1791, the Society denounced him as a Feuillant and an intriguer. He resigned as a deputy and retired from active life in August, 1792.

a turning point for the Revolution in Marseilles. The Municipality wielded great political power as ruler of the largest city in Provence. On February 15, 1790, as one of its first measures, it abolished the existing civic guard and authorized the sections to meet and form a provisional National Guard.

The National Guard soon numbered 14,000 men. Predictably, friction developed between it and the officers of the regular army in Marseilles. At 8:00 P.M. on March 20, the Marquis d'Ambert, colonel of the Royal de la Marine, a regiment garrisoned at Marseilles, arrived at the gate of Aix and insulted the national guardsmen on duty. The next day crowds assembled in the streets, and d'Ambert took refuge with the Municipality. The latter found itself caught between the fury of the populace and the cold hostility of the new governor-general of Provence, the Marquis de Miran. On April 2, 1790, a message arrived from Paris ordering that d'Ambert be tried by the seneschalsy of Marseilles. Five days later, on his own initiative, Jean-Pierre de Chomel, an aristocrat and lieutenant-general of the seneschalsy, released d'Ambert. Amid the furor caused by this arbitrary and illegal release, the Patriotic Assembly of Friends of the Constitution of Marseilles was born.[21]

[21] *Courier de Marseille*, Apr. 18, 1790, pp. 2–5. For copies of this gazette see BN, Lc[11] 635(94).

2

Origins

Only scanty records exist of the initial session of the Club, and there is no indication of which individual or individuals conceived the idea for its genesis. The best official source, the Regulations of the Society, drafted after long discussion during the months of April to August, 1790, simply states: "The eleventh of April of the first year of Liberty, 1790, a very great number of citizens met in the hall of the tennis court of the Rue Thubaneau. Their purpose was to establish a Society for the defense of the Constitution, the maintenance and the propagation of liberty." [1] Of the Revolutionary newspapers, only the *Courier de Marseille* provides an account of the Club's founding. At the end of April, 1790, the editors wrote:

This Assembly, of which we have not previously spoken in our *Courier*, was formed solely by patriotism. For two weeks, good citizens serving in the National Guard, the municipal administration, and other public offices, inscribed their names. . . . In the first general assembly seven municipal officers and many notables

[1] "Règlemens des amis de la Constitution de Marseille" (Marseille, 1790), pp. 1–2. For copies see AD, B-du-Rh, L 2076; AD, Var, L, supplement, Papers of the popular society of St.-Zacharie; AD, Basses-Alpes, L 856/2.

of the commune mingled among the members without any distinction of rank.[2]

The recollections of contemporaries and the researches of later historians do little to amplify our knowledge beyond adding that the founders elected Etienne Martin, the mayor, as their first president. In a single paragraph, written in 1838, the Orleanist historian, Charles Lourde, provides the best additional information.

This assembly which has left such terrible memories was, at first, only the continuation of the old Arquier reunion [see below]. Those who created it followed the example of the aristocrats who possessed several organizations of the same nature where they hatched audacious plots against the Revolution. In founding their assembly, the patriots were motivated by the need to meet together and to defend the principles enumerated by the National Assembly.[3]

The near-silence surrounding the conception of the Club is by no means unique. The origins of many Jacobin societies in France are shrouded in myth and mystery. In French Revolutionary historiography enduring controversies have arisen over this issue. Specialists have sought antecedents for the clubs not just in 1789, 1790, or 1791, but in the social and cultural milieu of the 1780's. Royalist historians, hostile to the Enlightenment, have traced the paternity of Jacobin clubs to pre-Revolutionary literary and cultural societies. In his study of Brittany, Augustin Cochin termed such organizations "thinking" societies (*sociétés de pensée*). He attempted to prove that they were political action groups rather than intellectual circles. More liberal historians have given qualified support to Cochin's theories; Crane Brinton, for example, has found many links between "thinking" societies and the clubs that followed.[4]

Marseilles had a welter of intellectual groups in the late eighteenth-century. There is no proof that any of these actually established the Society, but some common customs and personnel are apparent. A number of these associations enjoyed official status. The most prestigious royally-sanctioned institution, the Royal Academy of Belles-Lettres, Sciences, and Arts, dated from 1726 and enjoyed affiliation with the Academy in Paris. Meeting privately each Wednesday and holding only two public sessions a year, it was essentially nonpolitical in character. It awarded prizes annually for essays in the sciences and letters, but these dealt mainly with commercial topics and reflected the predominance of the wealthy merchants in the Academy.[5] While its aims and organization bore little resemblance to those of the later Club of the Rue Thubaneau, it provided some personnel. Letters patent of 1766 restricted the Academy to thirty regular members and thirty-five foreign associates. Of the twenty-five academicians listed in the *Almanach historique* of 1790 four can be said with certainty to have been members of the Club: Jean-Baptiste-Bernard Grosson, Claude-François Achard, Dominique Audibert, and Barthélemy Vidal. A fifth Club member, Jean-Raymond Mourraille, had served as the permanent secretary for sciences until his resignation in

[4] Augustin Cochin, *Les Sociétés de pensée et la Révolution en Bretagne, 1788–1789* (Paris, 1925); Brinton, p. 13.

[5] *Deux Siècles d'histoire Académique (1726–1926): Notice publiée à l'occasion du bi-centenaire de l'Académie* (Marseille, 1926), pp. 11–14; J.-B. Lautard, *Histoire de l'Académie de Marseille: Depuis sa fondation en 1726 jusqu'en 1826* (Marseille, 1826), I, 300.

1782.[6] All these men held positions of importance in the Society in 1790–1791 but had drifted away by 1793. When the Club elected Audibert as its president in April, 1791, he termed it "the most precious moment of my life." Less than a year later he fled to Paris to intrigue against his fellow members. Mourraille, who served both as mayor of Marseilles and as president of the Society in June–July, 1792, suffered denunciation and imprisonment at its hands in April, 1793.[7]

Additional members of the Society were associated in one capacity or another with other official institutions that promoted science and culture. The Royal and Marine Observatory, founded in 1702, ranked as one of the finest scientific institutes in Provence, and such prominent founders of the Society as Pleville-Lepelley regularly attended its meetings. Jacques Borély, the Society's second president, was a member of the Royal Academy of Painting, Sculpture, and Civil and Naval Architecture, established in 1753.[8] Several militant

[6] *Almanach historique de Marseille de 1790* (Marseille, 1790), pp. 252–253. Grosson, a royal notary, was the editor of the *Almanach historique* in 1789. Achard and Vidal were doctors; the former also deserves mention as being the author of several books on Provence and the founder of the first municipal library of Marseilles. The names of all three of these men appear regularly in the Club's minutes of June–July, 1790 (AM, I₂, carton 1790). Audibert belonged to a wealthy family of Protestant wholesale merchants and is particularly noteworthy for his correspondence with Voltaire. Mourraille (1721–1808) was a bourgeois and the mayor of Marseilles from November, 1791, to April, 1793.

[7] On Audibert see BM, 4717, "Second discours de M. Martin, Maire, prononcé dans l'Assemblée Patriotique . . . , avec le discours de M. Dominique Audibert" (Marseille, 1791); AN, F⁷ 4603, Emmanuel Beausset to Blanc-Gilly, Jan. 11, 1792. On Mourraille see AD, B-du-Rh, L 2071, session of Apr. 10, 1793.

[8] Georges-René Pleville-Lepelley (1726–1805) was born in Granville. For many years he captained a merchant vessel, but in 1789 he was

Jacobins also worked at this Academy as artists, models, and
teachers; four of them, Alexandre Renaud, Jacques Feissole,
Louis Chaix, and Jean-Nicolas Brard, led the band of fifty
patriotic Marseillais that seized the royal citadel, Fort Notre-
Dame-de-la-Garde, on the night of April 29–30, 1790.[9]

Unofficial societies also flourished in Marseilles in the
1780's, some of them overtly political. The *Journal de
Provence* sometimes advertised their meetings but unfortunately almost all their records have vanished. A Club des treize
convened during the American Revolution in a hall adorned
with portraits of Franklin and Washington. A mesmerist
Society of Harmony gathered periodically to discuss the
mysteries of animal magnetism. Another circle met in the
home of the Abbé Raynal, a minor *philosophe* in "exile" in
Marseilles from 1786 to 1791.[10] While no evidence connects

harbor master at Marseilles. From 1790 to 1793 he was a much respected speaker at the Society and held numerous posts, including
that of secretary in 1791 and May, 1793. He headed an important
commission of the Club to Arles in June, 1791. *Almanach historique,
1790,* p. 265. Borély was a wholesale merchant specializing in the
Levant trade.

[9] Renaud, a native of Dijon and a professor at the Academy, was
the sculptor-in-residence at the Club. In 1792 he cast a medallion commemorating the fall of the monarchy, and during the Terror he
sculpted a memorial to the victims of the Federalists. Brard, likewise
a professor at the Academy, came from Paris. He joined the Society
before June 13, 1790, when he is first cited in the debates. He co-
authored the address to the National Assembly in the name of the
men who had seized the fort. Feissole, originally from Braye-en-
Provence, was a model at the Academy, while Chaix was a painter and
professor; their signatures appear on petitions sent by the Club to the
National Assembly in 1791 (AN, C 127).

[10] See Robert Darnton, *Mesmerism and the End of the Enlightenment in France* (Cambridge, Mass., 1968), p. 52; Young, p. 260; Anatole Feugère, *Un Précurseur de la Révolution, l'Abbé Raynal (1713–
1796)* (Angoulème, 1922), pp. 232–234.

Raynal with the Society's founding, it is clear that the members initially regarded him with veneration, for on May 24, 1790, they resolved to place his portrait on the rostrum with the inscription "The Apostle of Liberty." [11] Marseilles boasted several salons, including one at the home of Dominique Audibert's wife. Young firebrands such as Antoine Brémond-Jullien [12] and Barbaroux frequented such gatherings, where they debated, read poems and essays, and discussed scientific problems.[13]

Many philanthropic associations functioned in the city on the eve of the Revolution, among them the Société philanthropique de Marseille, which originated in January, 1789, and was formally organized six months later. The founders, wealthy citizens of Marseilles, affiliated their "bureau of charity" with a mother organization in Paris. In 1790 alone they aided 120 indigent families. While the Philanthropic Society continued to exist until 1793, and thus was not just an earlier version of the Club of the Rue Thubaneau, there were parallels between the two in both activities and membership. In 1790 benevolent works consumed a great part of the Club's energies, as it contributed heavily to the support of the indigent and infirm and set up extraordinary treasuries

[11] *L'Observateur marseillais*, May 29, 1790. For copies see BN, Lc[11] 635 (95).

[12] Brémond-Jullien (1759–1792) was a lawyer from Marseilles. In March, 1789, he became secretary of the first citizen's militia. He was a secretary of the Society in the first month of its existence, May, 1790, and coedited the *Observateur marseillais*, the semiofficial journal of the Society, from May to August, 1790. On July 6, 1790, he became procurator of the District of Marseilles. He fled to Paris on November 6, 1790, after a dispute with the Club. Following his return he was hanged by a riotous mob on September 8, 1792.

[13] Barbaroux, pp. 38–39.

and committees to handle charitable activities. The *Almanach historique* for 1790 lists thirty-five directors of the Philanthropic Society, of whom at least twelve (34%), including the vice-president, were Club members.[14]

The majority of the educated and socially conscious Marseillais of the 1780's were the products of the city's clerically run schools. In 1789 Marseilles claimed two institutions of higher learning, of which the more prestigious by far was the Collège de l'Oratoire, founded in 1625. The Oratorians, renowned for their Gallicanism and Jansenism, had all but monopolized higher education in Marseilles since the expulsion of their rivals, the Jesuits, from France in 1763. In 1774 they taught 245 pupils. Boarders paid approximately 400 livres, but day students received their education free of charge. The Oratorians structured education around the study of Latin, but also provided a good grounding in science and mathematics. Historians have long acknowledged that the Oratorian colleges of France were training grounds for the future chiefs of the Revolution. To cite only one example, Danton received his education from the Oratory at Troyes. The Oratory of Marseilles was one of the most radical of these colleges in France, initiating a nation-wide rebellion in 1790–1791 against the authority of the central governing body in Paris. [15] Strong bonds tied the Oratorians of Marseilles to the Club; many college staff members doubled as Jacobins, and at least three of the eight professors of the college in

[14] BM, *2972, "Précis sur la société philanthropique établie à Marseille" (Marseille, 1789); *Journal de Provence*, Jan. 10, Nov. 28, 1789, Feb. 1, 1791; *Almanach historique*, 1790, pp. 358–361.

[15] Augustin Fabre, *Anciennes rues de Marseille* (Marseille, 1850), pp. 229–282; Masson, *La Provence au XVIII siècle*, pp. 470–481. A. M. P. Ingold, *L'Oratoire et la Révolution* (Paris, 1883), p. 20.

1790, Louis-Joseph Fabre, Alexandre-Louis Massol, and Decugis, became active members of the Society.[16]

Two Oratorians, Joseph Giraud and Louis-François-Dominique Isoard, merit special mention. The name of the former, who was born in Toulon about 1760 and moved to Marseilles before the Revolution, appears in the earliest records of the Club, and he became in time one of its most influential chieftains. The Society elected him as president twice (May–June, 1792, and June, 1794) and also as vice-president on two occasions (March–April, 1793, and October, 1793). Giraud became public prosecutor of the Criminal Tribunal of the Bouches-du-Rhône in November, 1792, and held the same position on the Revolutionary Tribunal in 1793–1794. Because of his avid Jacobinism, he was arrested three times in 1793–1794. The Federalists incarcerated him for three months during the rebellion of May–August, 1793. Fréron sent him before the Revolutionary Tribunal at Paris in February, 1794, but that body acquitted him of charges of corruption. Finally, on September 26, 1794, the reactionary representatives-on-mission, Auguis and Serres, ordered his imprisonment along with twenty-eight other chiefs of the Club, and he did not regain his freedom until 1795.

Of all the Jacobins of the Rue Thubaneau, Isoard had the most sinister and bloodthirsty reputation. He was born in

16 *Almanach historique, 1790*, pp. 283–284. AM, GG 166, List of the professors at the Oratory. Fabre taught logic. Born at Aups (Var) about 1734, he was a leading member of the Society from 1790 to the Federalist rebellion; between June and October, 1792, he served as secretary of the Club. The signatures of Decugis and Massol appear on several petitions of 1791–1792. (See AN, C 127; AM, I₂, cartons 1791 and 1792). Other Oratorians who became Club members included Jean-Pierre Camoin, Jean-Balthazard Turc, and Joseph-Benoît Almaric. Almaric was elected vice-president of the Society in early 1791.

1756, the son of a poor family of Marseilles. He matriculated at the College, where he was a friend of Barbaroux, and joined the Oratorian Order on the eve of the Revolution. He became director of the College after its nationalization in 1792. Although absent from Marseilles at the time of the founding of the Society, he enrolled in 1791 immediately after his return. On mission for the Society in the Basses-Alpes in 1792, he founded some forty new clubs. He served as secretary and vice-president in 1792–1793, and as president twice during the Terror. As chairman of the Club's dreaded central committee in the spring of 1793, he terrorized the city. He fled to Paris and joined the Jacobins during the Federalist rebellion, but returned in September, 1793, as an agent of the Committee of Public Safety. On September 24, 1795, this ardent revolutionary was guillotined as a Terrorist.[17]

There is some truth in the royalist Lautard's malicious remark that the "escapees" of the College fomented the Revolution in Marseilles.[18] The pupils of the Oratorians filled the ranks of the Club. Isoard, Barbaroux, and Brémond-Jullien were all graduates of the College, as was Alexandre Ricord. This young student-turned-revolutionary, born in Marseilles in 1770, had scarcely earned his degree when the Revolution erupted. He followed Mirabeau to Paris in 1789 and aided in the publication of the *Courrier de Provence*. After his return he coedited the *Journal des départements méridionaux et des débats des amis de la constitution de Marseille* in 1792–1793. In his capacity as Jacobin editor he proved himself a fervent disciple of the *philosophes*. One wonders if he learned his

---

[17] For pro and con viewpoints on the life of Isoard, see AD, B-du-Rh, L 3037, Trial of Louis-François-Dominique Isoard; *ibid.*, L 2076, "Vie politique de François Isoard" (Marseille, 1794).

[18] *Esquisses* . . . , p. 28.

Rousseau and Voltaire at the feet of the Oratorian fathers. In November, 1792, at age twenty-two, he was elected as an administrator of the department. During the Terror he became public prosecutor with the Military Tribunal of the French Army of Spain and edited a Jacobin journal at Perpignan. He died in 1829 near Marseilles.

Ricord's father, Charles-Alexandre (also an active Jacobin), was one of the most influential members of the masonic lodge Amateurs de la Sagesse. Almost every historian who has written on the Jacobins has had to deal with the problem of their masonic origins. Since the time of the Abbé Barruel, royalist writers have attributed the genesis of the clubs, and indeed of the whole Revolution, to a masonic plot. While generally scoffing at the idea of a conspiracy, republican historians have not denied the influence of freemasonry on the Jacobin movement. In a book published in 1915, Henri Labroue showed that approximately two-thirds of the masons of Bergerac (Dordogne) joined the popular society there. François Brégail provided evidence that the leaders of the masonic lodges in the Gers later directed the clubs in that department. For France as a whole, L. de Cardenal stopped short of affirming "a direct and premeditated line" between popular societies and masonic lodges; nevertheless, he noted "a community of thought, presence of some of the same individuals and common rites."[19]

[19] Augustin de Barruel, *Mémoires pour servir à l'histoire du jacobinisme* (Hamburg, 1798); Brinton, p. 14; François Brégail, "La Société populaire d'Auch," *Bulletin du comité des travaux historiques*, XXX (1911) 143–220; Henri Labroue, *La Société populaire de Bergerac* (Paris, 1915), pp. 6–8; L. de Cardenal, "Les Origines des sociétés populaires: Vues générales et faits," *La Révolution française*, LXXVII (1924), 210–211.

The first French masonic lodge was established at Paris in
1725, and during the remainder of the eighteenth century the
movement spread over the entire kingdom. A constitution
drawn up in 1773 created a national masonic organization.
The grand master was Philippe d'Orléans, the Duc de
Chartres, and over 500 lodges were affiliated by 1789. Initially, the founders of the lodges were exiled supporters of
the Stuart kings of England. It is not surprising, therefore,
that the first masonic temples in Provence should have sprung
up in the 1730's around the court of the Old Pretender
James III at Avignon. In Marseilles the first lodge appeared
in 1740, and Alain Le Bihan cites seventeen by the reign of
Louis XVI. There were in addition many obscure, unofficial
masonic groups of which no records remain. According to
Augustin Fabre, "There was one for the wigmakers, the
dockworkers, and every type of artisan." [20]

Freemasonry unquestionably influenced Jacobinism in
Marseilles. To a certain extent, both movements shared common practices and customs. The masons disseminated the
ideals of equality, liberty, and fraternity. The "temples" of
freemasonry and the Jacobin "temple of liberty" abounded
with seals, plaques, and banners. Both the lodges of Marseilles
and the Club of the Rue Thubaneau founded networks of
daughter organizations within Provence, and remarkable parallels can be seen in both the geographical extent of these net-

[20] Gaston-Martin, *La Franc-maçonnerie française et la préparation
de la Révolution* (Paris, 1926); René Verrier, *La Mère loge écossaise
de France à l'orient de Marseille (1751–1784)* (Marseille, 1950), pp.
19–20; Alain Le Bihan, *Loges et chapitres de la grande loge et du
grand orient de France (2ᵉ moitié du XVIIIᵉ siècle)* (Paris, 1967), pp.
120–126; Augustin Fabre, *Les Rues de Marseille,* II (Marseille, 1867),
416–417.

works and the methods of affiliation and correspondence that each used.[21] Finally, the evidence indicates that the Society had cordial relations with the masonic conclaves until 1793. On March 5, 1792, for example, the officers of a lodge called Egalité, newly formed by "laborious artisans," visited the Society. To lively and prolonged applause the masons vowed to "fight, live, and die for liberty." [22]

Some freemasons certainly became members of the Club, as is evidenced by the membership rosters of ten lodges that are preserved today in the Bibliothèque Nationale. Since biographical data are limited, identifying the Jacobins on these lists is difficult and risky.[23] From a total of 588 masons, I positively identified only 109 future Club members (a little over 18 per cent). Taken by itself, this percentage does not indicate a great overlap of personnel between the Club and the lodges. It is noteworthy, however, that almost all of the officers of the lodges, the individuals for whom the most biographical material is available, became influential Jacobins.

The roster of the Amateurs de la Sagesse, for example, dated 1787, is comprised of sixty-nine masons. The master

[21] The lodge of St.-Jean d'Ecosse founded daughter lodges at Salon, Martiques, and St.-Chamas (Bouches-du-Rhône), at Brignoles, Cuers, Draguignan, Hyères, and le Luc (Var), at Valensole, Barcelonnette, and Riez (Basses-Alpes), at Cadenet (Vaucluse), and elsewhere outside Provence. In these four departments the Club of Marseilles also formed numerous societies.

[22] *JdD*, Mar. 8, 1792, p. 7.

[23] See BN, FM² 282, 284, 285, 288, 289, 290, 291, 292. From a variety of sources I compiled biographies of 4,902 Club members; but this represents no more than five-sixths of the probable membership of the Society for 1790–1794, and the data on each member are by no means complete. The masonic lists themselves provide only names and professions. The entry "Pierre Martin, *capitaine de navire*," for example, might indicate any one of several citizens of Marseilles.

was Charles Le Peintre, a wholesale merchant. He attended the Club regularly in 1790. Etienne Seytres (parlementary attorney) held the office of orator in the lodge; in July–August, 1792, he served as president of the Society. Le Choix des vrais amis boasted forty-three members in 1788. Jean-Joseph Grasset, this lodge's orator, was the Club's secretary in October, 1792. Les Philadelphes, a sister lodge, had thirty-five active masons in 1785. The master at that time, Joseph-Claire Segond, later sat on many Club committees. François-Omer Granet, a wholesale merchant, had been the founder and first master of the lodge. This fiery Jacobin was elected to the Legislative Assembly in 1791 and to the Convention in 1792.

Le Nouveau Peuple éclairé was an elite temple of wholesale merchants and nobles, a substantial percentage of whom had their homes outside the city. Only two Club members can be identified as belonging to this particular lodge. One of them, however, was the master, François-Auguste Vieilh des Ambiez, a naval commissariat officer. Vieilh attended the Society assiduously until 1793 when he adopted the Federalist cause. In 1792, he wrote an address on patriotism which the Club published and distributed in the city.[24] La Parfaite Sincérité, by contrast, drew its membership from the petty middle class. Its master, François-Joseph Rouedy, was in the West Indies when the Club was founded, but when he returned to Marseilles he became a dedicated Jacobin. His prestige among the members earned him the position of judge of the Revolutionary Tribunal of the Bouches-du-Rhône during the Terror.

La Réunion des élus was a popular lodge with 101 members in 1788. Once again the master, Jean-Baptiste-Mathieu Dey-

[24] BM, 4717, "Discours prononcé par M. Vieilh, ci-devant Dezam-bies, à l'assemblée des amis de la Constitution" (Marseille, 1792).

dier, was a member of the Club. Deydier enrolled in the Society on July 28, 1790, and served as secretary in October, 1793. Other masons in this temple also held office in the Club, Jean-Pierre and Alexandre-Charles Cresp serving as secretaries in 1794 and Louis Long, a wholesale merchant from Cuges (Bouches-du-Rhône) as secretary in the autumn of 1791. The Disciples de St.-Jean, the Frères unis, and the Triple Union were smaller lodges. In other respects, however, they conformed to the general pattern; the masters of all three, Jean-François Arnoux, Pierre-François Janclerc, and Claude-François Achard, subsequently became Club members, and Joseph de Falconieri, orator of the Disciples de St.-Jean in 1788, was one of the Society's most respected early leaders.

In summary, it seems certain that the Club of the Rue Thubaneau was not the metamorphosis of a particular masonic lodge, and the dearth of evidence makes it impossible to say if there was a substantial overlap of rank-and-file masons and Jacobins. On the other hand it is clear that an extraordinary number of masonic officers later became leaders of the Society. In their positions as functionaries of the lodges the masters corresponded with each other, formed acquaintances, and shared ideas. It is possible that common masonic backgrounds and mutual allegiance caused some masonic dignitaries to become patriots in 1789 and chieftains of the Club in 1790.

While not underestimating the importance of the masonic movement, Maurice Agulhon has recently demonstrated that many elements of continuity also link the clubs of eastern Provence with lay religious brotherhoods called *confréries de pénitents*. They sometimes had a common membership and meeting place. Pre-Revolutionary intracity rivalries between

brotherhoods were reflected in the rivalries of hostile popular
societies that met in their chapels. Moreover, after 1792 the
Jacobins carried on many of the benevolent works formerly
performed by the brotherhoods.[25]

These religious organizations dated from the late fifteenth
and early sixteenth centuries. In Marseilles, where there were
fourteen brotherhoods in 1789, they purchased the freedom
of slaves and debtors, consoled condemned criminals, buried
paupers, aided indigents, and provided fellowship for members. Their membership had a broader base than did the
masonic movement, with artisans, petty tradesmen, clerics,
and shopkeepers predominating in many of the brotherhoods.[26]

The membership lists and minutes of some of these pre-
Revolutionary brotherhoods are still extant.[27] Generally speaking, they offer even less biographical data than do the records
of the masonic lodges. Comparisons of their personnel with the
Club's are even less profitable; in an examination of 586
members of three brotherhoods I could definitely identify
only 86 as Jacobins. These figures do not tell the whole story,
however; the actual number who became members of the
Club was probably higher. Certainly, many Marseillais retained a dual allegiance to the Society and to various brotherhoods until 1792. On April 18 of that year, Jean-Pierre Amy
informed the Society that the Legislative Assembly had suppressed the penitents; he publicly resigned from the Brotherhood of the Trinity and invited "every good citizen" to

[25] Maurice Agulhon, *La Sociabilité méridionale, confréries et associations dans la vie collective en Provence orientale à la fin du 18ème
siècle*, I (Aix, 1966), 492–501.

[26] *Almanach historique, 1790*, pp. 94–98; L. Fontanier, "Les Pénitents
noirs de Marseille," *Annales de Provence*, XIX (1922), 34–41.

[27] AD, B-du-Rh, XXIV F, nos. 58, 95 *bis*, 95 *ter*, 111; *AM*, GG 80.

imitate his example. At these patriotic words, the journal of the Society recounts, "an infinite number of members, penitents of diverse chapels, rushed to the tribune." [28]

Some brotherhood members, such as Amy, had great stature in the Society. François-Ferréol Galibert, a master cabinetmaker born in Marseilles in 1754, for example, wore the blue hood of the Confrérie des pénitents de Notre Dame de Pitié. He was a charter member of the Club and by 1792–1793 he and his brother, Pierre-Gabriel, ranked among the top echelon of leaders. He served as vice-president twice (February–March, 1793, and March–April, 1794). With the backing of his fellow Jacobins, he became a justice of the peace in 1793. Another Club figure, the renegade Abbé Emmanuel de Beausset, was a member of the Carmelin brotherhood. In 1789 Beausset was count of the ancient abbey of St.-Victor. On July 27, 1789, he led a band of Marseillais in freeing prisoners detained at Aix. In February, 1790, he became an officer of the first municipal administration, and during the Terror he renounced his vows and married.

Well before the foundation of the Club of the Rue Thubaneau its future members had shown a tendency toward sociability; they were joiners. But it seems clear that the Club was not the direct descendant of any pre-Revolutonary association or secret society to which they may have belonged. For the immediate origins of the Society one must look to the Revolutionary year 1789–1790. In Marseilles as elsewhere in France, the convening of the Estates-General encouraged the

[28] Amy, a ship owner, was born in Marseilles about 1758. In 1792–1793 he was one of the foremost chiefs of the Club. He served as secretary in May–June, 1791, president in September–October, 1792, vice-president in December–January, 1792–1793, and president again in May, 1793. He survived the purge of September, 1794 and was still active in the Society in 1795. *JdD*, Apr. 21, 1792, p. 84.

formation of innumerable public and private circles. Anonymous brochures tell us of their existence, but few documents
survive on their organization and composition. Some of the
larger among them developed from the first primary assemblies held prior to the Estates-General; others sprang up in
haphazard fashion. By the spring of 1790, the Bourgeois
Circle, the Phocaean Circle, and the Adelphian Circle, among
others, flourished in the city, and patriotic women had organized several local clubs.[29]

While one cannot go beyond speculation about the genesis
of the Club, it seems probable that it evolved, in an immediate
sense, from embryonic but semipermanent conclaves of the
leaders of the citizen's militia and National Guard. The chief
gathering places for the citizen's army in 1789 were the cafés
and bars of the city, where patriots met together informally
to exchange ideas and read the Parisian press. Two establish-
ments in particular acquired notoriety as the meeting places
of patriotic volunteers. The first, the Café de François, frequently mentioned in pamphlets, stood on the great Cours
Belsunce, only a few blocks from the Rue Thubaneau. After
March 24, 1789, it served as a formation point for the patrols
of the citizen's militia. Battalion leaders met together in cham-
bers above the barroom; rank-and-file volunteers congregated
below. "There," wrote Théodore de Lameth, who visited
Marseilles in March, 1789, "day and night, without interval,
orators gave interminable harangues."[30]

In more peaceful times the Marseillais had celebrated wed-
dings and festivals in the Arquier Tavern, in the allées de

[29] Lourde, I, 246–247; BM, 4717, "Etat et recette général des dons
faits à l'assemblée patriotique" (Marseille, 1790).
[30] *Mémoires*, published with an introduction and notes by Eugène
Welvert (Paris, 1908), pp. 44, 58.

Meilhon adjacent to the Cours. Here, an assembly of patriots formed the citizen's militia and established its headquarters. "The general staff sat there permanently, discussed and deliberated, and received communications and dispatches." Numerous delegations of citizens came to meet with militia leaders and thank them for preserving order. On July 23, 1789, a second great assembly, attended by some 6,000 citizens, took place there at the news of the capture of the Bastille. One year later the Club sponsored a fête in commemoration of this event, "the origins of liberty in Marseilles." [31]

After the formation of the National Guard on February 15, 1790, the Café de François and the Arquier Tavern continued to be its rallying points. Here the patriots heard the news of a great national awakening in the spring of 1790. Celebrations commemorating the patriotic unity of cities and national guardsmen took place in almost every province of France. Clubs sprang up spontaneously in emulation of the Paris Jacobins. In the Midi the month of April alone saw the formation of Societies of Friends of the Constitution at Nîmes, Bordeaux, and Valence. By August 16, 1790, 152 local clubs had affiliated themselves with the mother society in Paris.[32] The Marseillais could not have been unimpressed. Wishing to imitate the other great cities of the kingdom, some leaders of the National Guard apparently conceived the idea of founding a club in Marseilles. Only guardsmen and municipal officers could inscribe their names as members on April 11. Eight hundred national guardsmen attended the session of April 18.

[31] Vialla, p. 10. AM, I₂, carton 1790, session of July 8, 1790.

[32] Aulard, *Jacobins,* I, lxxxi; François Rouvière, *Histoire de la Révolution française dans le département du Gard,* vol. I (Nîmes, 1887); AD, Drôme, F 207; Pierre Flottes, "Le Club des Jacobins de Bordeaux," *La Révolution française,* LXIX (1916), 337.

With their pre-Revolutionary habits of association and their need to form a permanent organization to coordinate their activities, it was natural for the guardsmen to found the Patriotic Assembly of Friends of the Constitution of Marseilles.[33]

[33] *Courier de Marseille*, n.d. (no. 3), p. 18; BN, Lk² 3712 (32). "Adresse des membres de l'assemblée patriotique de la ville de Marseille, à MM. les officiers . . . et soldats du Regiment de Guienne" (Marseille, 1790). In one sentence in this address Brémond-Jullien stated that the National Guard founded the Club.

3

Organization of the Club

After its initial meeting, the Society's first order of business was to formulate a code of rules and regulations. A twelve-man committee, chaired by the Abbé Constans,[1] prepared the preliminary draft which the members debated article by article during the summer of 1790. The product of these debates, the Regulations of 1790, is the sole extant official document on the Club's internal organization. In its final form the Regulations showed marked similarity to the constitutions of other clubs. Certain articles were identical with passages in the Regulations of February 8, 1790, published by the Jacobins in Paris; and in its turn it often served as a model for Marseilles' satellite societies in Provence.[2]

The process of organization did not cease with the printing

[1] Constans (or Coustans), a twenty-five year old priest, was a prominent figure in the Club in 1790–1791. He signed nearly all the petitions, calling himself *"prêtre conformiste."* In 1792 he dropped from sight and apparently ceased to be an active member.

[2] For the debates of 1790, see AM, I₂, carton 1790. A copy of the constitution of the Parisian Jacobins can be found in BN, Lb⁴⁰ 569. Among others, the clubs of Cornillon, Apt, Solliers, St.-Zacharie, Riez, Pertuis, and Peynier modelled their constitutions on that of Marseilles. See AD, B-du-Rh, L 2040, L 2027; AM, I₂, carton 1791; AD, Basses-Alpes, L 856/2; AD, Var, series L supplement, St.-Zacharie. See also Chapter 2, footnote 1.

of the Regulations. Indeed, the internal structure of the Club went on evolving and changing throughout its existence, with the result that official guidelines came to vary considerably from parliamentary realities. Ultimately, on February 8, 1793, dissatisfied members appointed a commission to revise the outmoded rules.[3] There is no evidence that this revision was completed. It is possible that the Club rewrote its constitution on another occasion, in September, 1793, after the Federalist rebellion. Again, however, no records have survived. To reconstruct the regulations and procedures, it is, thus, essential to seek information in other records, particularly those of its meetings.[4]

Membership

In the debates of the Society few matters of internal organization attracted more attention than membership requirements. At the zenith of the Club's power, membership was a coveted privilege, a steppingstone to authority, and a matter of personal insurance. During the Terror it was essential to bearing arms. By 1792, citizens clamored to become Jacobins. On June 8 of that year, for example, a certain Chastel, sculp-

[3] *JdD*, Feb. 9, 1793, p. 596.
[4] Besides scattered published extracts, the longest chronicle appears in the *Journal des départements méridionaux*, extending over a period of fourteen months from March 4, 1792, to May 4, 1793. Although these accounts are scanty and replete with error, they provide invaluable information. For a period of two months (February 28, 1793–April 18, 1793) they are complemented by the official *procèsverbaux* (AD, B-du-Rh, L 2071). Two further sources, not widely known, are: Series I₂ of the Municipal Archives of Marseilles (an uncatalogued section of the classification general police), which contains minutes of the Club's meetings in 1790; and in the National Archives under W 86, where extracts survive of the meetings of August–September, 1794.

tor, made a colorful plea to the Antipolitiques of Aix for a letter of introduction to the Club. "I burn with desire," he wrote, "to count myself one of the members of that Society. . . . I would give up food and drink rather than be deprived of attending the sessions of the saviors of the Commonwealth."[5]

Initially, a citizen could attain the prize of membership by following a few easy steps. First, a member proposed his name. The assembly then accepted or rejected the nominee by voice vote, only a plurality being required for admittance. Next, an officer conducted all the candidates to the rostrum to pledge allegiance to the Club with the oath:

I pledge to be faithful to the Constitution of the Kingdom, to maintain it with all my power and to observe faithfully the rules of the Patriotic Assembly of Marseilles. I also pledge to defend with my fortune and my blood every citizen who has the courage to denounce traitors to the fatherland and enemies of liberty.[6]

After that, the nominee signed one of the great registers kept on display in the main hall. Finally, he received a membership card with his number and his name and became an official "brother" of the Society.

Gradually, innovations appeared in the admittance procedure. Strong recommendations from affiliated societies or from prominent local officials eliminated red tape. The club always rewarded acts of patriotism with membership; when Louis Gilly, "a brave lieutenant" of the National Guard was wounded while on duty on July 12, 1790, the clubbists admitted him immediately into their assembly. Oral nominations proved tedious and time-consuming, and the Society soon decided to regard "as a true presentation" the inscription of

[5] AD, B-du-Rh, L 2038. [6] AD, B-du-Rh, L 1980.

a nominee's name on a register kept at the *bureau* (central office). This system also had drawbacks, however, since some members covertly erased or marked out the names of those they disliked. (The Club finally determined to exclude anyone caught "scratching out, tearing, or making notations beside the names of the candidates.") At least 300 members had to be present to vote on the names inscribed in the register. After the balloting the candidates took the oath aggregately. The numbers doing so varied considerably; on June 24, 1790, for example, 80 candidates pledged their fidelity, on March 7, 1793, only 22.[7]

Entry cards had to be renewed every three months. Fearing the machinations of the ubiquitous "aristocrats," the Society adopted a rule on March 5, 1792, requiring members to pin them in their buttonholes for easy identification. However, this did not prevent suspicious persons from infiltrating the sessions. Lending entry cards was strictly prohibited; and the unfortunate individual who lost one had to follow a complicated procedure to acquire another. He took an oath pledging that he actually had lost the card; then, to prevent any unauthorized individual from using the lost pass, his name was entered in a register displayed prominently near the entrance. For a duplicate card, the inspection committee levied a fine of 3 livres, 12 sous.[8]

The Regulations of 1790 fixed the admission fee at 3 livres and dues at 12 sous per month thereafter. Elsewhere clubs charged entrance fees ranging from 3 to 12 livres and dues of up to 24 livres per year; the Jacobins of Paris, for example, charged 12 livres for admission in 1790 and 6 livres per quarter. But while the rates of the Marseilles Club may have compared

[7] AM, I₂, carton 1790; AD, B-du-Rh, L 2071.
[8] *JdD*, Mar. 8, 1792, p. 7. "Règlemens . . . ," chapter 3, article 2.

favorably with those charged by other societies in the early stages of the Revolution, they still made it impossible for the very poor to attend.[9]

Any change in dues had to be discussed in at least 3 Club sessions, and no amendment could be offered unless 300 were present. At the meeting of March 15, 1792, the president, deploring the financial state of the Society, proposed raising the dues for the following quarter by 24 sous. After acrimonious discussion the members passed this motion and also instituted a voluntary subscription. Three months later it was decided to fix the quarterly payment permanently at 3 livres. In 1793 and 1794 the Club drastically lowered membership fees; indeed, by May, 1793, the inspection committee had made it a regular practice to grant membership cards to all worthy citizens who could not afford the tariffs.[10]

In 1790 only two specific stipulations affected a man's ability to qualify for membership. Barring old age or infirmity, he must serve in the National Guard. In addition, a ruling of May, 1790, outlawed anyone who had worked for the provost Bournissac. Beyond the fees and these restrictions, the clubbists boasted of opening their assembly "to every honest citizen; we consider neither his means nor his state in life." [11] Theoretically, a Marseilles Jacobin could not belong to another society, but in fact many also joined the Antipolitiques

[9] "Règlemens. . . ," chapter 2, article 8; Brinton, p. 32.

[10] See *JdD*, Mar. 17, June 30, 1792, pp. 24, 210; AD, B-du-Rh, L 2076, "Discours prononcé par un membre de la société républicaine de Marseille" (Marseille, 1793).

[11] "Règlemens. . . ," chapter 2, articles 6 and 7; BM, 4717, "Aux Faux-témoins dans la procédure prévôtale: Discours prononcé par A. Mossy à l'assemblée patriotique dans la séance du 16 mai 1790" (Marseille, 1790). BM, 4717, "La Vérité ou seconde adresse d'un membre de l'assemblée patriotique" (Marseille, 1790).

of Aix, and commissioners such as Jacques Monbrion were often members of several clubs. If there ever had been any age restrictions, they had vanished by 1793–1794. On the membership roll of December, 1794, the youngest member was thirteen, the oldest eighty-one. On July 29, 1794, when a citizen Fiquet, aged fifteen, appeared at the Club with his certificate of citizenship and several attestations from true *sans-culottes*, his name was immediately inscribed on the rolls. On September 10, 1794, one Joseph Perret, aged ten, received an entry card.[12]

Like the other clubs of France, the Club of the Rue Thubaneau often accorded honorary memberships to outsiders, important personages, or visiting groups. On May 16, 1790, for example, when four representatives from the city of Les Baux came to praise the Marseillais for the capture of the Forts of St.-Jean, St.-Nicolas, and Notre-Dame-de-la-Garde, and to request "a confederation to defend the cause of the Constitution and of Liberty, jointly with the Marseillais," the Society, on the proposal of Barbaroux, received them as fellow members.[13]

Having joined the Society, a member could be removed by two means: exclusion or purification. Exclusion, the more common of the two, could involve, in its mildest guise, nothing more than censure in the Club's minutes and perhaps temporary suspension. In its extreme form, however, it could mean permanent banishment, and eventually imprisonment or death. In either case, it usually involved some type of written

[12] For the register of December, 1794 see AD, B-du-Rh, L 2073. On Fiquet and Perret see the *Tribune populaire*, July 29 and Sep. 10, 1794 (AD, B-du-Rh, L 2076, and BN, Lc[11] 635 72).

[13] BM, 4717, "Délibérations et adresses, tant de la garde nationale, que de la commune de la ville des Baux à la Municipalité de Marseille" (Marseille, 1790).

or oral denunciation. After such a denunciation a brother could be excluded by a majority vote of those present.

While every Jacobin had a "sacred obligation" to denounce enemies of the Revolution, it was wise to be circumspect in attacking other individuals. "A denunciation," pronounced a member in November, 1792, "is a civic act, but if it is not proved it is only a mere accusation." When one member at the meeting of May 13, 1790, imprudently compared the Abbé Constans with the infamous Abbé Maury, the Club voted to censure him publicly in the minutes.[14] Guillaume Carle, although later president of the Club (September, 1794), was censured in 1792 for a denunciation he had made on false information.[15] Members often replied to denunciations with counterdenunciations. In the summer and fall of 1792, Jean Beissière and François Moisson, two prominent clubbists, traded insults and charges. Their dispute terminated in the exclusion of Beissière; his suspension was only temporary, however, and when the Club reintegrated him on February 28, 1793, he embraced his former enemy, Moisson, amidst the applause of the Assembly.[16]

Purification (*épuration*), in contrast to exclusion, was col-

[14] On the "sacred obligation" see AN, W 86; BN, Lb⁴⁰ 996, "Profession de foi individuelle, de tous les membres de la société populaire et montagnarde de Marseille" (Marseille, 1794).

[15] *JdD*, Aug. 4, 1792, pp. 270–271. Carle, a militant at the Society throughout the Revolution, killed himself rather than be arrested by Auguis and Serres in September, 1794.

[16] AM, 4D₆, To the president of the Society, Nov. 10, 1792; AD, B-du-Rh, L 2071, session of Feb. 28, 1793. The name of Beissière, a maker of looking-glasses in 1789, appears on the earliest registers of the Club. During the Terror he was a member of the surveillance committee of Marseilles until his arrest by Auguis and Serres in September, 1794. During the White Terror of 1815 he was murdered by a royalist mob. Moisson commanded the "battalion of August 10" which helped overthrow the King.

lective and impersonal, and common to most of the Jacobin societies of France. The process involved the establishment of special club committees charged with examining the members over a period of time and weeding out "counterrevolutionaries." The Club of Marseilles appears to have had six such investigations between 1790 and the major purge of September, 1794. The first began on December 13, 1792, in the initial phases of the Girondin-Montagnard controversy, and lasted until February 4, 1793; during this period the admission of candidates temporarily ceased. Members might be removed from the assembly either if they had not signed an address of July, 1790, against D'André of Aix, or if they "had abandoned the society in times of danger." The second of these criteria was vague, and left ample room for pruning suspect Jacobins. A committee of 24, taken from the 1,449 names on the petition against D'André, directed the operation. Only weeks later, on April 10, 1793, the Club resolved "to purge the Society of all members suspected of Rolandism and Brissotism," but no records of this purification survive. Under pressure from the Federalist sections, the Club seems to have undertaken yet another purging operation at the end of May.[17]

After the Federalist rebellion the Club instituted a permanent examining committee to issue certificates of citizenship, receive denunciations, and manage purifications. The first of the three purifications that appear to have occurred under its supervision took place in September, 1793, when the committee purged the Club of Federalists and supervised a great influx of new members. On October 4, 1793, the *Journal républicain de Marseille* was able to warn counterrevolutionaries to beware, for "The Society is definitively purified." On

[17] *JdD*, pp. 552–591. For evidence of a May purification see AD, B-du-Rh, L 1980.

January 5, 1794. the *Journal* again reported a purge in the Club, but no records of this survive. A few documents exist on the last purification of the Terror, which followed an edict of March 13, 1794, issued by the representative-on-mission, Maignet, and extended over three months from April to June, 1794.[18]

Women

The Club never officially admitted women into its ranks. It allowed them to attend its meetings but compelled them to sit in the balcony, separated from the men by a balustrade. The segregation of the sexes was common in Jacobin clubs and had mixed results. De Cardenal writes, "In most of the societies the masculine and feminine elements were separated, but not always enough to prevent rapprochements from which the fatherland had nothing to gain, for the moment at least." [19] In Marseilles vigorous debates took place over the question of female participation. Opponents argued that the presence of women, even in the balcony, overcrowded the hall and disrupted the meetings, citing such incidents as that of March 4, 1793, when the president formally warned the *citoyennes* to cease nursing their babies. The profeminists defended their cause by pointing out that women added by their "beauty" and "virtues" to the "splendor of the Society," and that the "weaker sex" needed instruction. As a last resort they recalled the words of Jean-Jacques Rousseau: "If you want to make men grand and virtuous, teach women the meaning of virtue and of grandeur of the soul." [20]

[18] *Journal républicain*, pp. 15, 365; on Maignet see AN, AF II 91.
[19] *La Province*, p. 73.
[20] AD, B-du-Rh, L 2071, sessions of Mar. 4, Apr. 3, 1793; *JdD*, Mar. 17, 1792, Apr. 6, 1793, pp. 24, 691.

Despite their subordinate position, women still participated in the Club's activities in a variety of ways. Many contributed to its benevolent funds and voluntarily paid dues to the treasury. Others assumed the burden of rearing children orphaned by the Revolution. At the height of the war, on October 3, 1792, thirty women offered their services in making shirts, garters, etc., for the men at the front. Women also helped at fêtes and served as hostesses in greeting deputations to the Club. On February 28, 1793, for example, when a deputation from the corsair *Sans-Culotte* came to vow "irreconcilable hatred" to tyrants, a certain Magdelaine Chabert welcomed them to "the temple where equality has fixed its abode." On behalf of the women she vowed "to follow the path of the ancient Romans, to take for a husband only a true *sans-culotte*, to recognize no other master but God and no other sovereign on Earth but the people." [21]

From the galleries, women often intervened at crucial points in debates. On March 7, 1792, for example, a deputation from Apt in the Vaucluse came to seek the aid of the Marseillais against the non-juring priests of their region. During the debates on this petition a woman's voice rang out from the galleries taunting the members: "What! Gentlemen, you hesitate to consent to the wishes of your brethren. I am only a woman, but if I were free of all concern and if I were armed, I would give you an example to follow." Owing partly to this pressure, perhaps, the Marseillais sent a mission to root out the non-juring priests of Apt. [22]

The most celebrated of the women who frequented the Club was Thérèse Gaud, called "La Cavale" (the Claire

[21] *JdD*, Oct. 6, 1792, Mar. 2, 1793, pp. 380, 631. See also AD, B-du-Rh, L 2071.
[22] *JdD*, Mar. 10, 1792, p. 10.

Lacombe of Marseilles). She repeatedly spoke out in debates, and she surreptitiously signed the Society's petitions. On March 9, 1792, she headed a delegation of women sent to give a bonnet of liberty to the Antipolitiques of Aix. The same month she marched with the Marseilles army against the counterrevolutionaries of Arles. Because of her rabid Jacobinism the Federalists arrested and imprisoned her in 1793.[23]

Officers and Committees

Any member was eligible to become an officeholder of the Society. The Regulations of 1790 listed 41 official positions: president, vice-president, 4 administrative secretaries, 4 secretaries for correspondence, a treasurer, 8 commissioners of finance and administration, 8 commissioners of police, 8 commissioners of inspection, and 6 commissioners of surveillance. These figures did not remain static. New officers and committees came into being as the work load increased, and it is probable that the total number of offices rose by 50 per cent between 1790 and 1793.

Originally all posts were elective. Those present (in 1793 it was decided that the quorum should be 150) divided into groups of 30. Each group voted separately and reported the results to tellers appointed by the president. A plurality decided the election. In case of a tie, the eldest had priority. If an officer-elect declined to serve, the individual with the next highest number of votes took his place. Elections took place on the day the incumbent's term expired, which in the case of the president, vice-president, and treasurer, was usually the eleventh of each month; installation followed the day after. In the beginning the incoming and outgoing presidents gave speeches, but this practice was discontinued in 1792. Some installations were particularly splendid and proved of con-

[23] *Ibid.*, Mar. 14, 1792, p. 15. See also AN, C 127.

siderable propaganda value to the Club. The investiture of Etienne Martin as president, on the evening of March 12, 1791, brought 2,000 members to the hall, and a "prodigious concourse" of other citizens gathered in the vestibule and joined in the applause. The hall itself was brightly illuminated, and tar barrels lit the Rue Thubaneau and the Rue Tapis Vert while the installation ceremony was in progress. The Club had prepared a beautifully decorated *arc de triomphe*, inscribed with the Declaration of the Rights of Man, which a battalion of national guardsmen solemnly transported to Martin's home. The festive evening culminated with patriotic songs.[24]

Well-schooled in the political theories of the *philosophes*, the founders of the Society sought to guard against the excessive influence of individuals by limiting terms of office and by prohibiting re-election. In practice, however, the Club frequently violated these rules. The number of truly qualified persons was small, and some members proved particularly able in certain positions. For example, Pierre Trahan and Jacques Brogi[25] became perpetual secretaries of the correspondence committee in 1792 and 1793.

Theoretically, the presidency was the most important office in the Club. Up to 1793, however, it remained essentially a ceremonial position given to an important local dignitary whose duties barred him from regular attendance at meetings. For this reason the vice-president had to be chosen carefully; for the heaviest responsibilities rested on his shoulders. The presiding officer had many duties. He oversaw the work of the permanent committees and approved all the monetary transactions of the Club. He also appointed commissioners and

[24] AM, 4 D₁.

[25] Pierre Trahan was a wholesale merchant of Marseilles. Brogi was a clerk (*commis*) and a judge of the Revolutionary Tribunal during the Terror.

members of temporary committees and opened and closed the sessions. Necessity required him to be a good extemporaneous speaker, for he had the responsibility of welcoming the many delegations that entered the hall. When the commissioners of police could not control the sessions, it was his duty to bring order to the assembly. He accorded the floor to speakers and thus regulated the topics discussed. To check his influence a rule prohibited him from making a motion, but in fact he could circumvent this by giving up the chair temporarily and descending to the floor.

The treasurer ranked next to the president and vice-president in importance. Of necessity he had to be a man skilled in monetary matters; accordingly, at least until 1793, he was typically a wealthy merchant. The treasurer was accountable for dues paid into the Club. He paid all expenses and worked closely with the finance committee. Only he and the president had keys to the special charity box for patriotic donations from which funds were dispensed according to the instructions of the Society as a whole.[26]

Four administrative secretaries assisted the presiding officers. Initially these officials served for two months, with two of the four retiring each month. Their principal function was to record the minutes and read them at the beginning and end of each session, though they also administered the Club's archives and ordered the patriotic journals which it purchased. The personnel of this secretariat gradually became permanent. By 1793–1794 the Club employed at least two regular secretaries as archivists and stenographers.[27]

Like the other Jacobin societies of France, the Club vested

[26] AM, I₂, carton 1790, session of June 21, 1790.
[27] An undated edition of the *Manuel du laboureur et de l'artisan*, (no. 10), p. 77, discusses in detail the duties of a secretary. On the two permanent secretaries see AM, 10 H 10.

power in commissions rather than individuals. It developed an extensive network of committees which met before the sessions, directed policy, and often made decisions independently of the wishes of the rank-and-file. Ad hoc or temporary committees were the simplest type. A half-dozen might be formed in a single session; within a matter of days they would have disbanded. They typically consisted of from four to six people, appointed by the president, with the eldest among them presiding. The innumerable tasks of these ad hoc committees included aiding distressed persons, conferring with important authorities, and sifting through material too secretive or too time-consuming to be discussed at general meetings.

Some ad hoc committees endured for weeks and months and gained semiofficial status. Typical of these were the verification committee, established in 1790 to check the status of the needy destined to receive the charity of the Society, and the arms committee of March, 1792, which purchased and requisitioned pikes and rifles. Another example of a semipermanent committee was the constitution committee, created by a resolution of November 22, 1792, to aid the Convention in its work of writing a constitution for France. Initially it consisted of twelve members, but the Club added at least two more later. In late February, 1793, it began to hold public sessions in the former church of the Bernardines; in the following months it circularized the sections and neighboring clubs for their suggestions.[28]

Most Jacobin clubs in France had a permanent correspon-

[28] AM, I₂, 1790, session of June 12, 1790; *JdD*, Mar. 10 and Nov. 24, 1792, pp. 9, 461; AD, B-du-Rh, L 2071, sessions of Feb. 28, Mar. 1 and 4, 1793; *ibid.*, L 2076, "Les Membres composant le comité de constitution aux sections" (Marseille, 1793); *ibid.*, L 2038, "Les Membres composant le comité de constitution . . . à leurs concitoyens, salut" (Marseille, 1793).

dence committee and Marseilles was no exception. In 1790, it was served by four secretaries. Gradually its organization became more complex. On April 10, 1793, correspondence with affiliated societies fell so far in arrears that the Club decided to add five new secretaries. By 1794 the correspondence committee numbered at least twelve. Because of the nature of its work, a constant turnover of personnel proved impractical. Certain positions therefore became permanent, and its president became an executive vice-president of the Club. The committee had a multiplicity of duties, but its primary task was to receive and dispatch the Club's correspondence. Theoretically, every letter that it wrote had to be approved at the Society's meetings and signed by two secretaries. Representatives of the committee read incoming letters of sufficient interest to the full assembly. The committee was also responsible for sending and receiving certificates of affiliation.[29]

The finance committee, which in 1790 consisted of eight members, managed fiscal affairs and worked in close conjunction with the treasurer. Each month it made an official report to the assembly on the state of the budget. It also contracted with merchants for the maintenance and repair of furniture, the lighting and heating of the hall, etc. The inspection committee reported infractions of the rules to the president, examined the credentials of candidates, and issued entry cards. The members of this committee could refuse membership if the candidate did not meet the standards for admission. Between 1790 and 1792 its personnel rose from eight to twelve. It also became quasi-static in terms of the individuals who composed it. The eight commissioners of police were responsible for seeing that everything functioned properly in

---

[29] On the addition of April 10 see AD, B-du-Rh, L 2071; for the duties of the correspondence committee the "Règlemens . . . ," chapter 4, article 7.

the meeting place and, more importantly, for maintaining
order at the meetings. Police commissioners wore distinctive
tricolor armbands, and in theory everyone deferred to their
orders. They examined entry cards, prevented individuals
from standing on chairs or benches, from reading papers in
the meetings, or from taking Club property from the building.[30]

Other permanent committees of the Club included the
benevolence committee and the education committee. The
former distributed alms to the poor; the latter collected and
distributed patriotic materials, and during the Terror harangued the populace in the Temple of Reason every tenth
day. On July 12, 1790, the Society of Marseilles formed a
conciliation committee, "to terminate the disagreements between members of the Assembly and between other citizens."
Consisting of ten members, half of whom were lawyers, it
heard the complaints of disputants and gave legal support to
the individual who had "right" on his side.[31] Its first case
was a marital dispute. On July 16, 1790, Dame Rose-Michel
Reynoir, wife of the Venetian consul, Dominique-Barthélemy
Cornet, denounced her husband to the Club as a "monster
of nature" and accused him of defrauding her of her fortune. In the weeks that followed, the committee was bombarded with petitions from the women of Marseilles urging
it to come to the aid of "suffering and oppressed humanity."
"Among the victims of tyranny," they charged, "is a wife."
The conciliation committee ultimately obtained a satisfactory
settlement for Madame Cornet.[32]

[30] AM, I₂, 1790, sessions of June 22, July 1 and 4, Aug. 1, 1790.
"Règlemens . . . ," chapter 4, articles 1, 7, 9, 10, 15.
[31] AN, AF II 91, Decree of March 14, 1794. AM, I₂, carton 1790,
sessions of June 21, July 12, 1790.
[32] BM, 4717, "Dénonciation faite à la municipalité de cette ville de
Marseille. Par la Dame Rose-Michel Reynoir" (Marseille, 1790); *ibid.*,

In all the Jacobin societies of France one committee, a sort of steering committee, customarily dominated and directed the others. These steering committees had various names—surveillance committee (*comité de surveillance*), committee of investigation (*comité des recherches*), central committee (*comité central*)—but all had certain characteristics in common. The Club of Marseilles formed its first committee of investigation in the summer of 1790. Initially, it consisted of six elected commissioners plus the president of the Club. By early 1792 the positions on this committee had become appointive, and it was generally known as the "discretionary committee" (*comité de prudence*).[33]

Whatever its name, it engaged in a wide range of activities. As an administrative organ, for instance, it regulated the work of the finance committee. It also came to the aid of citizens in distress, either by recommending benevolence or by intervening on their behalf with the authorities. It had secret informers in a number of towns of Provence, and with the weight of the Club behind it, arbitrated disputes outside the city. In April, 1792, after troubles had disturbed the tranquility of Roves, Gignac, and Ansouis, it forced the Directory of the department to send commissioners to "enlighten" that region.[34]

On May 29, 1792, three new committees, two for internal and one for external affairs, superseded the discretionary committee. The new committees for internal affairs normally concerned themselves with matters within the district of Mar-

---

"Pétition faite par les citoyennes à l'assemblée patriotique, le 23 juillet 1790, en faveur de Madame Cornet" (Marseille, 1790).

[33] "Règlemens . . . ," chapter 4, article 12.

[34] AD, B-du-Rh, L 2075, Petition of a servant to the discretionary committee; *ibid.*, To the central committee of la Ciotat, July, 1792; *JdD*, Apr. 24, 1792, p. 88.

seilles. Their interests were wide. On June 6, 1792, for example, one committee examined a report presented by the sculptor Renaud on the best means to maintain liberty in Marseilles. Between July 6 and 9, 1792 the other intervened successfully on the side of the "generous cultivators" and "laborious artisans" of la Ciotat in their dispute with the Municipality of that city.[35]

The papers of the committee for external affairs survive only in the form of correspondence with daughter societies in Provence. Indeed, many societies of the region, like Aubagne, formed external affairs commissions in emulation of the mother club of Marseilles. The Marseilles committee's contact with rural communes enabled it to intervene in a wide variety of situations, although not always without provoking reaction; its encroachments into the internal affairs of Pertuis (Vaucluse), for example, drew complaints from the club of that village.[36] A letter to the club of St.-Zacharie gives a good picture of the peremptory and arbitrary attitude it often assumed:

Several patriots, guilty of no other crime than of having worked too avidly for the safety of the Fatherland, have been arrested; diverse persons have been threatened. We will not allow them to remain victims of their patriotism. . . . Every quarrel must cease, and animosities must end. Give up your jealous interests and think only of the public good. Let the constitution be your goal; let liberty alone triumph, and save your persecuted and threatened brethren.[37]

[35] *JdD*, May 31, June 9, 1792, pp. 158, 174.
[36] AM, I₂, carton 1792, To the external affairs committee of the Club of Marseilles from the external affairs committee of Aubagne, June 23, 1792; AD, B-du-Rh, L 2075, The club of Pertuis to M. Fabre.
[37] AD, Var, series L, supplement.

On February 12, 1793, after months of debate, the Club formed a powerful new central committee to conduct its secret affairs and work "for the triumph of liberty in the southern departments." The antecedents of this committee can be traced to the midsummer crisis of 1792, when central committees appeared in many parts of France. A central committee of the societies of the Var was convened at Toulon, for example, on July 20, 1792, and endured for four months. As early as July 27, 1792, the society at Manosque (Basses-Alpes) proposed that such a body be established at Marseilles. As befitted the great power of the Marseillais, the Manosquains urged that its sphere of interest should include all the departments of the Midi.[38]

As finally constituted, the central committee in Marseilles contained twelve members. The Society later named twelve alternates, but otherwise its composition altered little. In the beginning François Galibert was the president; but soon Isoard assumed this position, and he and two or three henchmen dominated the committee. It met every day, and Isoard reported, in its name, to the assembly every three days. A permanent secretary managed correspondence and kept a journal of the meetings.[39]

After February 12, a network of central committees blossomed in Provence, all of them dependent on Marseilles. Brignoles (Var) formed one in March to ferret out "abuses and treasons," and similar bodies arose at Manosque and Digne in the Basses-Alpes. In the spring of 1793, countless letters

[38] On Toulon see Labroue, pp. 30–35; on Manosque, *JdD*, July 31, 1792, p. 261.

[39] *JdD*, Feb. 14 and 16, 1793, pp. 605, 607; AN, AF II 90, "A Mes Juges"; AD, B-du-Rh, L 3014.

flowed in to Isoard and his assistants. From Velaux, on March 20, 1793, came a denunciation of a citizen who had insulted the justice of the peace. A letter from Tarascon on March 26, 1793, complained of an aristocratic song heard in that region. Societies from outside Provence, such as Perpignan, supported the efforts of the committee to foil the Rolandists.[40]

After the reception of minor complaints, the committee usually wrote to the local popular society to demand action. For more serious problems it ordered commissioners of the Club to the troubled regions. If neither of these courses succeeded, it employed the legal authority of the departments. Inside Marseilles its enterprises ranged from the ridiculous to the tyrannical. On the one hand it came to the assistance of a man whose assignats had been eaten by rats. On the other it tended the defense of the city and terrorized those it deemed to be counterrevolutionary. The actions of the central committee in 1793 were a major cause of the Federalist rebellion that followed.

After the collapse of the Federalist rebellion a public surveillance committee came into existence in Marseilles, subject to the Revolutionary Government in Paris. The clubbists staffed it, but otherwise it was not an official component of the Society. Within the Club, the correspondence committee seems to have expanded to assume the other tasks of the steering committees. By September, 1794, it approved discourses

[40] AD, B-du-Rh, L 2075, The popular republican society of Brignoles to the central committee of Marseilles, Apr. 11, 1793; *ibid.*, L 3037, Isoard to the secret committee of Manosque; AD, Basses-Alpes, L 856/2. On Velaux, Tarascon, and Perpignan see AD, B-du-Rh, L 2071, sessions of Mar. 7, 20, and 26, 1793.

given at meetings by nonmembers, directed benevolent activities, denounced suspects, appointed committees, and oversaw the work of the official administrations of Marseilles.[41]

The Meeting Place

The clubbists met in an indoor tennis court constructed at the end of the seventeenth-century. Arches and trees of liberty ornamented the entranceway. Immediately within the doorway was a small foyer where officers examined cards and the membership tables were placed. In June, 1793, when the Federalists temporarily closed the Society, they found twenty-two great tablets here. A balustrade divided the central assembly hall into a main floor and gallery. Great torches and chandeliers provided illumination. In the center of the hall stood the rostrum, the president's chair, and a central desk where the Society kept important documents. On a large table rested an iron charity box. All around, the usual Jacobin adornments were to be seen. On the walls hung plaques from other societies, portraits of Revolutionary heroes, and such patriotic inscriptions as the ubiquitous "*Vivre libre ou mourir.*" Busts of Brutus, Voltaire, and Rousseau stood on pedestals. Tablets engraved with the Declaration of the Rights of Man were prominently displayed, along with blunderbusses, cannons, and swords, symbols perhaps of the military prowess of the Marseillais. Until 1793 the English flag flew alongside the tricolor and the banners of numerous battalions, corsairs, and clubs.[42]

Like other large societies, the Club of the Rue Thubaneau had reading rooms for the enlightenment of its members. In

[41] *Tribune de la société populaire,* no. XII, sessions of Sep. 8–14, 1794.

[42] AD, B-du-Rh, L 1980, Closing of the patriotic society.

June, 1793, there were seventeen tables for public papers. Evidently the Society had a problem with readers taking papers away, for on June 18, 1790, it resolved to chain them in place. The Club members had an extraordinarily wide variety of materials to peruse, including collections of decrees from Paris, the procès-verbaux of electoral assemblies, and patriotic essays, poems, and speeches.[43]

In purchasing newspapers, the Club performed an invaluable service for its members. In June, 1790, it subscribed to the following twelve: [44]

Prudhomme's *Révolutions de Paris*
Desmoulins' *Révolutions de France et de Brabant*
Carra's *Annales patriotiques*
L'Observateur marseillais
Garat's *Journal de Paris*
Mirabeau's *Courrier de Provence*
Le Moniteur
Le Journal de l'assemblée nationale
Gorsas' *Courrier des 83 départements*
Le Journal patriotique
Linguet's *Annales politiques*
Le Courrier d'Avignon

Some of these lost favor during the Revolution, and others took their place. Carra's *Annales patriotiques* became extremely popular, as were all the journals of "that excellent patriot" Camille Desmoulins. During 1792, Robespierre's *Défenseur de la constitution* was held in high favor. For a long time the Club refused to subscribe to Marat, but it changed its policy in the spring of 1793. As the editors of the *Journal*

[43] *Ibid.* See also AM, I₂, sessions of July 23, Aug. 1, 1790.
[44] AM, I₂, carton 1790.

des départements méridionaux remarked: "Time, which is the father of truth, has demonstrated . . . that the bloody reputation of Marat was more the effect of intrigue and slander than the manifestation of his own opinions." [45]

The former tennis court on the Rue Thubaneau remained the meeting place throughout the Revolution, but growing pains caused the Society to consider abandoning this location in the spring of 1792. On April 19 it petitioned the Municipality and the district of Marseilles to grant it the church of St.-Homebon as a new assembly place. The petition cited the need for increased space to accommodate the growing number of members. It pointed out that the rent for the old location had risen exorbitantly since 1790 and that the tennis court was relatively unprotected from the nefarious plots of the "aristocrats." Appeal was made, too, to the precedent set by other cities and the Society's own utility as a patriotic institution: "In nearly all the cities where clubs are established, the municipalities have accorded to the Societies the enjoyment of a national domain. The utility of the clubs is no longer in question; they are, one and all, props of the Constitution." [46] The Municipality meekly acquiesced in the Club's request, but ultimately the Club members themselves decided against moving. Perhaps they realized that the fame of the Rue Thubaneau had spread far beyond the confines of Marseilles.

Initially, the Marseilles Jacobins assembled at their meeting place twice a week, every Sunday and Thursday evening. However, their zealous patriotism soon forced alterations in this schedule. By July 8, 1790, they had begun holding daily sessions. Later, during periods of crisis (for example, July–September, 1792, March, 1793, and August, 1794), the Club

[45] *JdD*, Apr. 13, 1793, p. 703. [46] AM, I₂, carton 1792.

members assembled twice a day and committees were in permanent session.

In 1790 its meetings began at 6:00 P.M. in the summer and 5:00 P.M. in the winter, but times varied drastically in the years that followed. During the spring of 1792, for example, the assembly opened at 8:00 A.M. and 4:30 P.M. In the Terror the evening assemblies met at 7:00 and morning sessions at 10:00 or 11:00. In troubled times, night meetings sometimes extended beyond midnight. On many occasions extraordinary sessions were added to the regular schedule. The president summoned a meeting at 6:30 A.M. on August 5, 1794, so that all the latest news on the Robespierrist conspiracy could be heard. The Society held public assemblies on Sundays and holidays devoted to the instruction of the general populace. On these occasions anyone could "practice the sublime art of speaking" as long as he took his text from the Declaration of the Rights of Man or from the "good decrees" of the National Assembly.[47]

Regular sessions commenced with the ringing of a bell. At this sound the members were supposed to go directly to their seats, they could not loiter in other rooms, enter the central office or obstruct the aisles. During the Terror the president opened and closed every session with these acclamations.

Long live the Republic! Long live the Mountain! Long live the Popular Societies! Long live the law of the maximum and its entire execution. Long live the brave defenders of the Fatherland! Let conspirators and traitors perish! . . . Citizens, you are encouraged to study the French language.[48]

[47] AD, B-du-Rh, L 2076, "Procès-verbal de la séance du 17 thermidor an II" (Marseille, 1794). BM, 4717, "Réponse de Jean Blanchard" (Marseille, 1790).
[48] AD, B-du-Rh, L 2076, "Procès-verbal du 17 thermidor."

After the opening ceremonies secretaries read the minutes of the last session. The reporting of correspondence followed; since the Society of Marseilles received an immense volume of correspondence, its presentation sometimes consumed the whole session. Secretaries also read the debates of the National Assembly and articles in popular newspapers. Often citizens who had received interesting personal letters rose voluntarily to read them to the meeting. The correspondence committee printed or recopied important letters and sometimes composed responses. French was always the favored language of the sessions; during the Terror the Club actively discouraged the use of Provençal.

After correspondence and business, the clubbists proceeded to the day's agenda. According to the rules, questions adjourned at preceding sessions had first priority for debate. The issues ranged over a wide spectrum. In April, 1794, for example, one of the topics debated concerned "the necessity of instructing the people on days of the decade." On March 2, 1793, the question at issue was whether the Bourbon family should be exiled, imprisoned, or put to death.[49] After the adjournment of the issue of the day, new members took the oath, and secretaries read the names of candidates and the preliminary minutes of the session. Often the meetings terminated with the singing of a hymn such as the Marseillaise.

Meetings were frequently interrupted by the arrival of deputations. Sometimes so many visitors entered the hall that no business could be conducted. These deputations can be divided for convenience into three main types. Some groups came merely to profess their support for the Club and for liberty. School children and their teachers, for example, were

[49] *Ibid.*, L 2076, *Tribune populaire*, Apr. 20, 1794; *ibid.*, L 2071, session of Mar. 2, 1793.

a frequent sight at the assemblies. The masters vowed to instruct their charges "in the love of the fatherland and the hatred of slavery and tyrants"; and the pupils themselves gave grandiloquent discourses. At the session of April 2, 1792, students drew an analogy between themselves and David: "David killed the giant Goliath with a slingshot and, thus, punished his insolent temerity. Our arms . . . too weak to bear the weight of arms can at least throw stones at traitors." [50]

Numerous delegations of soldiers, national guardsmen, and sailors appeared at the Society. Their visits all followed essentially the same pattern. The squadron entered the hall with drums beating. The commander ascended the rostrum, praised the patriotism of the Club, and vowed in the name of his men to live free or to die. The soldiers presented pennants or captured standards to the president, who replied with a speech praising the valor of the visitors. After this ritual servicemen and Jacobins embraced. Then the men left the hall as they had come, drums beating.[51]

A third category of visitors was the "V.I.P." Important personages rarely passed through the city without paying their respects to a club "so justly celebrated in all of France." General Paoli's visit on July 8, 1790, is typical. Selected commissioners conducted the General and his followers from their hotel to the hall. The president and a secretary formally greeted the distinguished Corsican, and he replied with a flowery speech of his own. The members then resolved to inscribe the names of Paoli and all his followers on the register of membership and to erect a marble plaque to celebrate the occasion. After an exchange of patriotic oaths, com-

[50] *JdD*, Apr. 5, 1792, p. 55.
[51] See AD, B-du-Rh, L 2071, session of Mar. 4, 1793; *ibid.*, L 2076, *Tribune populaire*, Apr. 14-19, 1794.

missioners escorted the General's party, with pomp and circumstance, back to their hotel.[52]

Spectacle and Propaganda

It would be a mistake to assume that the Jacobins of Marseilles never met outside the assembly hall. They were acutely aware of the importance of indoctrinating the ordinary citizens, and in the course of the Revolution sponsored scores of outdoor meetings, theatrical productions, public festivals, and parades. On April 27, 1790, barely two weeks after its birth, the Society organized a great public banquet for the National Guard. At the fête to commemorate the fall of the Bastille on July 14, 1791, it opened its assembly hall to the public as a gathering place and refreshment center. In December, 1791, it coordinated a brilliant ceremony to "unite" the French and English flags. At least seven units marched in a parade of May 2, 1792, organized to place a tablet inscribed with the Declaration of the Rights of Man in the bourse. In June an especially extravagant rite took place when the Club members planted a tree of liberty donated by the popular society of Mazargues. All the local officials, the constitutional clergy, and a large crowd of citizens witnessed the ceremony. Afterwards, a mammoth crowd chanted songs and snake-danced through the streets.[53]

During the Terror, the Club served as the official partner of the Municipality in organizing the festivals held every

[52] AM, I₂, carton 1790.

[53] On the fête of the federation see AM, 4 D₁, Letter of July 16, 1791. For the celebration of December 1791 see BN, Lb⁴⁰ 2773, "Relation de la fête de l'alliance des pavillons nationaux anglais et français (Marseille, 1791); AM, 1 D₉, session of Dec. 16, 1791. For the parade of May 2 see *JdD*, May 5, 1792, p. 111. On the tree of liberty see *JdD*, July 2, 1792, p. 214.

tenth day. It prepared the programs, canvassed its membership for artistic talent, and designated the people to take part
in these extravaganzas. At the fête of January 9, 1794, the
Club provided three contingents of members:

One hundred workers from various professions equipped with
their tools.
One hundred citizens clothed in white and wearing tricolor
sashes.
And all the old men who were members.

It also invited the victorious heroes of the siege of Toulon.
When the great day arrived, everything went perfectly. A
grand parade terminated at the Club, where Isoard, then president, harangued the participants and presented laurel crowns
to Dugommier and Lapoype, the two commanding officers at
Toulon.[54]

Spectacles of this nature attracted large crowds. They
offered an alternative to the usual pleasures of the promenade,
bowls, and café gossip, and the Club extracted the maximum
propaganda value from them. It organized a festival on April
29, 1794, for example, to dramatize the importance of the
requisition of saltpeter. The saltpeter makers carried in procession that day a block of saltpeter in the form of a mountain
topped by the head of Marat. The same evening the chief of
the saltpeter works in Marseilles came to speak at the Club.
After praising the Marseillais for their work in obtaining this
valuable substance, he concluded:

Citizens, while our brave brothers face the fatigues and dangers
of war, while they cross mountains, ascend cliffs . . . to give
liberty to peoples . . . we descend to the depths of the earth to

[54] AM, 4 D₇, To the president of the Society, Jan. 2, 4, 1794;
Journal républicain, Jan. 9, 1794, pp. 382, 386, 393–394.

tear away the powder that in their hands will finally avenge the men who are the slaves of kings.[55]

Such investment in celebration and spectacle undoubtedly brought great returns for the Jacobin movement. It represented only one part, however, of the Club's propaganda machine. The Society of the Rue Thubaneau was the nerve center of Jacobin publishing in the Midi. With its own press by 1792, it produced a torrent of printed propaganda. Wherever records of popular societies have survived, the Club's publications can still be found. The societies of Montpellier and Poitiers, to cite two examples, received dozens of circulars from the Club. In Provence, the Jacobins of Marseilles were in a position to insure their publications the widest possible dissemination. When the members voted to print a speech, such as the *Eveil aux français* of May 25, 1792, they sent instructions to affiliates to post it at strategic points in their communes and to propagate its "excellent principles in the countryside and neighboring villages." [56]

The publications of the Society may be divided into several categories. The first and most common type, the placard or poster, publicized forthcoming events and instructed the citizenry on important issues. The *Avis aux citoyens, amis de la liberté* (August, 1792), for example, counselled the Marseillais to elect only good clubbists as deputies to the Convention.[57] A second was the circular letter, a statement of policy drafted by a group of Club members with a preface by the correspondence committee appealing for approval from the affiliates.[58]

[55] AD, B-du-Rh, L 2076.

[56] AD, Hérault, L 5543; BM, Poitiers, S 15, S 22, S 26; AD, Var, series L, St.-Zacharie; *JdD*, May 29, 1792, pp. 155–156.

[57] AD, B-du-Rh, L 2076.

[58] For a sample of such a letter see *ibid.*, L 2065, "Les Républicains de Marseille à la Convention nationale" (Marseille, 1793).

A third type, the brochure or pamphlet, was normally the work of an individual who had secured the sponsorship of the Club for its publication and distribution. The *Préservatif contre le fanatisme* (1792), a dialogue between a peasant and the schoolmaster of a Provençal hamlet, is a typical example. In this pamphlet the author, the Abbé Aubanel, defended the reform of the clergy, "replied to all the arguments of the refractory priests," and elucidated such clerical "abuses" as the tithe and indulgences. The Society invited neighboring clubs to purchase this pamphlet (at a cost of 10 sous) and to instruct their members.[59]

Newspapers were the major carriers of Club propaganda. The Society of Marseilles, or its members, printed half a dozen gazettes between 1790 and 1794. Only one, however, the *Journal des départements méridionaux et des débats des amis de la constitution de Marseille* is widely known among Revolutionary scholars.[60] Copies of the others have been either destroyed or widely dispersed. The *Observateur marseillais*, for example, the most important Jacobin newspaper in

[59] *JdD*, Sept. 25, 1792, p. 362. Antoine Aubanel was born at Vence (Var) about the year 1753. He was a master of fine arts (*maître-ez-arts*) in April, 1790, when he joined the Club.

[60] J.-A. Bernard, "Les Journaux de Marseille pendant la Révolution de 1790 à 1797," *La Révolution française*, XXXVIII (1900), 161–166, the lone article purporting to examine the Revolutionary press in Marseilles, is largely devoted to the *Journal de Provence* (*Journal de Marseille* after 1792). Bernard makes a fleeting reference to the *Tribune populaire* (see below) and disposes of the *Journal des départements méridionaux* in a few lines. More recently, René Gerard, *Un Journal de Province sous la révolution; Le Journal de Ferréol Beaugeard 1781–1797* (Paris, 1964), has analyzed the *Journal de Provence* in depth. André Martin and Gérard Walter list the holdings of Marseilles newspapers found in the Bibliothèque Nationale in their *Catalogue de l'histoire de la Révolution française: Ecrits de la période révolutionnaire: Almanachs et journaux* (Paris, 1943), vol. V.

Marseilles prior to 1792, narrowly escaped extinction. Fifty-
one issues saw the light of day between May 16 and August
18, 1790; today, although fortunately the Bibiothèque Nationale has a complete holding, only the prospectus survives
in public collections in Marseilles itself.[61]

The *Observateur* was the successor to two earlier newspapers, the *Annales patriotiques de Marseille* and the *Courier
de Marseille.*[62] It appeared regularly, four times a week. Unlike later gazettes it was never the official mouthpiece of the
Society, nor was it subsidized or distributed by the members.
Though it reported some of the Society's meetings, the
greater part of its four quarto pages was devoted to political
affairs in Marseilles. A regular column discussed events in the
Midi, and a correspondent in Martinique provided colonial
news. Still another feature analyzed political trends in Vienna,
Turin, and London; and letters arrived periodically from such
French cities as Carpentras, Grenoble, Strasbourg, and Lille.
The prospectus consecrated the *Observateur* "to the defense
of liberty," but it did not neglect culture and the arts; a
supplement entitled *Littérature et beaux arts* regularly reviewed books and theatrical productions.

Of all the gazettes written by members of the Club, the
Observateur had by far the most sophisticated and lucid style.
It was edited by three clever young graduates of the Collège
de l'Oratoire, Barbaroux, Brémond-Jullien, and a self-styled

[61] See BN, Lc[11] 635 (95). Alfred-Chabaud, editor of the *Mémoires*
and correspondence of Barbaroux, never cites it as a source.

[62] The *Annales*, fourteen pages, octavo, appeared twice weekly
beginning February 17, 1790. Financial problems halted its publication
after issue number ten in early April, 1790 (BM, Toulon, 19665; BN,
Lc[11] 635 93). Shortly thereafter a "society of amateurs" began publishing the *Courier de Marseille* in cooperation with the editors of its
defunct predecessor. Six numbers appeared irregularly between
April 18 and May 12. The editors of the *Courier* belonged to the Club
and spoke of it as "our patriotic assembly" (BN, Lc[11] 635 94).

poet, Joseph-Alphonse Esménard. Barbaroux claimed credit for the idea of founding the new journal, but Brémond-Jullien's influence over policy exceeded his own. Initially, the trio took joint responsibility for the contents. By the end of June, 1790, however, a growing "diversity of opinions" had compelled Barbaroux to request the privilege of signing his contributions. The struggle for political supremacy in Marseilles between the Club and the commandant of the National Guard, Jean-François Lieutaud, occasioned the dispute between Barbaroux and his two colleagues. Brémond-Jullien and Esmémard championed the commandant and Barbaroux the Club. On July 29, 1790, Jean Beissière denounced Brémond-Jullien and Esménard before the Society; and after the fiftieth issue (August 14) Barbaroux, who had resigned from the *Observateur* in the meantime, likewise condemned it. The last number is dated August 18, 1790, the day after a Lieutaudist mob unsuccessfully attempted to close the Society.[63]

A journalistic drought of eighteen months followed the demise of the *Observateur*. In the spring of 1792, however, three new Jacobin sheets hit the presses, the *Mercure de Marseille*, the *Manuel du laboureur et de l'artisan*, and the *Journal des départements méridionaux*. Of the first, an ephemeral biweekly brochure, no copies have survived; nor do we possess the name of its author. All we know is that it furnished political news, literary criticism, and mercantile reports; that subscribers paid their bills to the concierge of the Club; and that its avowed goal was "to give the last bludgeon stroke to the cruel despotism that has devoured us so long." [64]

Jacques Monbrion, a little known but highly productive

---

[63] *L'Observateur marseillais*, pp. 121–122, 136. AM, I₂, ⌐ᵣton 1790, session of July 29–30, 1790. Barbaroux, *Mémoires*, p. 284.

[64] BM, 4717, "Prospectus, Mercure de Marseille."

Jacobin propagandist, edited the *Manuel du laboureur*. Born at Lourmarin (Vaucluse) in 1765, Monbrion settled in Marseilles in 1787. As a sergeant of the National Guard, he was one of the fifty patriotic Marseillais who seized Fort Notre-Dame-de-la-Garde on April 30, 1790. In May, 1791, he began to correspond with the Cordeliers in Paris, and by the spring of 1792 he was a ubiquitous "missionary of patriotism" in southeastern France, founding clubs at Pertuis (Vaucluse), Auriol (Bouches-du-Rhône), St.-Zacharie (Var), and elsewhere. In July, 1792, he recruited volunteers in the Vaucluse for the Marseilles battalion en route to Paris. He served as an agent of the Committee of Public Safety in the Var in the fall of 1793, and shortly thereafter left for the Hautes-Alpes to stimulate patriotism in that department.[65]

The publications of Monbrion, like most Jacobin writings, abounded in sermonizing and platitudes. Philosophically, they owed much to contemporary propagandists in Paris. An anti-Lieutaudist publication of 1791 entitled *Crimes de lèse-nation*, typifies his early works. In it he advocated the construction of gallows on the squares of all the great cities on which to hang the aristocrats. In 1792, as part of the antimonarchical campaign instituted by the Club, he wrote an *Adresse au Peuple, et aux défenseurs des droits de l'homme, . . . les amis de la constitution*. He read this twenty-three page bro-

---

[65] BM, 5136, "Adresse à l'auguste assemblée nationale, par les 50 citoyens qui se sont emparés . . . du Fort Notre-Dame de la Garde" (Marseille, 1790). For his letter to the Cordeliers see P.-J.-B. Buchez and P.-C. Roux, *Histoire parlementaire de la Révolution française*, (Paris, 1834–1838), X, 145. On his activities in 1793 see *Archives parlementaires*, LXXV, 249, LXXVI, 600. Apparently Monbrion returned to his ancestral home after the fall of the Club. The registers in Lourmarin indicate that a daughter, Marie, was born to him in 1796.

chure on his missions to neighboring societies. It called in
thinly veiled terms for a republic.[66]

Monbrion conceived the idea for the *Manuel du laboureur*
in early April, 1792. Whether the Society provided funds for
its publication is in doubt, but the members did agree to aid
in propagating it in the countryside. When Isoard founded
a society at Riez (Basses-Alpes) on May 14, he read a copy
of the prospectus at the initial meeting, and those assembled
voted to subscribe.[67] On June 4, the correspondence committee dispatched a letter to all the affiliates, saying:

The Society sends to you the first copy of a newspaper proper
for developing patriotic sentiments in persons of every age and
sex; if you feel, as we do, the need to enlighten the people, we
do not doubt that you will quickly subscribe to it, and recom-
mend it to the constitutional priests and the new educators.[68]

Largely owing to the Club's influence, the *Manuel* had a
fairly wide circulation in the departments of southeastern
France. The Antipolitiques of Aix read and discussed it in their
sessions. The clubbists of Buis (Drôme), pleased with its
"simple and instructive style," voted to purchase it and disseminate it among the people who had been "deceived for
too long a time," while the members of the Society of Valerne
(Basses-Alpes) lauded it as a work "truly worthy of our
brothers from Marseilles." Subscriptions were also entered by
clubs such as St.-Zacharie and Toulon in the Var.[69]

The *Manuel* appeared weekly. The first issue is dated June
6, 1792. The last issue of which this writer has knowledge

[66] BM, 4717. AD, Var, St.-Zacharie.

[67] *JdD*, Apr., 1792, p. 56. AD, Basses-Alpes, L 856/1.

[68] AD, B-du-Rh, L 2038.

[69] *Ibid.*, L 2027, L 2075; AD, Basses-Alpes, L 861; AD, Var, St.-
Zacharie.

was number twelve of mid-August; the Antipolitiques of Aix read a copy in their meeting of August 24, 1792.[70] Its avowed purpose was to instruct the people rather than to print news. "I undertook this work," said Monbrion in his prospectus, "believing that if men were in disagreement, it was primarily due to their lack of instruction." In his editorials he spoke as a primary teacher does to his pupils. The *Manuel*'s most popular feature was the weekly "conversation." The star of these dialogues was a fictional rustic sage named Anselme who loved to mingle among the peasants and explain "the fundamental points of the constitution." The conversations usually degenerated into attacks on Louis XVI. An explanation of the separation of powers led to this exchange:

Laborer: What do you mean by the powers?
Anselme: When I refer to the powers, I mean the legislative corps and the executive. . . . The King has the duty of executing the laws and decrees of the national assembly; this is why we call him the executive power. It is for this reason that we give him thirty million a year. . . .
Laborer: Why are you angry about giving him this revenue?
Anselme: Because we suspect him of having used part of it to support the enemies of the constitution.
Laborer: Thirty million and a bad king! [71]

The same antimonarchical zeal was also present in the *Journal des départements méridionaux*, but this newspaper was much more weighty and long-lived than the *Manuel*. One hundred and eighty-four issues (of four quarto pages) appeared triweekly from March 6, 1792, too May 7, 1793.

[70] Copies of the *Manuel* exist now, to this writer's knowledge, only in the AM, Toulon, L 56. On the Antipolitiques see AD, B-du-Rh, L 2027.
[71] *Manuel*, June 6, 1792, p. 6.

Purchasers paid their dues to the correspondence committee. At the outset three militant members of the Club, Joseph Giraud, Pierre Micoulin, and Alexandre Ricord, edited the *Journal*. Giraud ceased to be an editor after May 29, 1792, and thereafter, Ricord was the principal contributor until he went to Paris in January, 1793. Stylistically, the *Journal* fell far short of the *Observateur*, but the editors disavowed eloquence: "The austere truth presides over all our works, and the truth has no need of ornamentation." [72]

It is difficult to establish just how widely the *Journal* was distributed. The Club sent a prospectus to most of its affiliates in France. From the beginning many of the societies of Provence read it, and outside Provence clubs subscribed as far away as Montauban (Lot).[73] On April 9, 1793, the Society took over its distribution and increased its circulation substantially. Thereafter, it sent each issue to affiliates without charge. One way to gauge the impact of the *Journal* is to read the voluminous correspondence sent to it by the popular societies of Provence. Rural clubs found it an excellent means of obtaining information and of publicizing their activities. Now it is an invaluable source of information on the Jacobin movement in southeastern France.

The *Journal* had a standard format. The first two pages summarized recent sessions of the Society, though unfortunately the reporting of debates was extremely superficial. Readers often complained of errors in dates and names, and the editors glorified the role of themselves and their friends. On one occasion, April 23, 1792, the Club expressly disclaimed any responsibility for the authenticity of the

[72] BM, 1716–1717; BN, Lc[11] 635 (71); *JdD*, Mar. 6, 1792, p. 1.
[73] BM, Poitiers, S 26; AD, Hérault, L 5543; AD, Tarn-et-Garonne, L 403 supplement.

Journal's summaries. News reports customarily followed the debates. In addition, short poems were sometimes published and books and plays reviewed. Initially, the editors judged plays on their artistic merits, but soon morality and patriotism became the sole criteria of literary excellence.

The *Journal des départements méridionaux* died in May, 1793, during the Federalist rebellion. On October 1, 1793, a new *Journal républicain de Marseille et des départements méridionaux*, founded and operated under the orders of the representatives-on-mission in Marseilles, took its place. Sixty-two numbers of the *Journal républicain* (eight octavo pages) were issued before it ceased publication on February 8, 1794.[74] Although Alexandre Ricord collaborated in its publication until October 20, 1793, the principal editors were two Parisians, Sébastien Lacroix and Pierre Mittié.

Yet another new, and this time official, Club newspaper appeared in late April, 1794. The society of Mirabel-les-Baronnies (Drôme) received a prospectus on May 2. The lineal successor to the *Journal républicain*, the *Tribune de la Société populaire de Marseille* guaranteed authenticity as a "journal drafted in the name and under the observation of the Society." [75] In terms of content it amounted to little more than the printed minutes of the Society's debates. Responsibility for the contents rested with the secretaries. In length it averaged sixteen octavo pages. The Society probably published the *Tribune* every seven days, though it is difficult to be sure because of bewildering irregularities in numbering. It is similarly impossible to measure its distribution in France. The administrative authorities of the Bouches-du-Rhône appar-

[74] AD, B-du-Rh, L 1210 bis; BN, Lc[11] 635 (57).
[75] AD, Drôme, L 1100; only one number and scattered extracts survive today; see BN, Lc[11] 635 (72); AD, B-du-Rh, L 2076.

ently thought its audience was substantial since they placed notices and advertisements in its pages.[76] Philosophically, the *Tribune* was dogmatically Montagnard. For this reason it probably died with the arrest of the Society's leaders in September, 1794.

Printing presses and newspapers were not unique to the Jacobin Society of Marseilles. A few of the larger provincial clubs likewise published brochures and newspapers. What was unusual about Marseilles was the vast output of printed material. The Marseillais left no stone unturned in their efforts to indoctrinate the populace. All subscribed in principle to the motto of the *Journal:* "Men of every country, whatever your opinions, listen!"

[76] AD, B-du-Rh, L 129, To the editor of the journal of the Society, Apr. 24, 1794.

4

The Rise to Political Power

During the thirty-three months from April 11, 1790, to the execution of the king on January 21, 1793, the Club of the Rue Thubaneau rose from an obscure, provincial organization to a national political power. The infant society gave notice of its coming importance scarcely one month after its birth when it set off a severe local emergency. The shock waves were felt as far away as the capital. Underlying this crisis was an issue that had plagued Marseilles since February, 1790: whether the regular army or the National Guard should police the city. The Marquis de Miran and the minister of the interior, St.-Priest, supported the former, the Municipality and the Club the latter. As a compromise the National Assembly ordered the departure of two royal companies in mid-April, 1790, but left the Swiss regiments of Ernest and Vexin garrisoned in the city. The Vexin regiment, commanded by aristocratic officers, guarded the three principal forts of Marseilles, Notre-Dame-de-la-Garde, St.-Nicolas, and St.-Jean. For several weeks the Marseillais watched anxiously as quantities of provisions poured into the fortresses. In the cafés, dark rumors circulated of aristocratic plots to admit foreign troops by sea. Some way had to be found, the patriots felt, to neutralize these menacing citadels.

Throughout April, 1790, activists in the fledgling Club demanded that the fortresses be captured and demolished. Later, on May 5, 1790, the *Courier de Marseille* proudly boasted: "Our Patriotic Assembly composed of more than 4,000 citizens, had often resounded with these words, *delenda est Carthago*. The enterprise was perilous but we saw no other alternative to death or slavery." [1] In a letter to his brother dated April 27, 1790, Major de Beausset, an officer at Fort St.-Jean, voiced his concern over the Society's actions:

The Club National which assembles here at the tennis court and which is composed of all the scum of the city, has passed a motion calling for the National Guard to protect the forts jointly with the troops of the King. The motion was placed before the district assemblies. Approval is certain. The same people who compose the Club dominate the district meetings as well. [2]

The major's apprehension was well-founded. A conspiracy was afoot to seize the key fortress, Notre-Dame-de-la-Garde, which stood on the crest of a rocky hill, 520 feet above sea level. The plan, devised by Nicolas Doinet, Pierre Garnier, Jacques Monbrion, Louis Chaix, and Jean-Nicolas Brard, [3] members both of the twenty-first National Guard battalion and of the Club, had all the excitement and melodrama of a Hollywood scenario. During the night of April 29–30, 1790, fifty men stationed themselves at strategic points in the rocks

[1] BM, 4717, "Discours prononcé dans la salle des amis de la constitution par M. Maillet cadet, président" (Marseille, 1791). *Courier de Marseille*, May 5, 1790, p. 27.

[2] AN, F[7] 3659[1].

[3] Doinet, a mechanic, came from Reims (Champagne) and moved to Marseilles in 1776. The first reference to him in the Club's records appears in the minutes of June 13, 1790. Garnier, a mason, was born in Marseilles. He later served as an officer of the battalion of August 10. For a biographical sketch of Monbrion see Chapter 3.

around the fort. When the drawbridge was lowered at day-
break, two of the band, Alexandre Renaud and Jacques
Feissole, pretending to go to mass in the chapel, suddenly
overpowered the lone sentry on duty. The remainder of the
hidden band then entered the fort and disarmed the sleeping
soldiers. Marseilles woke to see the pennant of the twenty-
first battalion waving above the citadel.[4]

On April 30, battalions of national guardsmen and volunteers from neighboring towns hastily assembled to make an
assault on the other forts. Only the diligence of the Municipality and the sympathy of the common soldiers of the Vexin
regiment for the populace prevented bloodshed. The officers
of St.-Jean and St.-Nicolas, uncertain of their men, permitted
the national guardsmen to enter. In less than twenty-four
hours the "Bastilles of Marseilles" had fallen; and the confisca-
tion of 3,000 rifles at Fort St.-Nicolas further augmented the
might of the National Guard. Only one violent incident
marred the bloodless victory. On May 2, a crowd murdered
the haughty Beausset and paraded his head around the city on
a pike. The Club helped avert further reprisals on May 3;
when the Swiss soldiers of the Vexin regiment left their bar-
racks to celebrate with the citizens, they were harangued at
the Club by Brémond-Jullien and returned to their quarters
peacefully.[5]

In Paris, at the National Assembly on May 13, D'André
and St.-Priest lashed out at the Municipality and the "vaga-

[4] See P. Gaffarel, "La Prise des bastilles marseillaises," *La Révolution
française*, LXXII (1919), 314–325; Lourde, I, 249 ff.; *Journal de Provence*, May 4, 1790, pp. 3–8; *Courier de Marseille*, May 5, 1790, pp. 27–
40. The *Courier* boasted that the plan had been formulated behind
the Club's doors.
[5] *Ibid;* see also BN, Lb39 8730, "Evénement terrible arrivé à Marseille" (Paris, 1790).

bonds" who had captured Notre-Dame-de-la-Garde. A royal order countersigned by St.-Priest and written "in the style of the Ottoman viziers" arrived in Marseilles on May 17, demanding the surrender of the forts to the Swiss regiment of Ernest and castigating the "excesses" of the Marseillais. The Municipality replied by denouncing St.-Priest and dispatching Brémond-Jullien and Leroy d'Ambleville [6] to Paris to speak for the city. When the Club received the news of St.-Priest's letter, it sent sixty workmen on the night of May 17-18 to demolish the walls of Fort St.-Nicolas and Fort St.-Jean. The Municipality, learning belatedly of this step, managed to limit the demolition to those walls fronting on to the city.[7] On May 18, the Society started a patriotic campaign to pay the wages of the workmen involved. An anonymous correspondent of the ministry of the interior charged the "despotic club" with forcing the citizens to contribute; but on the whole the campaign was extremely popular and successful, raising 16,574 livres from sources as widely divergent as the shoemakers' guild, the Chamber of Commerce, and the bishop of Marseilles.[8]

In Paris the dismantling of the forts further roused the ire of D'André's party, but the intervention of Mirabeau saved

[6] Ambroise Leroy D'Ambleville, a barrister, was born about 1744. During the Revolution he held several offices in the Society including the vice-presidency in November–December, 1792. He was executed as a Federalist during the Terror.

[7] *L'Observateur marseillais*, May 20, 1790, pp. 9–10. *Réimpression de l'ancien Moniteur*, III, no. 133, 349–352, V, no. 150, 490–491; BM, 5220, "Discours prononcé à l'assemblée patriotique . . . par Maillet aîné" (Marseille, 1790); AM, 1 D₁, pp. 83–88.

[8] CC, I₇₀, To the deputies of the Chamber of Commerce of Marseilles; BM, 4717, "Etat et recette général des dons faits à l'Assemblée patriotique," *L'Observateur marseillais*, nos. 7, 9–11 (May 27–June 3, 1790); AN, F⁷ 3659¹.

Marseilles from punitive measures, and the question of the forts ultimately died in the committee of reports.[9] In Marseilles the Club's enemies accused it before the Municipality of "the intention of usurping legitimate authority." In reply the Society sent a deputation of six members, headed by Charles Barbaroux, to the municipal council-general on May 28, to restate its "true principles":

We vow, Gentlemen, to obey you, and to aid you with all our strength in maintaining public tranquility. . . . How can it be said that the Patriotic Assembly seeks to withdraw itself from your authority . . . ? Your empire is one of virtue and your power has brought only benefits.[10]

After this early success, the Society's strength multiplied, despite the exodus of many of the founders, who were disillusioned by the radicalism of May. Typical of the Club's increasing confidence in the summer of 1790 was the interest it took in the troubled affairs of Nîmes. Long-smouldering religious and political hatreds rent the capital of the Gard. At one pole stood a clerical-aristocratic party buttressed by its own armed troop, functioning independently of the National Guard. On the other extreme was a patriotic, anticlerical faction led by Nîmes' Club of Friends of the Constitution. Mutual antipathy culminated on June 13 in an armed attack on the latter by the aristocrats. In the next two days the patriots defeated their enemies, with the aid of volunteers from neighboring towns, but then abused their victory by executing some "aristocrats" and "fanatics" and by sacking monasteries and convents.[11]

[9] *Moniteur*, IV, no. 149, 483.

[10] *L'Observateur marseillais*, June 1, 3, 1790, pp. 38, 41–42; AM, 1D₁, session of May 28, 1790.

[11] Professor James Hood of Tulane University is preparing a book on this incident.

As early as May 9, the Club of Marseilles had received a letter from the Friends of the Constitution in Nîmes reporting troubles caused by "presbyterians." On May 10, at 1:00 a.m., Brémond-Jullien and one Roustan departed on the orders of the Club to offer assistance to the patriotic citizens of Nîmes. In a published address the Society vowed to defend the Nîmois to the death against the "fanatics and counterrevolutionaries." For its part, the Municipality authorized the Club to organize a confederation of the National Guards of Marseilles and the rest of Provence.[12]

The news of the mid-June troubles arrived too late for the Club to render military aid. Instead, on June 18, Barbaroux proposed sending fifty wagon loads of wheat, in care of the Jacobin Club of Nîmes, to nourish "the hungry victims of patriotism." An address of June 20, the day after the grain was dispatched, begged forgiveness for the "weak tribute when we owe our blood"; should the "fanatics," like hydras, grow new heads, however, the Club demanded that a special courier be sent to inform them. The Jacobins of Nîmes acknowledged their gratitude to their "brothers" in Marseilles with a flood of correspondence, both public and private. In the session of August 8, a special deputation publicly thanked the Marseillais for their generosity and support.[13]

At Marseilles the Society channelled its energies into a

[12] On the mission of May 10, see *Courier de Marseille*, May 12, 1790, p. 47; *L'Observateur marseillais*, May 18, 1790, pp. 6–8; *Moniteur*, IV, no. 133, 346. The "Adresse . . . au régiment de Guienne" is contained in BN, Lk² 3712 (32). A description of the "confederation" exists in BM, 4717, "La Prédiction accomplie: Adresse aux Marseillais par Sans-Souci" (Marseille, 1790).

[13] AM, I₂, carton 1790. *Journal de Provence*, June 26, 1790, pp. 183–184. *L'Observateur marseillais*, June 22, 1790, pp. 85–86, and June 26, 1790, p. 96. *Moniteur*, V, no. 187, 45. BM, 4717, "Discours de MM. les députés du club à Nîmes, prononcé à l'assemblée patriotique" (Marseille, 1790).

wide range of enterprises. It manifested great interest in the election of the first administrators of the district of Marseilles in early July. It was not yet strong enough simply to name the officers itself, as it would do later, but it did send numerous petitions and deputations to the electoral assembly. On July 12, 1790, those elected attended that day's meeting of the Club to thank the Society for its support. The Society also stepped up its surveillance of suspected counterrevolutionaries and others it deemed to be enemies. When French nationals were expelled from the Kingdom of the Two Sicilies, some members demanded the arrest of the Neapolitan consul in Marseilles. On August 3, 1790, the so-called plots and maneuvers of D'André and ministers "leagued with the tyrants" caused the Club to adopt a series of emergency measures proposed by Barbaroux. Delegations of clubbists consulted with the Municipality, the commandant of the National Guard, the officials of the merchant marine, the commander of the Château d'If, and the soldiers of the regiment of Vexin. The Society also formed a special committee to oversee defense preparations and sent commissioners to confer with the patriots of Toulon on problems of regional defense.[14]

The Club's fundamental problem in 1790 was its mortal struggle with Jean-François Lieutaud, the commandant of the National Guard in Marseilles. This episode must be regarded as a watershed in the Club's short political history. Control over the city's powerful National Guard was the central issue, but economic and social discontent, caused by a slackening in commercial activity and rising unemployment, provided a

[14] AM, I₂, carton 1790; AD, B-du-Rh, L 1021. BM, 4717, 'Lettre de M. Barbaroux, en réponse à celle de M. Esménard" (Marseille, 1790). *Ibid.*, "Motion de M. Barbaroux, avocat" (Marseille, 1790).

significant backdrop. The propaganda of both sides exacerbated class tensions; the Club depicted Lieutaud as an agent of the rich, while the Lieutaudists berated the Club for destroying Marseilles' commerce. The importance of Marseilles insured that the struggle had national repercussions. D'André and the ministers supported the Lieutaudists. The affair caused much embarrassment to Mirabeau, for Lieutaud had earlier been his friend and disciple. It also sired serious divisions within the Society, and many early militants resigned over the issue.

The Club had a powerful ally in the Municipality. Despite the disagreement of May over the demolition of the forts, amicable relations remained the norm. Many municipal officers were also members of the Society. Some, like Etienne Martin, tried to straddle the fence when the crisis came, but only a few took the side of the commandant. They probably did not realize that the Club of the Rue Thubaneau represented, potentially, a greater threat to their authority than did Lieutaud. Indeed, the self-confidence of the municipal officials is revealed by two letters sent to the commune of Brignoles (Var) concerning the formation of a popular society there:

The assembly that is formed in your city with the title of patriotic club can only exist with the authorization of the municipality. It must be forbidden to interfere in the affairs of the commune. . . .

We have one at Marseilles that is truly patriotic; its statutes, regulations, and deliberations are submitted for our inspection and to our censure. We enjoin it to respect the decrees and operations of the elected administrations; these should never be the object of its deliberations and examinations.

If it defied our authority, we would dissolve it.[15]

[15] AM, BB 293, Letters of Aug. 7, Oct. 7, 1790.

Lieutaud himself was born in Marseilles in 1754, the son of a rich hardware merchant. Lourde contends that he practiced no profession but was an educated man with superior intelligence. Almost everyone concurs on his vices, one of which was his addiction to gambling. Lieutaud had been a patriotic activist since the riots of March, 1789. He helped to organize the first civic guard, and, along with five other patriots, fled to Paris when it was dissolved. His exile earned him election to the first Municipality in January, 1790. He became chief of the Guard on May 3, 1790, after the original commandant, the Chevalier de Greling, resigned.[16]

As commandant, Lieutaud proved arrogant and imperious. Without authorization from the Municipality he created a military council and began to issue illegal decrees and proclamations. Through six handpicked aides-de-camp he administered the National Guard despotically. By mid-June, complaints about the would-be czar had become profuse. On June 22, François-Trophime Rébecquy openly castigated Lieutaud at the municipal council.[17] When the deputation to the fête of the federation in Paris, headed by Lieutaud, returned to Marseilles on August 10, 1790, a petty incident took place which further strained relations. The city's officials refused to break protocol and descend the steps of city hall to welcome the deputation, so the commandant haughtily marched the group away.[18]

Within the Club discontent surfaced slowly. Until the end

[16] Lourde, I, 267. AN, DXXIX bis 28.

[17] AM, BB 293, Letter to Mirabeau, Sep. 8, 1790; *L'Observateur marseillais*, June 24, 1790, p. 89. François Rébecquy was born in 1744 in Marseilles, the son of a wine merchant. In 1789 he was one of those arrested by Bournissac. In 1792 he was elected to the Convention, where he supported the Rolandists. He committed suicide in Marseilles during the Terror by throwing himself into the port.

[18] *Ibid.*, Aug. 14, 1790, pp. 197–200.

of July it published Lieutaud's letters, praised him in song and verse, and erected statues in his honor. On June 20, 1790, on a motion by Barbaroux, a twenty-four man deputation went to express the Club's devotion to him. The next day, to prolonged applause, he thanked the members from the rostrum. Only at the end of July was there evidence of an estrangement. By August 1 Lieutaud was refusing to see deputations from the Society and no longer appeared at its sessions.[19]

The catalyst in the political struggle was the National Assembly's decree of June 12, 1790, specifying uniforms for all national guards. The law, which Lieutaud insisted on applying, aroused apprehension in the Society because of memories of the bourgeois guard. Moreover, it discriminated against the poor by not setting aside funds for the purchase of uniforms. In August, the Club disseminated brochures and placards accusing Lieutaud and his adherents of plotting to re-establish the bourgeois guard, of speculating with the uniform manufacturer, and of hobnobbing with the selfish rich. The commandant's reply warned the populace against the "frenzied ones" who slandered him and defied the decrees of the National Assembly. On August 16, a motion was made in the Club, and "greeted with the universal applause of the great number attending." It requested the convening of an assembly of active citizens to press for the replacement of officers of the guard. With the prior approval of the Municipality, 150 active citizens duly met, drafted a petition calling for new elections, and presented it to the Municipality the next day.[20]

[19] BM, 4717, "Discours prononcé par M. J. F. Lieutaud . . . à la tribune de l'assemblée patriotique" (Marseille, 1790). BN, Lk² 3712 (41), "Hommage héroique: Ode à Monsieur Lieutaud" (Marseille, 1790). AM, I₂, carton 1790.
[20] AN, DXXIX bis 28. BM, 4717. Several propaganda leaflets and placards survive: see "Vie de Phocion, Général Athénien" (Mar-

On the morning of the seventeenth, Lieutaud's agents went to work "especially in the old quarters . . . to excite the people to rise up and attack the patriotic assembly." The same day at 2:00 P.M., Jean-Joseph Arnaud, the commandant's aide-de-camp, made a motion in an assembly of captains calling for the Club's dissolution. Two hours later the Municipality expressed its concern to Lieutaud over rumors that the Society was to be closed that evening. Lieutaud promised to do everything necessary to prevent disorders, but the action which he took was to send Arnaud, who had already threatened the Club, to protect it. That evening an armed mob forced its way into the hall where between 600 and 900 members were gathered. It demanded the petition calling for elections and threatened its authors with the gallows. Only the arrival en masse of the Municipality prevented bloodshed. The crowd agreed to retire, and the Club closed its doors; with one exception, no further meetings were held for nearly a month.[21]

In the succeeding weeks the Society's fate rested in the hands of the Municipality, composed largely of Club members hostile to Lieutaud. In a letter dated August 20 to the deputies of Marseilles at the National Assembly, it blamed the commandant for the riot and condemned his dictatorial practices. Subsequent epistles outlined the ways in which he had usurped the Municipality's authority. Faced with the hostility of the communal officials, Lieutaud found allies in the Direc-

seille, 1790); "Adresse aux habitans de la campagne" (Marseille, 1790), and other pieces. *L'Observateur marseillais*, Aug. 7, 1790, pp. 185-186.

[21] AM, BB 293, Letter of Aug. 20, 1790. See also AM, I₁, 73 and 1D₉. BM, 4717, "Adresse de Blanc-Gilly . . . , portant plainte et dénonciation d'un libelle diffamatoire" (Marseille, 1790). *Ibid.*, "Lettre de Barbaroux."

tories of the district and department. He sent addresses to each administration excoriating the "dozen men" who had "intimidated" the Society's members into breaking the laws and advocated the Club's permanent closure. Both administrations attempted to intervene in the investigation of the riot, but the Municipality stoutly defended its jurisdictional prerogatives.[22]

After a preliminary investigation the Municipality issued a proclamation on August 28 which was openly antagonistic to the commandant. It also called for the Club to hold a special meeting on August 30. At this assembly the members sent their registers to the Municipality and resolved "in the interests of peace and union" not to meet again until the Municipality ordered. In fact the resumption of sessions came very soon and was foreshadowed by a number of events in early September. On September 2, the Municipality designated the militant Jacobin, Barbaroux, as its new clerical secretary; on the sixth it removed Lieutaud from his seat on the council. On September 13, a group of clubbists formally requested the reopening of the Society; and the same day a decree was issued to this effect. As its first act the triumphant Society purged all the Lieutaudists who had formerly been members.[23]

In the next few weeks the Club's puppets, the sections, resurrected the petition of August 16. As a countermeasure Lieutaud tried to convene meetings of the separate National Guard battalions, but the Municipality issued two curt orders forbidding such convocations. Ultimately, on September 28,

[22] AM, BB 293; AD, B-du-Rh, L 122.

[23] AM, 1D₉, session of Aug. 27, 1790. BM, 4717, "Dépend de la délibération de l'assemblée patriotique de Marseille: Du 30 août 1790" (Marseille, 1790). See also "Eloge de M. Cabrol Moncoussou" (Marseille, 1790).

1790, groups opposing the Club assembled, without official permission, at the Arquier Tavern and at Château-Gombert (a suburb). These assemblies, composed of "moneyed people" and wholesale merchants, drafted a note to the National Assembly.[24]

Undeterred by the meetings of these two rump assemblies, the sections met on September 30, 1790, and, by an overwhelming majority, elected Cabrol de Moncaussou, then president of the Club, as the new commandant of the National Guard. François d'Hilaire de Chamvert, another militant member of the Society, became second-in-command. Both were officially installed on October 2.[25] The election of the new commanders left the Club and the Municipality in full control of the National Guard. In Marseilles the Club's position was fairly secure. In the next few months it focused its attention more and more on Paris and Provence.

The alliance of Club and Municipality sealed the defeat of Lieutaud. In the twelve months from October, 1790, to the end of the Constituent Assembly this powerful combination dominated Provençal politics. In 1790, the Municipality clearly ranked as the senior partner, but by October, 1791, it had been eclipsed by the Society. With increasing justification, enemies charged the Club with manipulating municipal

[24] AM, BB 293, To the commandant of the National Guard, Sep. 24, 1790; and To the deputies of Marseilles, Sep. 29, 1790. Later, at the end of December, 1790, the Club deprived those who had signed the petition of the right to serve in the National Guard. BM, 4717, "Petition à la municipalité de Marseille: A l'effet que les anti-patriotes signataires de l'adresse des Carmes et d'Arquier soient désarmés" (Marseille, 1790).

[25] De Moncaussou, a wealthy bourgeois, was born at Revel in 1735. He was executed as a Federalist during the Terror. De Chamvert, a chevalier, was fifty-nine years old at the time of his election. His signature appeared regularly on the Club's petitions. See AM, BB 293, several letters.

administrators. On the Society's command the sections, staffed and officered by clubbists, were convoked and their decisions adopted. The petitions of the Jacobins rapidly assumed the weight of law.

At the same time relations deteriorated between the Club and the moderate mayor, Etienne Martin. In the first six months after Lieutaud's ouster there were few hints of friction. In a letter of November 15, 1790, for example, Martin stoutly defended the Society against the slanders of D'André in Paris. The Club, in turn, honored the mayor in its sessions and elected him again as its president in March, 1791. A breach only became apparent after the king's flight to Varennes. Republican feeling ran high in the Society, and Martin remained a constitutional monarchist. On July 7, 1791, when a deputation from the Society insulted the mayor during a municipal council meeting, he resigned and suddenly disappeared. Fearing disturbances, the Club declared itself in extraordinary session and sent out patrols to locate Martin. He was eventually found and escorted to the Rue Thubaneau, where a tearful reconciliation took place. A month later the Society chose him as its president for the third time, but the reunion did not endure for long.[26]

The Club generally collaborated with the Municipality in 1790–1791, but it harassed and intimidated the "unpatriotic" district and departmental administrations, which had supported Lieutaud. This pattern was not unique to Marseilles. The municipalities of France in 1790–1791 were generally more democratic and prorevolutionary than the district and departmental governments. In an effort to end the old jumble

[26] BM, 4717, "Lettre détaillée de M. Martin, . . . en réponse à celle de M. D'André" (Marseille, 1791); in this collection there are several eulogies written by members of the Club to Martin. See also AM, 4D₁, To the deputies of Marseilles at the National Assembly, July 11, 1791.

of overlapping administrations, known variously as *bailliages*, *généralités*, and *gouvernements*, which had existed before 1789, the National Assembly had partitioned France into eighty-three departments, subdivided into districts, cantons, and communes (municipalities). Election of officers in the communes was direct and relatively popular: every citizen who paid a direct tax equivalent to three days' work was eligible to vote for the mayor, municipal officers, and notables. By contrast, the officials of the districts and departments were elected indirectly by electoral assemblies. Moreover, to qualify as a district or departmental officer one had to pay a tax equal to ten days' work. Both the district and departmental administrations consisted of an elected council which met one month out of the year, and an eight-man executive committee, the Directory.

The essentially undemocratic nature of their election insured that the district and departmental administrations often became centers of conservatism, and later of counterrevolution. This was particularly true in the Bouches-du-Rhône. The problem here was compounded by the fact that Aix, and not Marseilles, had been chosen as the departmental capital, a decision that the Marseillais attributed to political intrigues in Paris. Under continual attacks from the Club, the departmental Directory at Aix became increasingly dependent on the royal government. By September, 1791, it had virtually confessed its inability to control the Society.

The Club also interfered audaciously in the affairs of the districts of the Bouches-du-Rhône. In January, 1791, in the Club, Chompré formally rebuked Etienne Martin, *fils* d'André, the president of the district of Marseilles. Under pressure Martin retracted a letter written to the National Assembly "libelling" the National Guard. Shortly thereafter, he emigrated from France and the district ceased to challenge the Club's authority.[27] In August, 1791, after complaints from the patriots of the village of Velaux, the Society dispatched two deputies to browbeat the Directory of the district of Aix:

Gentlemen! Public opinion has been rising against you for some time; . . . it is by oppression, through deceit that you wish to dominate. . . .

Faithful to our oaths, we will sustain the constitution with all our strength, and we will no longer allow perjurous and ungrateful administrators . . . to propagate the cause of the enemies of the Revolution. . . . We declare to heaven and earth that if you do not return within the limits of the constitution, we are ready to defend it.[28]

The Directory, fearing the "exemplary justice" the Club promised, immediately appealed to the minister of justice, Duport. On August 21, 1791, he censured the Club of the Rue Thubaneau in the National Assembly.[29]

If the Society was keeping one watchful eye on local affairs in 1790–1791, it had the other fixed firmly on the national capital. The clubbists devoured reports from the National Assembly and regularly debated issues which concerned the kingdom at large. Necessity demanded this, for the National Assembly enacted a series of ordinances designed to curtail the waxing power of the clubs. Conjointly with its affiliates, the Club of the Rue Thubaneau protested vehemently against

[27] AD, B-du-Rh, L 2026, Antipolitiques of Aix, session of Jan. 3, 1791; BM, 4717, "Mémoire justificatif de la Société des amis de la Constitution séante à Marseille" (Marseille, 1791).

[28] Lourde, II, 34–37; AD, B-du-Rh, L 2071, Letter from the Antipolitiques, Aug. 30, 1791.

[29] *Procès-verbal de l'Assemblée Nationale*, XXVIII, 18–19.

the "odious" legislation. An address of June 8, 1791, for example, challenged the constitutionality of a law forbidding societies to petition collectively and advised the National Assembly to reform itself rather than the clubs.[30]

In the minds of Society members, a sinister counterrevolutionary coalition in the capital was working to undermine liberty in France. The nucleus was the so-called Austrian committee clustered around Marie Antoinette. In early 1791 the Club sent an address to the National Assembly demanding an end of royal marriages to foreigners; a strong, united nation no longer needed "entangling alliances" or "shameful marriages." The strongest blasts, however, were reserved for D'André and the king's ministers. In 1790–1791, this group attacked the Marseillais at every opportunity. The Club replied with petitions like that of November 4, 1790, bearing 1,200 names and circulated in all the departments, which indicted the current ministry and demanded its removal. Subsequent addresses reiterated this theme.[31] The cold war between the Society and the royal government flared up in every major regional crisis of 1790–1791. With the certainty of a scientific law, they invariably took polar positions.

After the election of the new officers of the National Guard on October 2, 1790, the Club's foremost concern was to liquidate the last vestiges of power that Lieutaud and his supporters retained. In the environs of the city, agents of the ex-commandant still sowed discontent. Barthélemy Lambarini, former aide-de-camp to Lieutaud, bragged of having 400

[30] AM, I₂, carton 1791.

[31] BM, 4717, "Adresse de la Société des amis de la Constitution de Marseille à l'Assemblée Nationale" (Marseille, 1791); *ibid.*, "Pétition faite . . . par 1200 citoyens actifs de Marseille" (Marseille, 1790); *Moniteur*, VI, no. 281, 67. See also BM, 5213, "Ce que sont les ministres" (Marseille, 1790).

armed retainers at his disposal. In October, many Lieutaudists fled to Paris to enlist support. Joseph-Alphonse Esménard attracted a national audience when he defamed the Club in Desmoulins' *Révolutions de France*. In early November, Brémond-Jullien also decamped for the capital to defend liberty against what he called the "daggers of license." [32]

Troubles at Aix in December, 1790, offered the Club the opportunity to take further measures against Lieutaud. The aristocracy, more deeply rooted at Aix than at Marseilles, had formed plans for a new society called the Friends of the King, of Peace, and of Religion. Alarmed, the two patriotic clubs of Aix, the Antipolitiques and the Friends of the Constitution (the Bourbon Club), temporarily united against this menace. On December 12, street fights before an aristocratic café resulted in several injuries. The following day three aristocrats, including the parlementary lawyer Pascalis, were arrested. On the fourteenth a mob snatched the hapless trio from their cells and lynched them.[33]

The discovery of a letter from D'André among the papers of Pascalis caused consternation in the Club of Marseilles. The letter slighted the Marseillais and defended a speech by Pascalis predicting the reappearance of the parlements, more glorious and powerful than before. In a published discourse, a Marseilles Jacobin, Blanc-Gilly, cited this correspondence as "authentic proof" of a confederacy composed of D'André, Pascalis, and "the vile conspirator, Lieutaud." From that day forward Lieutaud claimed that he "lived . . . under the fear

[32] AN, DXXIX bis 28. AM, BB 294, To the deputies of Marseille, 15 octobre 1790; BM, 4717, "Adresse aux citoyens de Marseille: Touchant le renvoi et les éclaircissements de l'affaire de M. Lieutaud, par M. Esménard" (Marseille, 1790); *ibid.*, "Copie de la lettre écrite au district de Marseille par M. Brémond-Jullien" (Marseille, 1790).
[33] AN, BB[16] 86; *Ibid.*, F[7] 3659[1]; Ponteil, XIII, 39–47.

of assassination." On the night of December 17, 1790, the ex-commandant, together with his wife and Lambarini, surreptitiously set sail for Genoa. Contrary winds forced them to land at Bandols (Var), however, where they were arrested, eventually to be returned to Marseilles.[34] The affair at Aix had acquired, abruptly, great regional significance.

On December 20, 1790, the National Assembly named three royal commissioners to re-establish order at Aix. This ordinance provoked an immediate protest from the Friends of the Constitution of Aix, Marseilles, and Toulon. (The correspondence of Pascalis had also incriminated a Toulonese lawyer, Cyprien Granet). They rebuked it as further evidence of a counterrevolutionary conspiracy. On January 15, 1791, on the motion of D'André, a new decree reserved to the Investigations Committee the prerogative of trying Lieutaud and other prisoners detained at Aix, Marseilles, and Toulon. The predictable reaction came from the clubs. Only the district courts, elected by the people, they argued, had the right to judge the prisoners: "No, Gentlemen! No citizen can be removed from his natural judges." [35]

The royal commissioners reached Aix in January, 1791, and spent the best part of the next six months verbally jousting with the Club. The latter's unswerving aim was to compel the interlopers to return to the capital. Along with its satellite societies in Provence it sent repeated addresses to the National Assembly urging the "recall of those whose presence is use-

[34] BM, 4717, "Lettre de M. Blanc-Gilly . . . à l'assemblée patriotique de Marseille" (Marseille, 1790); AN, DXXIX bis 28.

[35] *Moniteur*, VI, no. 356, 689, VII, no. 17, 138. BN, Lb[40] 991, "Adresse à l'Assemblée Nationale par les Amis de la Constitution . . . de Marseille: adhérée par les Amis de la Constitution d'Aix et de Toulon" (Marseille, 1790).

less." [36] The commissioners responded by opposing the
Marseillais in every major issue occurring in the Midi. They
diagnosed the disturbances at Aix as "three public assassinations," forwarded the voluminous memoirs of Lieutaud to
Paris, sought the release of the prisoners at Aix, Marseilles,
and Toulon, and supported the papal party in the Vaucluse.

In February and March, 1791, the political barometer
dropped ominously. The commissioners advised the minister
of the interior of the impotence of the authorities in the
Bouches-du-Rhône and asked for more powers. They reported "murmurings" in the countryside and alarming deliberations in the Club: "The rumor spread yesterday," they
wrote on March 12, "that a mob of armed people was to
arrive today from Marseilles to advise us to leave." [37] On
April 2, the National Assembly authorized the commissioners
to requisition regular troops without the prior approval of
local officials. In a terse statement the Club denounced this
decree as another example of "tyrannical oppression . . .
despotism and fanaticism," and made strenuous efforts to
combat it. It sent two petitions to the National Assembly and
long justificatory addresses to Carra, editor of the *Annales
patriotiques*. On April 10, two Club members accompanied
the mayor and a municipal officer to Aix to protest to the
Directory of the department. When the visit terminated unsuccessfully, some speakers at the Society called for an armed
expedition to Aix. Instead, on April 13, a circular letter was
drafted, to be sent to all the clubs of France, branding the
decree of April 2 as the treacherous work of D'André and

[36] See AN, C 127, "Adresse des trois sociétés réunies . . ." (Marseille, 1791).
[37] AN, F⁷ 3659¹.

the "infamous commissioners" of the executive branch.[38]

On April 12, the commissioners issued a formal proclamation denouncing the Club. "The Constitution is completed," they contended; "only criminals oppose it." They also attempted to promote dissension between the Society and its ally the Municipality. Their letters warned the municipal officers that they were treading on a volcano: "The people who are accustomed to dominate now will soon recognize no law at all." The commissioners matched their speeches and letters with diligent attempts to obtain troops. On April 18 they reported erroneously to the ministry that the Club had placed a bounty on their heads and was organizing an army of 6,000 men to send against them.[39]

Despite the arrival in Aix of 400 marines sent by the military governor at Toulon, one of the commissioners hurried to Paris to lobby for additional political and military support. His efforts were partially successful. On May 21, 1791, he secured a royal edict freeing Lieutaud and the prisoners detained at Aix, Marseilles, and Toulon since December. On hearing this news, on May 28, the Society sent off a defiant letter to its affiliates saying: "We have resolved to hold ourselves on the alert and to perish rather than see ourselves overwhelmed by despotism." The vigilance of the Society, however, did not prevent the escape of its bitterest enemy, Lieutaud. On May 31, dressed as a Swiss soldier, and with the connivance of the regiment of Ernest, he eluded the Club and set off for Paris.[40]

Serious troubles in the two papal enclaves north of the

[38] *Moniteur*, VIII, no. 93, 18–19. AN, F[7] 3659[1]; AM, 20D; *Annales patriotiques*, May 4 and 21, 1791, pp. 1370–1371, 1441.

[39] AN, F[7] 3659[1]; AM, 1 D$_9$, session of Apr. 13, 1791.

[40] AD, B-du-Rh, L 2038, To the society of Antipolitiques of Aix, May 28, 1791. Barbaroux, pp. 78–80.

Durance further exacerbated the Club's quarrel with the commissioners. Since its foundation the Society had watched carefully the events transpiring in that region. Its sympathies lay
with the pro-French patriots of Avignon and against the
papists at Carpentras. On October 28, 1790, the clubs of Aix
and Marseilles had jointly proposed a federation of national
guardsmen from the Bouches-du-Rhône, Basses-Alpes, and
Var to march against Carpentras. Two months later the Antipolitiques took the initiative in advocating the formation of a
regiment of 1,200 Jacobins to be sent to Avignon. Marseilles
was to contribute 800 men. Both these projects were stymied,
however, by the intervention of the departmental Directory
at Aix.[41]

In April, 1791, open warfare erupted between Carpentras
and Avignon. Carpentras was supported by both the Directory
of the department and the royal commissioners. The latter
used the situation as an argument in their appeals to Paris for
troops and bemoaned the coalition between "the Avignon
brigands" and the Club of Marseilles. The Society, for its
part, printed innumerable addresses demanding union of the
Vaucluse with France. In May it contributed 1,000 louis and
several wagon loads of wheat to Avignon. Ultimately, at the
request of mediators dispatched by the National Assembly,
500 national guardsmen from Marseilles marched to Avignon
to restore order. The part the Club played in organizing this
expedition is obscure, although it must have been extensive;
François D'Hilaire de Chamvert, a militant member of the
Society, commanded the battalion.[42]

[41] BM, 4717, "Contre-Révolution et meurtres arrivés à Carpentras
et Cavaillon" (Marseille, 1790); AD, B-du-Rh, L 122, Correspondance générale, Dec. 30, 1790.
[42] AN, F7 3659₁; Vialla, pp. 74–77; see also AD, Hérault, 5498, 5543.

The Club's struggle with the royal commissioners in Provence did not diminish its interest in events in Paris. In national politics the period from October, 1789 to mid-1791 was relatively uneventful. However, in the late spring and summer of 1791 developments in the capital assumed a new significance. Three incidents in particular profoundly stirred the Jacobins of the Rue Thubaneau: the death of Mirabeau, the flight of the king to Varennes, and the schism between the Feuillants and the Jacobins.

On April 1, 1791, Mirabeau died after a short illness in Paris. A sorrowing National Assembly voted to place his body in the Pantheon, and huge throngs attended his funeral. When the news of his death reached Marseilles on April 8 the city was plunged into deep sorrow. The Municipality proclaimed a day of mourning on April 11. The bourse and the theaters closed, and citizens attended requiem masses in the churches. At the Club, elaborate memorial ceremonies were held on April 11 and April 12. A bust of Mirabeau was crowned in the assembly hall, and speakers gave solemn eulogies. On April 13, the Society sent an address to the National Assembly which opened: "We no longer have Mirabeau. . . . One of the torches of the French Empire has been extinguished." [43]

To twentieth-century historians the death of Mirabeau no longer seems such a momentous and tragic occurrence. It is still generally acknowledged, however, that the flight of Louis XVI to Varennes on June 20, 1791, "was one of the most important events of the time—for Europe as well as for the

[43] *Journal de Provence*, Apr. 12, 1791, p. 355; BM, 4717, "Proclamation de la Municipalité sur la mort de Mirabeau" (Marseille, 1791); *ibid.*, "Eloge à Honoré-Gabriel-Riquetti-Mirabeau" (Marseille, 1791); BN, Lb^{40} 2771; AN, F^7 3659^1, "Nous n'avons plus Mirabeau" (Marseille, 1791).

Revolution."[44] It "unmasked the true character of Louis XVI" and prepared the way for the cataclysmic events of August 10, 1792. One day after the incident, on June 21, 1791, a manifesto drafted by the Cordeliers in Paris called for the establishment of a republic.[45]

The news of the king's betrayal reached Marseilles on June 25 and caused "much agitation." Crowds smashed busts and portraits of the monarch. On the Rue Thubaneau the clubbists met in permanent session from June 26 to June 29 to digest the latest messages from Paris.[46] These anxious days fundamentally altered majority opinion in the Society. In 1790 every member had taken an oath to defend the constitutional king. In speeches they referred to Louis XVI as "the best of kings," the "friend and father of the people." As late as March 27, 1791, they attended a Te Deum to celebrate the king's recovery from an illness.[47] Monarchist sentiment disintegrated after June 25, 1791. Addresses sent to the National Assembly reflected the mood of anger. They avoided the use of the harsh word "republic," but they were plainly republican in nature and demanded the deposition of Louis de Bourbon. "Legislators!" concluded one petition, "Louis XVI has irrevocably lost the confidence of the French people; can he reign in this state any longer?"[48]

The National Assembly ignored the wishes of the Marseillais and the radicals in Paris. On July 15 and 16, it exonerated Louis XVI and restored him to the throne. The king,

[44] Georges Lefebvre, *The French Revolution*, trans. Elizabeth Moss Evanson, I (London and New York, 1962), 206.

[45] Alphonse Aulard, *The French Revolution*, trans. Bernard Miall, I (New York, 1910), 260–299.

[46] *Journal de Provence*, June 30, 1791, pp. 202–203; AM, I₂, carton 1791, To the Friends of the Constitution of Aix, June 25, 1791.

[47] *Journal de Provence*, Mar. 29, 1791, p. 307.   [48] AN, C 127.

for his part, agreed to accept the constitution. On July 17 occurred the celebrated massacre on the Champ de Mars, when national guardsmen under Lafayette fired into a crowd assembled to protest the decrees. Over the next two days most of the moderate Jacobins, including Lafayette, Barnave, and Sièyes, seceded from the original society and formed a new Society of Friends of the Constitution based at the former convent of the Feuillants. Only Robespierre, Pétion, and a handful of radical Jacobins stayed on in the old club on the Rue Saint-Honoré. On July 19, they notified the affiliates of the schism, news that shook the foundations of the Jacobin network. The provincial clubs had to choose between "a Pope and anti-Pope" competing for their allegiance.[49]

As one of its first acts in 1790 the newly formed Club of Marseilles had sought affiliation with Paris. The earliest formal record of this affiliation is a list of March 7, 1791, published in the *Moniteur*, but the Society had received correspondence from Paris as early as June 24, 1790. In September and October, 1790, it dispatched warnings to the Jacobins in the capital about certain Lieutaudists who had fled there, warnings which the Paris club respected by rejecting two of the "intriguers" when they presented themselves as prospective members. In 1791 communications were regularized. Delegations from Marseilles to Paris grew in number, and one of the founders of the Club of Marseilles, Malherbe,[50] proposed an

[49] The phrase is that of J. M. Thompson, *Robespierre*, I (New York, 1936), 65.

[50] François Boursault-Malherbe (1752–1842) was director of the theater at Marseilles. A speech that he gave in April, 1790, is the earliest address at the Club of which this writer has found record. In 1791 he moved to Paris, where he opened a new theater, the Salle Molière. He became a deputy to the Convention from Paris in 1793.

oath at a meeting of the Jacobins in Paris on January 24.[51]

Members of the Club avidly read the debates of the Jacobins published in the Paris newspapers. The position that the Marseillais took on issues in the mother club varied, but they generally supported the opinions of the radicals. Indeed, there developed a veritable cult for the high priest of Jacobinism, Robespierre, after he defended the Club in April, 1791, in its dispute with the royal commissioners at Aix. Following the death of Mirabeau, the Municipality implored the Incorruptible to replace the Great Tribune as the defender of Marseilles.[52] After the flight to Varennes the Society rushed to defend its new idol. On June 21, Robespierre announced that conspirators planned to assassinate him. On learning that Robespierre's life hung in the balance, the clubbists addressed an impassioned manifesto to the entire kingdom vowing to protect him against his enemies:

Frenchmen! Truly free men of the eighty-three departments, your brothers and friends, the Marseillais, invite you to render homage to Robespierre, the apostle of national liberty. . . . Be warned, Frenchmen, that your brothers of Marseilles have vowed to watch over the safety of those few courageous men that the capital is fortunate to possess. . . . The Marseillais, at the least shadow of danger, will fly to their aid.[53]

[51] *L'Observateur marseillais*, June 24, 1790, p. 92; Aulard, *Jacobins*, I, lxxxi-lxxxv, II, 510, 549. BM, 4717, "Lettre écrite par l'assemblée patriotique de Marseille, au club des Jacobins à Paris" (Marseille, 1790); *ibid.*, "Fameuse réception des sieurs Esménard et Fournier au club des Jacobins à Paris" (Marseille, 1790).

[52] AM, 4D₁, To M. Robespierre, deputy; see also Robespierre's "Discours sur l'organisation des gardes nationales" (Marseille, 1791), printed and distributed by the Club: AD, Drôme, F 207; BM, Poitiers, S 15.

[53] BN, Lb⁴⁰ 2779, "Adresse au peuple francais" (Marseille, 1791).

Despite the Club's idolatry of Robespierre, its course in the Feuillant-Jacobin schism was by no means preordained. Before the Terror, allegiance within the Jacobin network rested on mutual confidence and trust. The provincial clubs were inferior to the mother club of Paris in strength, and generally subservient in the formulation of doctrine and policy. Yet, the larger among them sometimes questioned the authority of the central club and initiated movements which the leaders in Paris did not wholly support. Faced with the schism of July, 1791, the provincial societies reacted in a variety of ways. Initially, a great many supported the Feuillants; some, such as Toulouse, refused to ally themselves with either faction and demanded their reunion; and a few societies were faithful to the Jacobins. The Club of the Rue Thubaneau, in an address to the Feuillants dated August 2, vowed to remain united with the Jacobins but urged a reunion of the two factions on grounds of public interest. "Gentlemen," the Club wrote, "your schism rends the hearts of the patriots . . . the fatherland is in danger and our friends are separated. Hasten, zealous citizens, true defenders of liberty, hasten to . . . dissipate our alarms; your union alone can reunite France." [54] The Feuillants failed to heed this request. By November, 1791, the Marseillais had severed all ties with them. Like "all true revolutionaries of the Kingdom," they henceforth esteemed only the Jacobins.[55]

The Feuillant-Jacobin schism coincided with the last days of the National Assembly. Throughout France in August, 1791, active citizens gathered to elect deputies to the forthcoming Legislative Assembly. On August 25, the electoral

[54] AD, B-du-Rh, L 2038, "Circulaire des amis de la constitution de Marseille" (Marseille, 1791).

[55] AN, F⁷ 4603, Ferroul *et al.* to Blanc-Gilly.

assembly of the Bouches-du-Rhône convened at Aix. From the outset it was dominated by Marseilles. The Club had pressed for its "prompt convocation" since mid-July. During its meetings members were there to observe the electors. Representatives from the Club visited the Antipolitiques "almost every day" to discuss "the most suitable means to bring about good choices in the electoral assembly." When electors were negligent in attendance, the Society prodded the missing to attend. In the meantime the Club and its affiliates bombarded the meetings with propaganda, urging the election of "the defenders of the rights of the people," that is, those individuals who had their approval.[56]

One of the principal topics of concern for the electors was burgeoning civil strife at Arles, a district capital of the Bouches-du-Rhône. In that ancient city, two factions, the counterrevolutionary "Chiffonnists" (Chiffonne club) and the patriotic "Monnaidiers" (Mint society) stood poised for battle. The former included scores of non-juring priests and "aristocrats." Since early 1791 each side had committed provocations. Monnaidiers had forcibly ejected rebel priests from their homes and expelled them from the city. On June 8, 1791, the Chiffonnists disarmed many of the "Monnaidiers" and drove others into the countryside. These events were the occasion for angry debates on the Rue Thubaneau. At least once, in June, the Society sent a deputation of inquiry to Arles, headed by Pleville-Lepelley and Jean-Pierre Amy. Throughout the dispute it staunchly supported the Monnaidiers. Under pressure from the Club, the Directory of the de-

[56] Aulard, *Jacobins*, III, 63; B-du-Rh, L 2071, Letter written by our brothers the Antipolitiques of Aix, Aug. 30, 1791; *ibid.*, L 2038, The Antipolitiques to the Club of Marseilles, Sept. 8, 1791; *ibid.*, L 277, Electoral assemblies of the Bouches-du-Rhône.

partment had grudgingly issued a decree on July 20, 1791, ordering two of its officials and 400 troops to Arles to restore order. This commission reintegrated the Monnaidiers into the National Guard, but did little more than patch up wounds temporarily.[57]

Trouble flared up once more on September 1, 1791, when the Chiffonnists again seized power at Arles. On this occasion the electoral assembly, dominated as it was by Jacobins of Marseilles, provided a convenient tool to usurp legal authority. It declared itself to be a permanent body and, on September 12, compelled the dilatory department to call up 4,000 national guardsmen. This decree, announced at an extraordinary session of the Club at 10:00 A.M. on September 13, provoked the "utmost joy." The Society helped recruit and organize the contingent from Marseilles. Within a few days more than 2,000 Marseillais were encamped at Tarascon, where an incident occurred that illustrated the considerable authority the Club wielded over this force. On September 15, the guardsmen arrested the public prosecutor of Arles who was on his way to Aix with letters libelling the Society and Municipality of Marseilles. The department immediately ordered his release, but the Marseillais refused to comply until they received special confirmation from the Club.[58]

The projected invasion of Arles miscarried. The minister of the interior, Delessart, intervened in favor of the Chiffonnists, meted out sharp reprimands to the Club and the electoral assembly, and forced a willing Directory to rescind its decrees and disband the army it had called up. The abortive invasion

[57] AD, B-du-Rh, L 2079, Minutes of the extraordinary session in 1791; AN, F[7] 3659[1], To the Minister of Justice, July 11, 1791; AD, B-du-Rh, L 289, "Extrait des délibérations des amis de la constitution séante à Marseille, 8 août 1791" (Marseille, 1791).

[58] AD, B-du-Rh, L 123; *ibid.*, L 277; AN, F[7] 3659[2].

was, nevertheless, a clear indication of the Club's strength. So too were the pitiful letters sent to Delessart by the members of the Directory. Debourge, the royal commissioner at Arles, stated the overall situation most cogently. In his opinion, one great obstacle blocked peace in the Bouches-du-Rhône:

The center that we must cleanse is Marseilles. It is the most important city of the department. The Club that we must destroy is likewise that of Marseilles; it is the one that has done so much evil. . . . The Club of Marseilles has dominated too long. Now, no local administration dares not regard it as inviolable.[59]

After September, 1791, the tension between Marseilles and the Directory at Aix heightened perceptibly. The Club charged the Departmental administration with betraying the constitution, excluding patriots from appointments, and trafficking with the interests of the people. On January 31, 1792, the Municipality of Marseilles denounced the Directory of the department to the Legislative Assembly, deputizing Barbaroux and Jean-Baptiste Loys to present its views in Paris.[60] Hints of an approaching expedition to Aix began to appear with startling regularity. "Our department is rotten with aristocracy," wrote Moyse Bayle to Blanc-Gilly from Aix on January 31, "each day I expect to see our Marseillais arrive here to execute justice; it will undoubtedly inspire and motivate the remainder

[59] AN, F⁷ 3659².

[60] Loys, a lawyer, was born at Arles in 1757. In 1791 he moved to Marseilles, where he became procurator of the district and a leader at the Society. After his trip to Paris in 1792 (except for a brief period when the Club excluded him), he acted as liaison between the Jacobins of Paris and Marseilles. In 1794 he was a member of the surveillance committee of the department of Paris. See Charles Barbaroux, *Correspondance et mémoires*, ed. Claude Perroud and Alfred-Chabaud (Paris, 1923); *Moniteur*, XI, no. 52, 427–430.

of the Kingdom. This purification is of the most urgent necessity." [61]

About 10:00 P.M. on February 25 approximately 800 national guardsmen left Marseilles for the long-awaited showdown. The informers of the ministers believed that the project originated in the Society. It is difficult to say with absolute certainty. The Municipality apparently had no prior knowledge of it, but the march was too well organized to be spontaneous. The Marseillais arrived at Aix at 9:00 A. M. on February 26. During the next thirty-six hours volunteers swelled the force to more than 8,000. The department relied for its armed support on the royalist regiment of Ernest, recently transferred from Marseilles. Twice it ordered the Swiss to march on the Marseillais, but the patriotic Puget de Barbentane, brigadier general,[62] refused to execute its orders. Eventually the majority of the Directory fled, and on February 28, 1791, the Swiss consented to disarm and departed for Toulon. Pierre Baille,[63] a member of the Club, called a rump councilgeneral of the department which then elected a new Directory, one that became simply an instrument of the Marseilles Society. In a letter to the minister of the interior dated

[61] AN, F⁷ 4603; Moyse Bayle was born in Geneva in 1757. His name appeared on the Club's registers as early as June, 1790. He drafted several addresses in 1790–1791 and served as secretary in March, 1791. In 1792 he was elected to the Convention, where he voted consistently with the Montagnards.

[62] Barbentane was born in Paris in 1754. After his patriotic actions in Aix the minister of war suspended him from his command. The Club angrily condemned this suspension and demanded that Barbentane be given a promotion. Eventually he was promoted to lieutenant-general.

[63] Baille was born at Marseilles in 1753. In 1792 he became a deputy of the Bouches-du-Rhône to the Convention. While on mission at Toulon in the summer of 1793 he was arrested by the Federalists. He committed suicide on September 2, 1793.

March 12, 1792, the former president of the Directory bemoaned the department's fate: "It will be unfortunate so long as it trembles under the despotism of Marseilles." [64]

With the department under its control and the Swiss in Toulon, the Club began to prepare for a second expedition against the Chiffonnists. Moyse Bayle and Pierre Baille, two leaders of the rump council-general, conferred with the Society in Marseilles and departed for Paris on March 8, 1792. At the Legislative Assembly on March 18, they lauded the "burning patriotism" of the Marseillais and rebuked the aristocratic Chiffonnists. Their arguments bore fruit. On March 19, the Legislators ordered the Marseillais to march on Arles.[65]

The Club spent the month of March, 1792, feverishly preparing for the approaching campaign. The newly formed *Journal des départements méridionaux* pressed for haste on the supposition that the Chiffonnists were corresponding with the Spanish and the Germans. A myriad requests poured in from clubs and communes seeking to march alongside the Marseilles army. The correspondence became so voluminous that the Society formed a special committee to oversee it. The organization of the troops required ceaseless activity. The Club sent missions to affiliates to whip up patriotism and began fund-raising subscriptions for the purchase of arms and the payment of wages. On the day of their departure, March 22, the commanders of the expedition, François-Trophime Rébecquy and Romuald Bertin visited the Rue Thubaneau to pledge their patriotism. During their mission they mailed regular progress bulletins to the Club.[66]

[64] AN, F⁷ 3659³.   [65] *Moniteur*, XI, no. 70, 624, no. 81, 681.
[66] Joseph-Romuald Bertin was a wood merchant from Velaux (Bouches-du-Rhône); *JdD*, Mar. 6–Apr. 3, 1792, pp. 8–49.

The Marseillais won a bloodless victory. On March 30, 1792, 6,000 national guardsmen marched triumphantly into Arles. The successful termination of the expedition greatly enhanced the prestige of the Society, whose members now styled themselves "saviors of the Midi." On April 12, 1792, a deputation appeared in the Club from the Monnaidiers "thanking the Assembly" for delivering them from "a frightful and unsupportable yoke." [67]

Less than one month after stamping out counterrevolution at Arles, the Marseilles army marched on Avignon. This region had remained troubled despite a decree of September 15, 1791, uniting it with France. On October 17, "300–400 unknowns," among whom was Jourdan, executed sixty counterrevolutionaries in one of the towers of the papal palace. This event, the Massacres of la Glacière, led to the entry of 3,000 French troops into Avignon and the arrest of Jourdan and other revolutionaries. The Club provided asylum for those who escaped. In Marseilles they formed a Society of the Imprisoned or Exiled Friends of the Constitution of Avignon. During the march on Arles, Wittgenstein, the royalist French commander at Avignon, threatened the flank of Bertin and Rébecquy. This danger was removed, however, when Barbaroux helped secure the appointment of the Marquis de Montesquiou-Fezenzac as Wittgenstein's replacement. The new commandment cultivated the friendship of the Club, personally visiting it on May 1, 1792, to pay homage to the masters of Provence.[68]

[67] *JdD*, Apr. 14, 1792, p. 72.

[68] See two articles by Pierre Vaillandet, "Les Massacres de la Glacière et l'opinion publique," *Mémoires de l'Académie de Vaucluse*, XXXII (1932), 27, and "Lettres inédites de Barbaroux," *Annales historiques de la Révolution française*, X (1933), 338–353; see also Barbaroux, *Mémoires*, p. 98; *Moniteur*, X, no. 322, 27–47, XII, no. 142,

With Wittgenstein replaced, Rébecquy and Bertin decided to aid the oppressed patriots in Avignon. In April a band of 200 Marseillais forced the cells of Jourdan and his fellow revolutionaries, and on April 29, 1792, the released prisoners accompanied the Marseilles army in triumph into the city. Angered at the Marseillais for taking matters into their own hands, the Legislative Assembly ordered Rébecquy and Bertin to Paris to answer charges. Before leaving, both went first to the Club to justify their conduct. The Society blamed their persecution on the Feuillants and on May 22 sent a petition, bearing 10,000 names, to the capital in support of Rébecquy and Bertin. The two appeared before the Legislative Assembly on June 8 and June 15 and were ultimately exonerated.[69]

The forceful elimination of its enemies at Arles, Aix, and Avignon earned the Club of Marseilles the leadership of the democratic movement in France. "From that time," wrote Georges Lefebvre, "Marseilles represented the highest hopes of the Patriots." [70] It was to the "heroes of the South" that the Jacobins and *sans-culottes* of Paris looked for support. In turn, the club gave unwavering support to the "good" Jacobin deputies in the Legislative Assembly, the *sans-culottes,* and revolutionary heroes such as Pétion and Danton. The cult of Robespierre grew to enormous proportions. When he founded his gazette, the *Défenseur de la constitution*, the Society's *Journal* printed the entire prospectus. Marseillais who went to

430; BM, Poitiers, S 22, "Recueil des pièces concernant Avignon et le Comtât" (Marseille, 1791); BM, 4717, "Discours prononcés . . . dans l'assemblée des amis de la constitution à Marseille, . . . par MM. Montesquiou et Puget-Barbentane" (Marseille, 1792).

[69] BN, Lb⁴⁰ 993, "Adresse à l'assemblée nationale" (Marseille, 1792); *JdD*, 22, 24 mai 1792, pp. 141–144, 146; *Moniteur*, XII, nos. 105, 108, 130, 162, pp. 117, 139, 334–335, 613.

[70] Lefebvre, I, 230.

Paris sought out Robespierre at the first opportunity. The Incorruptible, reported Barbaroux in one of his letters, "supported Marseilles as if it was his fatherland." [71] At the Legislative Assembly the authority and prestige of the deputies from the Bouches-du-Rhône rested on their adherence to Jacobin ideology. The Club insisted that every deputy of the Bouches-du-Rhône join the Jacobins, and it carefully scrutinized their voting records. Absenteeism at crucial votes resulted in reproval; voting on the wrong side of the ledger meant denunciation. Over the heads of the representatives hung the perpetual threat of exclusion from the Society, and exclusion meant political death in Marseilles.[72]

Etienne Martin, the ex-mayor, was the first to suffer disgrace. His widening divergence from the Society had only been patched over sufficiently long enough for his election as a deputy in September, 1791. "He accepted the post with all the more haste," wrote Lourde, "because his role in Marseilles had ended. He feared, without daring to avow it, the Club of this city which was already more powerful than he." [73] Personal differences also played a part in his downfall. The new mayor, Jean-Raymond Mourraille, was jealous of his predecessor.

On December 12, 1791, when an "unsealed" letter arrived at the town hall addressed by Martin to a certain Spigne, clerk in the archives, Mourraille opened it and forwarded it to the Society. The incriminating document criticized Mourraille's inability to maintain order and made disparaging remarks about the Legislative Assembly. "It is a club more than

[71] Barbaroux, *Correspondance*, p. 58.

[72] AN, F⁷ 4603, Chabaud to Blanc-Gilly, Feb. 12, 1792, and other letters.

[73] Lourde, II, 50.

an assembly of legislators," said Martin. In a rage, the Society accused Martin of "eating the soup of the ministers," destroyed all his portraits and memorabilia, and scratched his name from the registers. Martin's letter of defense made matters worse, for in it he deplored the schism between the Jacobins and the Feuillants. From that time forward the Club lumped the former mayor with the "blacks" of the Assembly. "Who would have believed," moaned the *Journal des départements méridionaux* in May, 1792, "that the Martin that we called the Just, was the greatest enemy of the Marseillais and the Clubs." [74] His power lost, Martin retired from political life in August, 1792.

Mathieu Blanc-Gilly,[75] one of the most energetic leaders and pamphleteers of the Club in 1790–1791, also fell from grace. In 1791–1792, while the Society was shifting to the left, he adopted a moderate stance in Paris. His friend Henri Chabaud constantly warned him of his increasing isolation from the Society and of the growing influence of such rivals as Barbaroux. "Try, if not in the name of friendship, then in the name of God," urged Chabaud on one occasion, "to put yourself in the spirit of the people." Discredited already, Blanc-Gilly threw off his Jacobin mask completely in the summer of 1792. In a published letter, he described the attack on the Tuileries which occurred on June 20 as an "atrocious . . . event which dishonored the Revolution." In his famous *Réveil d'alarme d'un député de Marseille, aux bons citoyens*

---

[74] BM, 4717, "Lettre du Sieur Martin . . . au Sieur Spigne" (Marseille, 1792); *ibid.*, "Lettre de M. Martin . . . aux Amis de la Constitution de Marseille, suivie de la réponse à ladite lettre" (Marseille, 1792); AN, F⁷ 4603, Chabaud to Blanc-Gilly, Dec. 28 and 30, 1792. *JdD*, May 24, 1792, p. 147.

[75] Blanc-Gilly (1747–1804) was a bourgeois of Marseilles. He was elected in 1791 as a representative to the Legislative Assembly.

de Paris, he warned the Parisians about the approach of "five hundred brigands" from Marseilles. The Club learned of the first letter on July 2, 1792. On confirming its authenticity on July 5, it sent a circular address to all its affiliates warning them that Blanc-Gilly was in league with the king and La Fayette, and vowing vengeance. The Revolutionary career of Blanc-Gilly had terminated. After August 10, the former president of the Club of the Rue Thubaneau fled to Switzerland.[76]

One of the chief characteristics of the year 1792 was the rise of republican sentiment in France. Nowhere was this more true than in Marseilles. The Club's dislike of the constitutional king was clearly evident from the beginning of the Legislative Assembly. When the legislators adopted a rule of protocol on October 6, 1791 stipulating that the king was to be addressed as "sire" or "majesty" in its sessions, the Society published an address by Barbaroux condemning the regulation as an attempt to "further the royalist cause" and to "revive feudalism." [77] Sullen obedience yielded to defiance after the king's vetoes of November 12 and December 19, 1791, annulling legislation against émigrés and non-juring priests. In their private correspondence members of the Club began to speak of revolutionary action. On February 12, 1792, Chabaud wrote to Blanc-Gilly:

We await a coup from the Parisians whom the Marseillais will second marvelously; . . . provided that the patriotic deputies are informed of it, my friend, is it not essential that the Tuileries suffer the same fate as the Bastille? Perhaps I am deceiving myself,

[76] AN, F[7] 4603; *JdD*, July 5 and 7, 1792, pp. 117–121; AD, Var, L, supplement, St.-Zacharie.
[77] Lourde, II, 53.

but pardon a patriot *enragé* who sees all the evil that the veto is doing.[78]

In early 1792 the Club inaugurated a campaign to wean Provence away from the monarchy. Three new newspapers began publication, replete with indictments of the veto, the civil list, and royal inviolability. "Be persuaded," editorialized the *Journal des départements méridionaux* after the surprise appointment of a Brissotin ministry on March 10, 1792, "that to deceive you better the King would become a Jacobin if it was necessary." The motto of the *Mercure de Marseille* read.

> If man is born free, he ought to govern himself,
> If man has tyrants, he must dethrone them.

For its peasant audience, the *Manuel du labourer et de l'artisan* compared the royal veto to releasing a "devouring wolf" in a sheep pasture. Commissioners of the Club travelled in force to affiliated societies to encourage support of republican principles. At St.-Zacharie, in April, Jacques Monbrion proudly declaimed: "Let me be called a republican; I glory in this title if you mean by republican the enemy of kings." [79]

Reverses in the War strengthened the republicanism in France in general and on the Rue Thubaneau in particular. The Club linked the defeat of Dillon at Tournai on March 28, 1792, with "a traitorous king" and the Austrian committee. In letters to the Jacobins in Paris, it began to lobby for the formation of an armed camp of 100,000 federalists (*fédérés*) to protect the capital. A circular of May 28, 1792, asked the affiliates of the eighty-three departments to join the Marseillais in their efforts.[80] An epistle of June 1, to Pétion, "father of

[78] AN, F⁷ 4603, Chabaud's use of the word *enragé* was probably not accidental. This was the period of the Legislative Assembly in which the Robespierrists called themselves by this term.

[79] *JdD*, Apr. 3, 1792, p. 51.   [80] AD, B-du-Rh, L 2075.

Paris," outlined the arguments for a national federation and warned the Parisians that they would "always be in mortal peril as long as a treasonous national council exists in Paris."[81]

On June 4, under pressure from the clubs and the Parisian *sans-culottes*, the Brissotin minister of war, Joseph Servan, proposed a convocation of twenty thousand federalists in Paris to observe the second anniversary of the fête of the federation. At the news of Servan's bill, passed on June 8, the Club of Marseilles composed an address to the National Assembly warning that the peril facing liberty was too great for a mere 20,000 men; but while this message was on its way to Paris the king dismissed Servan and his Rolandist colleagues in the ministry. On June 19, he vetoed the convocation of federalists. The next day a crowd of Parisians marched on the Tuileries, where they harassed and insulted the king. The courageous behavior of the monarch and his refusal to revoke the vetoes drew expressions of support from many parts of France. At this point the sections of Paris appealed to the Jacobins of Marseilles for assistance.[82]

On June 19, 1792, Mourraille received a now famous letter from Barbaroux and forwarded it to the Club. "Send six hundred men who know how to die," wrote the young lawyer. On June 20, the clubbists petitioned the Municipality for a register wherein citizens might volunteer for the battalion. On June 23, after consultation with the Society, the Municipality voted to send 500 men to Paris. Twelve clubbists supervised the selection of volunteers, many of whom were fellow Club members; the Commandant, François Moisson, was a

[81] *JdD*, June 5, 1792, p. 166.
[82] For the address of June 8 see BN, Le[34] 92. See also a circular letter in AD, Var, series L, supplement, St.-Zacharie, beginning "Frères et amis."

militant and had served several times as an officer of the Society.[83]

On June 22, while preparations were being made for the battalion, a banquet was held on the Rue Thubaneau. A Jacobin from Montpellier, François Mireur, who had come to confer with the Society, sang a hymn written by Rouget de Lisle in Strasbourg on April 25. The next day the *Journal des départements méridionaux* printed the text under the title *Chant de guerre de l'armée du Rhin*. Each of the Marseillais in the battalion received a copy. On their march to Paris they immortalized this song, the famous "Marseillaise."[84] On July 2, the day of their departure, the vice-president of the Club, Maillet the younger, charged them to uphold the name of Marseilles: "Go brave citizens! blend your courage with that of the Parisians. Frighten the tyrant on a throne that he no longer merits! Tell him that the sovereign people has come to sanction the decree that he has struck down with his monstrous veto!"[85]

The details of the formation of the battalion of August 10

[83] Joseph Pollio and Adrien Marcel, *Le Bataillon du 10 août: Recherches pour servir à l'histoire de la Révolution française* (Paris, 1881), p. 48. *JdD*, June 23, 1792, p. 197.

[84] *JdD*, June 23, 1792, p. 200; AD, Hérault, 5500.

[85] Augustin Maillet (Maillet the younger), a master of fine arts, was born at Purse (Basse-Alpes) about 1757. He served on at least four occasions as president of the Club. He was chosen as a justice of the peace in 1791 and as president of the Criminal Tribunal of the Bouches-du-Rhône in 1792. The Federalists imprisoned him in May, 1793. After his release he became president of the Revolutionary Tribunal of the Bouches-du-Rhône. In February, 1794, he was tried (on the orders of Fréron) before the Revolutionary Tribunal in Paris, but acquitted. His avid Jacobinism eventually led to his arrest by the reactionary representatives-on-mission, Auguis and Serres, in September, 1792. He remained a prisoner at Ham until 1795. See *JdD*, July 5, 1793, p. 218.

in Marseilles are well known. What is less recognized is the concerted effort that the Club made to mobilize auxiliaries from its affiliates. Fiery orations were sent to all eighty-three departments begging for assistance in overthrowing the monarchy. Of more significance were the recruiting campaigns of veteran commissioners in the Bouches-du-Rhône and neighboring departments. In late June, Monbrion journeyed to the Vaucluse to recruit federalists. Isoard later claimed that he had conscripted 400 volunteers in the Basses-Alpes between June 19 and August 10. Other commissioners visited Nîmes, Orange, Avignon, and Montpellier to invite "subscriptions." [86]

The visit and speech of one of these envoys, a certain Dlionville,[87] has been preserved in the papers of the popular society of St.-Zacharie (Var). On July 10, Dlionville arrived in this commune accompanied by two volunteers recently recruited at Peynier. In his address he began by declaring that liberty was in mortal peril. The king, he contended, was a traitor who had accepted the constitution only after betraying it and then had set about corrupting "a great part" of the deputies to the National Assembly by means of the civil list. He continued:

His many forfeits have obliged the citizens of the great cities to march to the capital. Five hundred have left from Marseilles. . . . We reckon that there will be around 150,000 citizens at Paris. . . . Come brothers and friends, come join us. . . . Citizens, the moment has arrived; . . . let us demand that the royal family be proscribed, that this family which is the cause of our troubles be annihilated.[88]

[86] *Ibid.*, July 3 and 14, 1792, pp. 213, 233. AD, B-du-Rh, L 2075, Letter of the Club of Pertuis to M. Fabre, July 3, 1792; *ibid.*, L 2076, "Vie politique d'Isoard."

[87] Dlionville was a Parisian who attended the Club in the summer of 1792 and frequently served as a commissioner in Provence.

[88] E. Poupé, "Les Papiers de la société populaire de St.-Zacharie,"

Dlionville's entreaties bore fruit. Two federalists from St.-Zacharie accompanied those from Peynier to join the battalion in Paris. Elsewhere, the evangelism of the Club also had significant results. Communes such as St.-Maximin, Montpellier, Trets, Langres, Niort, St.-Paul-Trois-Châteaux, and Manosque all announced monetary subscriptions or the registration of volunteers. As early as June 21, representatives from the club of Toulon appeared at the Club to announce their readiness "to fly to the aid" of their country with fifteen federalists. By mid-July twenty-four communes of the Var had contributed their sons.[89]

The aim of the Marseillais was to dethrone the king. An address by the Municipality (read and approved in the Club on June 30) proclaimed it openly to the Legislative Assembly on July 12; and other pamphlets outlined the best means to reorganize the executive after this object had been achieved. In case of the expedition's failure or the capture of Paris by the Austrians, a southern republic was to be formed, with Marseilles as its capital. On July 23, 1792, the Directory of the district, the Municipality, and the Club of Marseilles decided to send thirteen representatives into the southern departments to propagate these ideas and to raise 6,000 men for the armies of the Midi.[90]

The overthrow of the monarchy on August 10 made these preparations superfluous. The news of these events reached

---

Bulletin de la Société d'études scientifiques et archaéologiques de Draguignan, XXV (1907), 59–74.

[89] *JdD*, June 23–July 5, 1792, pp. 198–218; E. Poupé, "Les Fédérés varois du 10 août," *La Révolution française*, XLVII (1904), 305–325; AD, Hérault, L 5500; AD, Drôme, L 1085, especially July 8, 1792.

[90] *Moniteur*, XIII, no. 196, 26; BM, 4717, "Adresse du Conseil-Général de la Commune de Marseille" (Marseille, 1792); *ibid.*, "Adresse des autorités administratives" (Marseille, 1792).

Marseilles on August 16, a day of triumph for the Society. In succeeding weeks the Club erected a monument to the fallen heroes of August 10 and celebrated the new era with splendid public ceremonies. Its orators boastfully claimed credit for overthrowing the king, and it accepted without hesitation the plaudits of its admirers. Typical of such praise was a speech given in the Club on September 7 by Thomas-Augustin de Gasparin, a national commissioner: "It is to the Marseillais, it is to the popular society of this city . . . that the universe owes its liberty founded on equality." [91]

The last months of the moribund Legislative Assembly were eventful ones in Marseilles. Between July 21 and September 8, roving bands murdered fifteen "counterrevolutionaries." At first the Marseilles Jacobins, meeting by now twice a day, justified these popular executions.[92] By mid-September, however, they had begun to urge the protection of persons and properties; and they helped form a Popular Tribunal on October 1, to give those suspected of counterrevolution a fair trial.[93] On August 22, 1792, a band of 800 Marseillais returning from Manosque kidnapped the entire Directory of the department and conducted them from Aix to Marseilles. After

[91] *JdD*, Sept. 15, 1792, p. 346. Thomas-Augustin de Gasparin of Orange was a deputy of the Bouches-du-Rhône to the Legislative Assembly and the Convention. He died on a mission in the Midi in the fall of 1793.

[92] See a letter of August 6, 1792, written to St.-Zacharie, AD, Var, series L.

[93] AD, B-du-Rh, L 2076, "Adresse des amis de la Liberté, et de l'Egalité de Marseille aux citoyens du département" (Marseille, 1792). The Popular Tribunal tried a number of the Jacobins of Marseilles during the Federalist rebellion, but in the beginning all the judges were members of the Club. See P. Albert Robert, *La Justice des sections marseillaises* (Paris, 1913); AN, AF II 90, "A Mes Juges" (Marseille, 1793).

consultation with the Society, the Municipality provided the Directory with a permanent meeting place in Marseilles. Henceforth, it was little more than an appendage of the Club; indeed, on November 30, 1792, its members went en masse to the Club to pay homage to their liege lord: "True republicans, you are our models; you are our masters, and you will be our strongest prop." [94]

On September 2, the electoral assembly of the Bouches-du-Rhône convened at Avignon to elect representatives to the forthcoming National Convention. Like the assembly of the previous year, it declared itself permanent and organized expeditions into the Bouches-du-Rhône. Moreover, it too was dominated by the Jacobins of Marseilles. Prior to the assembly the Society had begun to propagandize the voters. A placard drafted by Maillet the elder and Ricord advised them to choose only men who had proved their patriotism over the last four years.[95] After the assembly had opened, the electors from Marseilles designated those who were to be chosen. According to one of the deputies elected, Durand de Maillane: "The four hundred electors of Marseilles permitted no one to raise a voice against them." [96] Of the six Marseillais selected, all were militants of the Society. Before their departure for Paris, each took an oath acknowledging the right of the people to recall any representatives who "betrayed the

[94] AN, F⁷ 3659³; AM, 4D₆; *JdD*, Dec. 1, 1792, p. 475.

[95] François Maillet (Maillet the elder), a master of fine arts, was born at Purse (Basses-Alpes) about 1752. He served as secretary of the Club in October, 1790, as president in August–September, 1792, and as vice-president in June, 1794. He was arrested by the Federalists in May, 1793. After his release he became an administrator in the department. He suffered imprisonment at Ham during the Thermidorian Reaction. AD, B-du-Rh, L 2076, "Avis aux citoyens, amis de la liberté" (Marseille, 1792).

[96] *Histoire de la Convention nationale* (Paris, 1825), p. 31.

fatherland." This "right" was soon claimed by the Club.[97]

The months of August and September, 1792, saw the fortunes of the French reach their nadir in the War. In Marseilles, at the morning session of the Club on September 3, 1792, a secretary read an alarming letter from François-Omer Granet in Paris telling of the capture of Longwy by the Prussians and forecasting an enemy march on Paris. On a motion by the acting president, Barthélemy of Toulon,[98] the members resolved "to fly to the aid" of the fatherland. Several patriotically offered themselves, their sons, and their silver to staff and equip a new battalion. The Municipality charged all citizens to emulate the Club's patriotism and invited the Society to name eight commissioners to procure arms. After feverish preparations, 594 Marseillais left the city for Paris. By the time they arrived on October 20, however, Dumouriez had turned the enemy's advance into a retreat. Instead of guarding the capital, the volunteers found themselves being used as pawns in the deadly political game being played by the Jacobins and Girondins.[99]

In describing the first months of the Convention, historians have traditionally concentrated on the power struggle between the Girondins and the Montagnards. The Girondins, according to the classical accounts, were moderate republicans and representatives of the provinces; the Montagnards (who sat on the left in elevated seats) believed in radical re-

[97] AD, B-du-Rh, L 278. The six deputies were Rébecquy, Barbaroux, Moyse Bayle, François-Omer Granet, Pierre Baille, and Bernard Laurent.

[98] Barthélemy, a lawyer, was born in Toulon on January 12, 1752. He was a municipal officer of Toulon from 1790 to August, 1791, when he fled into temporary exile at Marseilles. He was executed by the Federalists of Toulon in 1793.

[99] *JdD*, Sept. 11, 1792, pp. 335–337; AM, 4D₆, To the President of the Society, Sept. 3, 1792.

publicanism and represented Paris. More recently, however, M. J. Sydenham has cast doubt on the very existence of a Girondin party.[100] While his theories may go too far, he has caused historians to re-examine the question. It is clear that the issues dividing the two groups were based on personal rivalries more than political or geographical principles. The Jacobins of Marseilles certainly recognized the existence of two parties in Paris and identified them with individuals. They called the Girondins "Brissotins" or "Rolandists." The leaders of the Mountain they believed to be Marat and Robespierre.

The Girondins planned to use the ten thousand federalists in Paris as a counterweight against the Jacobins and the sections. The federalists had a club of their own in the headquarters of the Marseilles battalion. Under the influence of Barbaroux, who was by now an archenemy of Robespierre, the battalion harassed the Montagnards and served as a sort of praetorian guard for Roland. In the beginning Barbaroux was able to carry the delegation from the Bouches-du-Rhône with him. On October 1, he persuaded nine members to endorse a public indictment of Marat and the Commune of Paris. In the Convention he repeatedly attacked prominent Montagnards. Gradually, however, dissension appeared in the ranks of the twelve deputies, and in early January, 1793, four of the Marseilles representatives, Granet, Moyse Bayle, Pierre Baille, and Bernard Laurent,[101] accused Barbaroux of breaking his oath and of leading the battalion of Marseillais to the brink of an abyss.[102]

[100] *The Girondins* (London, 1961).

[101] Laurent (Laurens) a surgeon, was born at Barrême (Basses-Alpes) in 1742 and died at Paris in 1802.

[102] Barbaroux, *Mémoires*, pp. 186–190. F. Portal, *Le Bataillon marseillais du 21 janvier* (Marseille, 1900), pp. 4–7. AD, B-du-Rh, L 2076,

Both factions had partisans in the Club of the Rue Thubaneau. Barbaroux and Robespierre were regarded with high favor, but neither Marat nor Roland had the respect of the members. The clubbists generally regarded Marat as a bloodthirsty demagogue; and Roland had lost favor through his interference, as minister of the interior, in the affairs of Provence. Throughout the autumn the Society tried to follow a neutral course. As late as December 22 it was urging the deputies from the Bouches-du-Rhône to be "neither Maratists nor Brissotins." When the Jacobin society in Paris denounced Barbaroux, the Marseilles Club sent it in reply an address written on December 16, lamenting the "intrigue and ambition" in the capital and peremptorily requesting a profession of faith: "Although it would grieve us very dearly to separate from you, we warn you that we will break off all liaison and correspondence until you prove yourselves still the same Jacobins of '89." [103]

The threatened rupture did not materialize. By January 23, 1793, when a reply to the letter of December 16 arrived in Marseilles, the Montagnard position had triumphed in the Society. Since the electoral assembly the Marseilles Jacobins had consistently demanded that the "traitor Louis" be judged and put to death. The Girondins sought to delay the execution by the device of appealing to the primary assemblies to decide the king's ultimate fate. Pro-Montagnards in Marseilles, including Ricord and Jean-Baptiste Loys, utilized this issue to discredit Barbaroux and his cohorts. On January 4, with Loys presiding, the Society voted against indulgence for Louis XVI. Astonished murmurs filled the hall on January 9, when

"Discours que prononca Granet, accompagné de Moyse Bayle, P. Baille et Laurens" (Marseille, 1793).

[103] *JdD*, Dec. 13–22, 1792, pp. 495–512.

a letter from Barbaroux was read that argued for the appeal to the people. Charles Guinot [104] drafted an address condemning Barbaroux's opinions and warned that those who voted for the appeal to the people would be declared traitors. In a long speech on January 13, Loys urged every good citizen to unite with the Jacobins and *sans-culottes* in Paris. Shorty thereafter the Club began to expel members who supported the Girondins. On January 23, it formally excluded Barbaroux and his close ally Rébecquy. [105]

In the ensuing weeks the Club began a nationwide grass roots campaign to remove the "perfidious deputies" who had voted on January 15 for the appeal to the people. Letters to the societies of southeastern France urged new electoral assemblies to recall the deputies who had broken their oaths. After lengthy discussion the Club mailed out to the 83 departments 2,000 copies of an address drafted on February 7 by Maillet the elder and Guinot demanding the convocation of electoral assemblies and the recall of "traitors and disturbers." This letter set off a groundswell of public opinion which, before it had run its course, had almost propelled the Jacobins into actions detrimental to their best interests. [106]

On February 17, 1793, in Paris, Ricord informed the mother society of Marseilles' proposal. Jeanbon Saint-André, later a member of the Committee of Public Safety, opposed it,

[104] Guinot, a master of fine arts, was one of the most important leaders of the Club in 1792–1793. He was secretary on several occasions and served as president in March–April, 1793. With the support of the Society, he became chief instructor of the National Boarding School in 1792.

[105] *JdD*, Jan. 3–26, 1793, pp. 539–571. See also BN, Le[38] 180.

[106] AD, Basses-Alpes, L 856/2, "Les Marseillais à tous leurs amis de la République, salut" (Marseille, 1792). Commissioners of the Club journeyed as far west as Castres urging the recall of the unfaithful deputies; AD, Tarn, L 1531.

condemning the movement as federalism and pointing out that new elections might be turned against the Montagnards. A motion to support the proposal of Marseilles was tabled; however, the Paris Jacobins found themselves hard-pressed to stem the floodtide in support of the Marseillais. Innumerable clubs sent addresses of support. In the southeast their names read like a roll-call of the popular societies. This tidal wave compelled the Paris society to reconsider the question in its session of February 27, 1793. For a time the issue hung in the balance. Desfieux rose to point out that the majority of the affiliates favored the recall of the unfaithful deputies. Only the intervention of Robespierre seemingly blocked adoption of this program. The Incorruptible argued against the "rash measures" urged by Marseilles; while the fatherland was in danger it would be foolhardy, he reasoned, to engage "in a new arena of cabal and intrigue." The motion, as finally passed, simply stated that unfaithful deputies would be excluded from the clubs and subjected to civic censure.[107]

The Marseillais failed to stampede the Jacobins into their ill-conceived project. Nevertheless, the attempt illustrated the great prestige and power of the Club in February, 1793. Even more important, it marked the definitive triumph of Montagnard republicanism on the Rue Thubaneau. Moderates ceased to have any important voice in the Club's deliberations. The groundwork was laid for the Federalist rebellion of 1793.

[107] Aulard, *Jacobins*, IV, 30–31, 46. For samples of the addresses of affiliates see AN, DXL 18; AD, B-du-Rh, L 2071, March–April, 1793. For the reaction of a club outside the Midi see *Délibérations de la société populaire de Lons-le-Saunier*, ed. H. Libois (Lons-le-Saunier, 1897), session of April 19, 1793.

5

The Decline of the Club

On Saturday, January 26, 1793, a bulletin from Alexandre Ricord in Paris informed the Marseillais of the death of Louis XVI. Upon learning the news, businessmen closed their shops, the Municipality illuminated the city, and three days of street demonstrations began. The Republic was welcomed by the Club, where control had passed into the hands of such militant Jacobins as the brothers Maillet, Joseph Giraud, Etienne Chompré, Charles Guinot, Pierre Micoulin,[1] and, above all, Isoard. In their speeches and messages this group immodestly referred to themselves as the "Mountain of the Midi."[2]

During the spring of 1793 the Club's militant nucleus adhered closely to the ideology of the Montagnards in Paris. Politically, they urged a "third uprising" to expel the "trai-

---

[1] Pierre Micoulin was an oil merchant. He coedited the *Journal des départements méridionaux* in 1792–1793. He was imprisoned by the Federalists in May, 1793. During the Terror he served for a time as an administrator of the department. After Thermidor he underwent a change of heart and began to entertain royalists and non-juring priests in his home. In 1799 he became a member of the Academy of Marseilles. He died in 1840 at Marseilles.

[2] Danton also used the phrase "Mountain of the Midi" in a speech at the National Convention; see *Moniteur*, XV, no. 87, 808.

torous Rolandists." Socially, the central theme was an outspoken hatred of the "rich." The six Jacobin representatives of Marseilles to the Convention corresponded with the Society almost daily, as did Marseillais in Paris like Alexandre Ricord. The most important liaison with the Montagnards, however, was Jean-Baptiste Loys, who had returned to the capital. During the spring of 1793 a special courier carried his letters to Marseilles. In them he reported in detail the program of the *sans-culottes*. Revolutionary armies were to be formed; the rich must be taxed; all suspects, Feuillants, and moderates were to be incarcerated; and, above all, the "guillotine must be permanent and ready to strike." [3]

The month of March, 1793, was characterized by acute tension in France. The news of the defeat of Miranda in Belgium had much the same impact as the bulletins from Longwy in August, 1792. During the days of March 8–14, 1793, the Convention created a Revolutionary Tribunal and ordered eighty-two of its members into the provinces as representatives-on-mission with wide powers. On March 16, five letters arrived from Paris apprising the Society of these developments and announcing continued "plots" by the Rolandists. Moyse Bayle reported Parisian preparations for a third insurrection and asked for help from Marseilles. The Club immediately declared itself to be in permanent session. Amy urged sending a new battalion to Paris to expel from the convention those who had voted for the appeal to the people. Ultimately Maillet the elder, Chompré, and Guinot drafted addresses to the Convention and to the sections of Paris threatening the Rolandists with the "vengeful sword" of the people, and urging the *sans-culottes* to drive them from the capital. On the same day, discussion began over an "unlimited

[3] See AD, B-du-Rh, L 1980.

levy" of men, and the president appointed a special treasurer to receive "contributions" from the rich for war expenses. On March 25, at Chompré's suggestion, the central committee named twenty-four "good republicans" to visit the southern departments "to ready them to rise en masse when the decisive moment comes."[4]

When the Club declared itself in permanent session on March 16, the central committee did likewise. Dominated by Isoard, it became for a short time the virtual dictator of the city. Isoard and his lieutenants hounded the Municipality, raising the specter of counterrevolutionary plots. After meetings on March 15 and 16, 1793, the city fathers abolished all associations in the city except the Club and instituted a Revolutionary Tribunal and a committee for forced contributions. "You will soon see," boasted Isoard in a letter to the club of Digne, "a law which will tax the rich to subvent the expenses of the War."[5] Behind closed doors at the Municipality on March 18, Isoard proposed a general disarmament of all suspects in the city. He also drew up a list of several hundred Marseillais who were to be incarcerated. The enemies of the Club later contended that the arrests were planned as a prelude to "September massacres" in Marseilles. The Mayor, Mourraille, the procurator, Seytres, and other municipal officers opposed the arrests but acquiesced in a disarmament which took place on March 19.[6]

Between March 24 and March 28, four of the representatives-on-mission newly named by the Convention, Moyse Bayle and Boisset for the Bouches-du-Rhône and Drôme, and Fréron and Barras for the Hautes-Alpes and Basses-Alpes, arrived in Marseilles to recruit volunteers, arrest suspects, and

[4] AD, B-du-Rh, L 2071. [5] AD, B-du-Rh, L 3037.
[6] AD, B-du-Rh, L 3104.

"dismiss gangrenous administrators." The Club, which had often disputed precedence with Parisian representatives in the past, at first opposed the decree of March 9, 1793, but then worked closely with the representatives after their arrival. The four deputies approved the twenty-four commissioners named on March 25 and counselled them to "take money and horses from the selfish rich." In the evening session of March 28, Barras outlined the reasons for a "third revolution" in Paris and asked for support from the Club. "Paris has need of a push from Marseilles in order to rise a third time." [7]

The presence of these proconsuls offered the Society an opportunity to remove two potential enemies, Mourraille and Seytres (both former presidents of the Club), from their positions as mayor and procurator. Their friendship with Barbaroux and their opposition to some of the plans of the Society had compromised both these officials. In February, Emmanuel de Beausset and Charles Guinot charged Mourraille with being a Rolandist. The rift was briefly closed after the latter defended himself in the session of February 23, but by March 16 it had opened again. On that date Pierre Peyre-Ferry [8] proposed that the office of mayor be abolished. Finally, on April 10, "an infinite number of members disputed the glory of denouncing the tyranny and vexations of the mayor and of the procurator of the commune." On April 12, 1793, Bayle and Boisset ordered the arrest of the two hapless municipal officers. [9]

[7] AD, B-du-Rh, L 2071.

[8] Peyre-Ferry was the son of a wealthy wholesale merchant. Both father and son were militant members of the Club. Pierre was president of the revolutionary committee of Marseilles during the Terror. In 1796 he edited a Jacobin journal, *L'Observateur du Midi de la République*.

[9] AD, B-du-Rh, L 2071. *JdD*, Feb. 26 and 28, 1793, pp. 623–624, 629.

On April 11, 1793, a courier from Paris brought news of the evacuation of Landau by the French. This fresh reversal prompted the Club to take new measures to ensure the safety of the city and its own preeminence. It asked the Municipality to assemble all the national guardsmen and hold them ready to march, and it also promised a bounty of 10,000 livres to anyone who would bring to Marseilles, dead or alive, those who had supported the appeal. Finally, it resolved to form a committee of general security to oversee the defense of the Midi. The blueprint for this committee was no less than a plan for the government of the southern departments by the Club of Marseilles. It was to include two deputies from every department of the Midi and representatives from the Jacobins of Paris. Local popular societies would be its administrative agents. In fact, the committee of general security never left the drawing board, but the idea resurfaced in October, 1793, when a general assembly of popular societies gathered at Marseilles.[10]

At the moment when the Club had apparently reached the pinnacle of strength and prestige, a popular movement originating in the sections overturned it. The sections were first formed as electoral districts, each with roughly 4,000 inhabitants, within the municipalities. Every electoral district had a legal assembly of electors, but originally the assemblies could be convened only on the orders of municipal officials. Prior to 1792 the thirty-two sections of Marseilles acted almost wholly as electoral organs. Meetings were infrequent, and only a few citizens bothered to attend. In the turbulent days of July-September, 1792, however, a sharp rise in attendance took place, and the assemblies, which met daily, lost their purely electoral character and became deliberative bodies.

[10] *Moniteur*, XVI, no. 122, 272; AD, B-du-Rh, L 2071.

When a new crisis developed in March, 1793, a massive push began until, by April, there were often 500 participants in each section.[11]

The uprising of the sections was part of a large "Federalist rebellion" taking place in France in the spring of 1793. Historians have traditionally viewed the Federalist movement in Marseilles as a sort of class struggle between the rich bourgeoisie of the sections and the poor *sans-culottes* of the Club, an interpretation that was re-enforced by the violent verbal assaults of the central committee against the rich and by the fact that many wealthy wholesale merchants were executed during the Terror. However, the social composition of the Society and the sections was much more similar than this stereotyped picture indicates. Indeed, a great many sectionnaires were former members of the Society. Pierre Laugier, president of the Club in January-February, 1793, was the first Federalist executed during the Terror. The decisive schism had taken place at the time of the expulsion of Barbaroux from the Club. The engineer Couedic, himself a secretary of the correspondence committee, declared publicly that the Society had gone insane. At the same time the triumphant Montagnards in the Club began a purge of suspected Brissotins.

A powerful undercurrent of resentment toward the Society had always existed in Marseilles. As the Club became more arbitrary and autocratic in the spring of 1793, resentment mushroomed into outright rebellion in the sections. By April, control of the sectional assemblies had passed into the hands

[11] Professor Vovelle at the University of Aix-en-Provence has been directing a group project on the sections of Marseilles. See also John B. Cameron, "The Federalist Movement in the Bouches-du-Rhône" (unpublished dissertation, University of North Carolina at Chapel Hill, 1971).

of republican opponents of the Montagnards in Paris, secret monarchists, and former Jacobins alarmed by the actions of the radicals in the Society. The royalist Fonvielle, for example, tells us that he began attending the sections when he learned that his name was on a list of citizens the central committee wanted to arrest.[12] As early as March 9, 1793, concern had been voiced in the Club over "doubtful citizens" in the sections. As a preventive measure the Society urged all members to attend the sectional meetings. It soon became clear, however, that the formerly docile sections had become too powerful for the Club to contain. Charges began to be heard in the sectional assemblies that the Society was building a "rolling guillotine" and planning to massacre the citizens. Ultimately, the sectionnaires bound themselves together under a general committee to coordinate action. Bayle and Boisset fled to Montelimar on April 28, 1793, taking with them a few members of the Club. From there they charged that the sections had fallen into the hands of the rich and ordered the abolition of the two basic instruments of sectional government, the general committee and the Popular Tribunal.[13]

The sectionnaires ignored this order and demanded the closure of the Society, charging its leaders with plotting "murder and carnage." On May 4, the Club was reduced to beseeching the Municipality for support. Some clubbists called an emergency assembly at Salon to galvanize the patriots of the Bouches-du-Rhône. During the sickness of

[12] M. Vovelle, "Essai d'analyse idéologique des sections marseillaises," *Bulletin. Institut Historique de Provence*, no. 2 (1963), pp. 138–140; A. Genta, "La Vie des sections marseillaises de juin 1791 au 25 août 1793" (unpublished dissertation, University of Aix, 1959); Chevalier de Fonvielle, *Mémoires historiques* (Paris, 1824), I, 399–450.

[13] G. Guibal, *Le Mouvement fédéraliste en Provence en 1793* (Paris, 1908), pp. 92–95.

Ricord, now returned from Paris, Isoard assumed the presidency of the Society and directed its defense. In an address placarded about the city, he decried the "black calumnies" circulated by the "aristocrats" in the sections. On May 11, Guinot drafted an oration denying the presence of intriguers in the Club.[14] Several entreaties were sent to the Paris Jacobins; a letter of May 13 complained that:

The sections filled with the rich patriots of August 10 and January 21, have vowed to annihilate our society. They denounce our orators as intriguers. . . . Our poor society is lacerated and put on the wheel by the "honest people" . . . who have become so patriotic in the last month.[15]

The Club's efforts failed. On May 16, 1793, the Federalists enjoined it from holding meetings on the same day as the sections. Between May 14 and 20, the general committee of the sections ordered the arrest of twenty leading members of the Club, including the brothers Maillet, Beausset, Guinot, Micoulin, Joseph Giraud, Isoard, Chompré, Joseph Tourneau, Louis Barthélemy, Frederick Hughes, Beissière, Trahan, and Ricord.[16] Formal protests availed little. In despair, Hughes killed himself in his cell. Trahan also attempted suicide but without success. On May 25, a meeting of the frightened rump

[14] AM, 1 D11, session of May 4, 1793. AD, B-du-Rh, L 1980, L 3104, L 2075–2076.

[15] AD, B-du-Rh, L 1980.

[16] Hughes was an entrepreneur and a member of the central committee in 1793. Louis Barthélemy, a soap maker, was elected a notable of the Municipality in 1790. The Federalists executed him in 1793. Tourneau, a clerk from Aubagne, accompanied Isoard to the Basses-Alpes in April–May, 1792, and served as his chief assistant in the central committee.

of the Society retracted its criticism of the sections and condemned the jailed "extremists." [17]

Despite this betrayal, the general committee of the thirty-
two sections abolished the Club. At 7:00 P.M. on June 3,
1793, a deputation of sectionnaires entered the old tennis
court on the Rue Thubaneau, seized all papers and posses-
sions, and sealed the doors.[18] The Federalists justified their
actions on the grounds that the Republic could not tolerate
the "existence of a society of intriguers and anarchists . . .
which, down to the least administration, disposed of everything, pronounced on everything, and arrogated to itself universal power." [19] After May 29, 1793, the general committee
also refused to recognize any decrees of the Convention. For
nearly three months Marseilles was in a state of insurrection
against the French government.

June 4 to August 28 is a period of interregnum in the Club's
history. Many of its rank-and-file probably joined the sections. Most of the chiefs of the Society languished in their
cells; a few (François-Paul Grimaud, Jean Bazin, Sébastien
Abeille, and Louis Barthélemy) were tried by the Popular
Tribunal and executed.[20] The fortunate ones escaped. Charles

[17] AN, AF II 90, "A Mes Juges" (Marseille, 1793); *ibid.*, AF II 91;
AD, B-du-Rh, L 1980, "Les Républicains du club de Marseille, à leurs
frères de toutes les sociétés et sections de la République, salut" (Marseille, 1793). See also BN, Lb[40] 2781.

[18] AD, B-du-Rh, L 1980, Closing of the patriotic society.

[19] *Ibid.*, L 2076, "Le Comité général, au nom de ses commettans"
(Marseille, 1793).

[20] As commissioners of the Society in 1792–1793, Grimaud, Abeille,
and Bazin terrorized the commune of Salon. Grimaud was born in
1759 at Sisteron. He attended the Club as early as March, 1791, and
served as judge of the district tribunal of Marseilles until his arrest
and execution in 1793. Abeille, a tailor, was born in Béziers in 1756.

Guinot fled to Toulon, where he offered his services to Pierre Baille and Beauvais, representatives with the army of the Midi. The clever Isoard went to Paris, where he aided in the overthrow of the Girondins on June 2 and joined the Jacobins. On July 1, 1793, he and other refugees from the Midi formed a small exile society of which he was president.[21]

On August 24, 1793, a government force under General Cartaux defeated the last remnants of the Federalist army at Septèmes, a small village just north of Marseilles. The following day at 9:00 A.M., accompanied by five representatives-on-mission, Cartaux marched into Marseilles; and the representatives set to work immediately releasing prisoners, re-establishing the purged local administrations, and ordering the arrest of Federalists. The National Convention received the news on August 31, when Danton arose to denounce "the merchant aristocracy" of Marseilles and to demand that they be guillotined. On September 4, the Convention decreed that the rebels should be punished, their property confiscated, and the persecuted patriots reimbursed. The Terror had begun in Marseilles.[22]

The representatives solemnly reopened the Club on the day of their entry into Marseilles, but it did not begin to meet regularly until some days later. Meanwhile faithful Club members inventoried the effects of the sections, denounced suspects, and volunteered to serve in the siege of Toulon.

Bazin, a notary public, born about 1760 in Lambesc (Bouches-du-Rhône), was active in the Society in 1793.

[21] AN, AF II 90, 664, nos. 5, 7, 18; AD, B-du-Rh, L 2076, "Les Patriotes du Midi réfugiés à Paris, à leurs concitoyens" (Marseille, 1793); *ibid.*, "Vie politique d'Isoard."

[22] Alphonse Aulard, *Recueil des actes du Comité du salut public* (Paris, 1889–1933), VI, 112–113, 158–161, 272–273; *Moniteur*, XVII, no. 249, 572–574.

Several of the small exile band in Paris became agents of the Committee of Public Safety. On August 28, the Committee gave Loys 20,000 livres to fulfill a special mission in the Bouches-du-Rhône. It also ordered Isoard, Jacques Monbrion, Jean-Joseph Ferru, Charles Ehrmann, Antoine Réquier, Libre Morel, and Romuald Bertin to Provence "to resurrect the popular societies, especially that of Marseilles." Under their direction a major purification of the Society took place. On September 12, under its new president, Isoard, the Club formally notified its affiliates of its re-establishment.[23]

During the Terror, the Club of Marseilles no longer dared to defy the Government in Paris. Its addresses to the Convention were innocuous pledges of support and loyalty. Like the other clubs of France, it functioned as a quasi-official unit of administration. "Any authority, any individual," stated a decree of the Convention of July 25, 1793, "who under any pretext whatsoever obstructs the meeting of Popular Societies or employs any means to dissolve them, will be prosecuted as guilty of a criminal offense against liberty and punished as such." As a legal assembly, the Club formed a subsidiary link in a chain of command descending from the Committee of Public Safety. This great committee quarried the Society for

[23] Aulard, *Comité du salut public*, VI, 85, 160, 186, 204, 295; *Moniteur*, XVII, no. 63, 560, no. 271, 759; AD, B-du-Rh, L 3037.

Réquier, a schoolmaster, was a founder of the Society in 1790 and a secretary three times after January, 1793. He served as public prosecutor of the Revolutionary Tribunal for a time during the Terror.

Ehrmann, a wholesale merchant, was secretary of the Club in July, 1792, and throughout the Terror. He was also judge of the Revolutionary Tribunal for a time. Auguis and Serres had him arrested in September, 1794. Morel was vice-president of the Society in August, 1794. At that time he was a departmental administrator. He too was arrested by Auguis and Serres. Ferru, born in Toulon about 1759, attended the Club for about nine months in 1791–1792.

republicans deemed "suitable for public office" and for workers in the wartime industries.[24] Only after Thermidor did the Club recover sufficient courage to challenge the rule of the committees and the "moderates" in the Convention.

After August, 1793, disputes between the Club and the administrations of the city, the district, and the department were noticeably absent. In order to serve in any of these, one had first to be a Jacobin. The representatives-on-mission, with the exception of Barras and Fréron, consulted the Club before making new installations to these administrations. Isoard became procurator of the Municipality on October 25, 1793. In this position "he always took to heart the interests of the society of which he was the idol." The fact that positions on the Municipality were monopolized by the Club's members did not restrict the clubbists from scrutinizing its conduct. When a deputation from the Society found no one present at the city hall one night in October, 1793, it vigorously reproved the Municipality for its negligence.[25]

During the Terror the Club and the Municipality worked in tandem. The Society publicized decrees and proclamations and functioned as an employment bureau for a wide variety of patriotic projects. When duties overburdened the municipal officials, they often turned to members of the Society for assistance. On September 18, the Municipality asked the Club to name twelve commissioners to scour the countryside for mules, draft horses, and saddle horses. Two days later, a commission of Club members and local officials visited the prisons to verify health standards and make lists of those detained. The clubbists also cooperated by staffing municipal commit-

[24] Brinton, pp. 74–75; AM, 4 D₇, To the popular society, Nov. 29, 1793.

[25] AM, 1 D₁₁, sessions of Oct. 20, Dec. 28, 1793.

tees. One such committee approved petitions for certificates of citizenship. Another, the twelve-man committee of émigrés, half of whom were named by the Society, examined cases of emigration.[26]

Under the Revolutionary Government the national agent of the district became for a time the most important local official. Throughout most of the Terror Elzear de Mongendre, an ardent member of the Society, held this position. Mongendre employed the Club both to disseminate propaganda and instruction and to implement the decrees of the Committee of Public Safety.[27] Clubbists also staffed the instruments of revolutionary justice. Through the surveillance committee, whose members included such Jacobins as Beissière, the Club kept an observant eye on suspects and helped guide the investigations of the public prosecutor. Leaders of the Club officered the Revolutionary Tribunal of the Bouches-du-Rhône: from August 28, 1793, to January 18, 1794, and again from March 10 to April 25, 1794, Maillet the younger was president, Joseph Giraud public prosecutor, and Étienne Chompré secretary; from March 15 to April 18, 1794, Étienne Bompard served as president and Antoine Réquier as public prosecutor; judges included Jacques-François Brogi, Leclerc, and François-Joseph Rouedy.[28]

Having once possessed extreme power, the leaders of the reincarnated Club of the Rue Thubaneau found anything less

[26] AN, AF II 90, 661. AD, B-du-Rh, L 129, Letter of Sep. 22, 1793. See also various letters and other pieces in AM, 4 D₇, 1 D₄, 1 D₁₂.

[27] AD, B-du-Rh, L 1061, L 1035.

[28] Bompard, a wholesale merchant, became a notable in 1792. During 1791–1792 he served on several occasions as secretary at the Club. Michel-François Leclerc, an associate of Barbaroux, was a lawyer in 1790. He acted as vice-president of the Club in July–August, 1792.

intolerable. In the Terror the Club may have been a shadow of its former self, but it was a shadow seeking substance and form. The vehicle it attempted to ride to power was a general assembly of popular societies which met in Marseilles in October, 1793. Even before the Federalist rebellion, the Society had broached schemes for regional governments based on the Jacobin network. As early as February 27, 1793, Hugues had proposed that the societies of the Bouches-du-Rhône send permanent commissioners to Marseilles to form a committee to "work together for the safety of the Republic"; [29] and the committee of general security envisaged in April would have expanded this proposition to include all the departments of the Midi.

Blueprints for Jacobin party government were by no means limited to the fertile minds of the Marseillais. Indeed, the general assembly that convened at Marseilles in October, 1793, resulted from two previous congresses called by the popular society of Valence (Drôme), both of which had sought to unify the clubs in the face of the Federalist menace. [30] The second of these conventions, which met on September 7, 8, and 9, 1793, included deputies from seventy-one clubs in the Isère, Bouches-du-Rhône, Drôme, Vaucluse, Gard, Ardèche, Nièvre, and Basses-Alpes. Jean-Baptiste-Antoine Boutin and Emmanuel de Beausset represented Marseilles, while Sébastien Lacroix and Isoard attended in the name of the Jacobins of Paris. [31] A motion unanimously adopted at this congress pro-

[29] *JdD*, Mar. 2, 1793, p. 631.

[30] BN, Lb⁴⁰ 3057, "Procès-verbal de l'assemblée du 42 sociétés populaires" (Valence, 1793). BN, Lb⁴⁰ 3058, "Procès-verbal de l'assemblée de soixante-onze sociétés populaires" (Valence, 1793).

[31] Boutin, a curé, was born at Brignoles in 1746. He was president of the Club in November–December, 1792, and again in October, 1794.

Marie-Sébastien Bruneau de Lacroix came from Châtillon-sur-

posed "successive reunions of popular societies in order to
. . . revive the revolutionary spirit and to take measures for
the public safety." It assigned an eight-man group (including
the omnipresent Isoard) to organize the first such assembly at
Marseilles.

Isoard returned to Marseilles on September 10, 1793. Two
days later the Club drafted an address to all its affiliates announcing a congress at Marseilles on October 1. It is impossible to say precisely how many of them attended. Pierre-
Stanislas Mittié, an agent of the minister of the interior at
Marseilles in 1793–1794, counted about 60 on October 6, but
later reports boasted representation from 400 clubs. The general assembly held its initial session on October 3, 1793, at
9:00 A.M. and thereafter convened every morning at the same
time. In the evenings deputies attended the regular sessions
of the Club. On October 3 those assembled elected Isoard
president and Alexandre Ricord vice-president. A committee
of twelve was chosen to prepare the agenda; since they included Isoard, Ricord, Loys, Giraud, and Maillet the elder,
little could be undertaken without the Club's sanction.[32]

One of the main interests of the congress was the struggle

Marne. Prior to 1789 he studied law at Paris. In 1792–1793 he acquired notoriety as an ardent petitioner of the Paris sections. He
served as an auxiliary of Fréron and Barras at Marseilles in the fall
of 1793, editing the *Journal républicain de Marseille*. He died on the
guillotine in Paris on April 13, 1794.

[32] For the announcement of September 12 see AD, Basses-Alpes,
L 856/2, "Frères et amis" (Marseille, 1793). The report of Mittié is
in P. Caron, *Rapports des agents du Ministre de l'Intérieur dans les
départements, 1793-an II* (Paris, 1951), II, 279. See also BN, Lb^{40} 2782
(1–5), "Procès-verbal de l'assemblée générale des sociétés populaires"
(Marseille, 1793); AD, B-du-Rh, L 2076, "Précis des opérations des
sociétés populaires . . . réunies en assemblée générale à Marseille"
(Marseille, 1793).

against counterrevolution and federalism. In delegations and addresses to the National Convention, it demanded the trial of the "traitors" then in the hands of the Revolutionary Tribunal and the arrest of the deputies who had protested against the coup d'état of May 29–June 2. On the local level it urged death for all Federalist functionaries and worked for the recapture of Toulon. It named an eight man commission to investigate the condition of the troops, the citizenship of the generals, and the honesty of the entrepreneurs supplying the besieging force. Finally, it created a revolutionary army, the Montagnard Legion, whose mission, proposed originally at Valence, was "to pursue counterrevolutionaries" and to aid in the siege of Toulon. With mixed results the congress sent commissioners and letters to the clubs of the Drôme, Vaucluse, Hautes-Alpes, and the Basses-Alpes seeking recruits for the legion. Economic matters also occupied an important part in the debates; as one of its measures, the congress drew up a plan for the national organization of food supplies.[33]

The most significant project undertaken was an attempt to expand the power and influence of the clubs. The congress demanded privileges for popular societies heretofore reserved for legally sanctioned administrations. Even more important, it asked the Convention to organize annual national and departmental councils of clubs. National councils would meet for two to four weeks each year, in alternating cities. The Convention would provide the necessary funds for travel and lodging except in rebel areas where counterrevolutionaries would foot the bill. The departmental assemblies would meet

[33] *Ibid*. See also BN, Lb[40] 2788, "Adresse des sociétés populaires du Midi, réunies à Marseille, à la Convention nationale" (Marseille, 1793). Aulard, *Jacobins*, V, 481. AN, C 285. AD, Basses-Alpes, L 861. *Archives parlementaires*, LXXVI, 655–660.

yearly and always in the same city. One of their tasks would be to select a committee of nine popular society members to exercise "active surveillance" over the departmental administration. Similar observers would be selected for each of the districts of the department. On the communal level every society would select watchdogs for its particular municipality. Detailed reports would be sent to the ministry of the interior.[34] It is easy to see that these measures, had they been enacted, would have created a parallel party hierarchy alongside the official government agencies, reminiscent of that which exists in some totalitarian countries today. The clubs would have had life and death power over functionaries. It is small wonder, therefore, that the representative-on-mission, Fréron, did not approve of the plans and eventually dissolved the congress.

The most celebrated proconsuls of the Terror in Marseilles were the Vicomte Paul de Barras and Pierre-Marie-Stanislas Fréron. Neither of them possessed the highest moral character, nor have they found many defenders among historians. Conservatives have denounced both as bloodthirsty tyrants; Robespierrists have labelled them corrupt intriguers. Barras was an "aristocrat by birth, education, and tastes, and a demagogue by profession." [35] Fréron was the son of a *philosophe*, corrupt, and the famous chief of the "gilded youth" of Paris. Mathiez described him as a "*débauché* who shed torrents of blood at Toulon and Marseilles . . . being devoid of ideas, he substituted abuse for arguments." [36] The rule of these representatives began on October 12, 1793, and ended in February, 1794. On the day of their arrival they proclaimed

[34] AD, B-du-Rh, L 2076, "Précis des opérations."
[35] *Memoirs of Barras: Member of the Directorate*, ed. Georges Duruy, trans. Charles E. Roche (London, 1895), I, xlv.
[36] A. Mathiez, *After Robespierre* (New York: A. Knopf, 1931), pp. 11, 36, 69–70.

terror the order of the day. Typically, they spent their first week criticizing the preceding representatives in Marseilles. In a letter to his old schoolmate, Robespierre, Fréron boasted: "If Barras and I had entered Marseilles [on August 24], the houses of the rich would be razed and Toulon taken." [37]

To begin with, Barras and Fréron were highly popular with both the Club and the delegates at the assembly of popular societies. They attended the sessions of both and often utilized members to carry out important missions. When two Dutch ships, said to be filled with munitions, were compelled to seek harbor at St.-Nazaire and Bandols, the two representatives sent deputies from the congress to investigate. In turn, the Club and the assembly praised the representatives lavishly in addresses to Paris. As late as November 8, the united clubs rushed to Fréron's defense when Hébert denounced him at a meeting of the Jacobins in Paris.[38]

Despite such evidence of support, Fréron found the existence of the congress intolerable. In letters to Paris he condemned it as "a new species of federalism" and charged it with usurping legal authority. Bringing it to an end, however, required some skill on his part. His predecessors at Marseilles had issued a decree promising the deputies ten francs per day, thus tying them to the city. He finally paid out 100,000 francs to the delegates "to extirpate the federalist wolf." On November 22 the congress formally dissolved itself.[39] Fréron

[37] Aulard, *Comité du salut public*, VII, 404. See also AN, AF II 185.
[38] On the Dutch ships, see AN, AF II 185. On Hébert see Aulard, *Jacobins*, V, 481, 492–502.
[39] Poupé, *Lettres de Barras et de Fréron*, pp. 45–52, 66–67. AN, AF II 186, Barras to the Committee of Public Safety, Dec. 2, 1793; AD, B-du-Rh, L 2076, "Les Membres des sociétés populaires . . . , réunis en assemblée générale à Marseille, à la Convention nationale" (Marseille, 1793).

then turned on the "intriguers" in the Club who had dominated it, accusing them of using every conceivable strategem
to keep it in operation. It is perhaps not coincidental that accusations charging Fréron and Barras with counterrevolution,
sumptuous living, and corruption now began to filter into the
Committee of Public Safety with increasing frequency. A
letter bearing their forged signatures, dated December 1, 1793,
implied that the representatives were plotting with the English.[40]

The hostility between the leaders of the Club and the two
representatives was the underlying cause of a series of disturbances which broke out in Marseilles on December 2, 3, and
4, 1793. The immediate spark was the application of a decree
issued by the Committee of Public Safety on November 4,
1793, placing Marseilles under martial law. The army commandant at Marseilles, Nicholas-Benoît Montmeau, executed
this order without prior notification to the Municipality or
the Club. The Society's reaction was to declare itself in permanent session; turbulence broke out in the city. Fréron later
charged that Isoard planned the troubles as an excuse to lynch
imprisoned suspects. Under Isoard's direction the Municipality arbitrarily lowered the price of bread in order to secure
the allegiance of the people. At 2:00 A.M. on December 3
eight Jacobins armed with sabers and pistols appeared at
Montmeau's residence and escorted him to the Club, where he
was interrogated and threatened by its officers. Without the
authorization of Barras and Fréron, the Municipality coun-
termanded the orders of a battalion of 1,200 *sans-culottes*,
who were scheduled to march to Toulon, and told them to
remain in the city. The Club asked all the official administra-

[40] Poupé, *Lettres*, pp. 55, 65, 75, 80; *Moniteur*, XVIII, no. 80, 623–
628.

tions to meet with it. Faced with rebellion against their authority, the representatives called for re-enforcements from the Var and the Drôme. On December 4, the representatives dissolved the Municipality and the surveillance committee and established new ones in their place. La Poype, brother-in-law of Fréron, was named the new commandant of Marseilles.[41]

Having taken these steps, the two representatives dispatched justificatory letters to Moyse Bayle, who was now in Paris, complaining of "a continual struggle" with fifteen to twenty "ringleaders" in the Society who "defied national authority and sought to lead the popular societies astray." Fréron named Isoard, Loys, Maillet the younger, **Giraud**, Réquier, Guillaume Carle and others as the principal culprits. He hesitated to arrest them or to dissolve the Society for fear of being denounced as a counterrevolutionary. On the other hand, if he allowed them to meet in the name of "liberty of opinion" then "anarchy would reign." He requested that Bayle formulate some pretext to remove them from the city.[42]

Between December 12, 1793, and January 12, 1794, Barras and Fréron retired from Marseilles to preside over the capture of Toulon and the execution of approximately 800 Federalists. On January 6, from Toulon, they issued a tripartite decree divesting Marseilles of its name and inviting the Convention to give it another; arresting the municipal officers removed on December 4; and establishing a military commission in Marseilles in place of the Revolutionary Tribunal headed by Maillet and Giraud. During the first three weeks after their return to Marseilles, they ordered a general disarmament and arrested more than eighty members of the Club. Maillet

[41] *Moniteur*, XVIII, no. 83, 647–648, no. 84, 654; Poupé, *Lettres*, pp. 55–57, 66–81; AN, W 329.

[42] Poupé, *Lettres*, pp. 61–81.

the younger and Giraud were sent for trial to the Revolutionary Tribunal in Paris. A letter to the public prosecutor, Fouquier-Tinville, charged them with corruption and favoritism toward the rich and with being the "principal leaders" of the disturbances of December.[43] A proclamation to all the communes of the Midi outlined the "criminal plots" of the Marseillais:

Some intriguers avid to dominate have duped the Popular Society to the point of transforming it into a sovereign tribunal, summoning public functionaries to the bar, making them suffer interrogations, and holding them in a state of arrest. In secret councils composed of men that they call ringleaders, they even considered laying sacreligious hands on the National Representatives.[44]

In defiance the Club elected Isoard president again on December 21, 1793. Shortly thereafter he published a justificatory memoir condemning "the system of calumny directed against the purest patriots." Faced with the prospect of certain imprisonment, some members of the Club went into hiding, while Isoard and Loys fled to Paris. Barras and Fréron urged the Committee of Public Safety to arrest them, warning that Isoard was "the most dangerous of all." On February 6, 1794, Loys appeared at the Jacobin club in Paris at the head of a deputation from Marseilles and accused the representatives of promoting factionalism by arresting "eighty-six patriots." Simultaneously he drafted a letter to Camille Desmoulins, which the Club published on February 14; Marseilles, said Loys, was crushed under "the cruellest type of tyranny." [45]

[43] *Ibid.*, pp. 117, 123, 132; AN, W 329.   [44] AN, AF II 90, no. 29.
[45] AD, B-du-Rh, L 2076, "Vie politique d'Isoard." For the warning against Isoard see AN, AF II 186, Jan. 13, 1794. On Loys see Aulard, *Jacobins*, V, 641–642; AD, B-du-Rh, L 2076, "J.B. Loys à Camille Desmoulins" (Marseille, 1794).

Ultimately, the Club and its leaders won a temporary triumph. This was due in no small part to the rift which had appeared between Fréron and Barras on the one hand and the deputies of the Bouches-du-Rhône to the Convention on the other. Omer Granet and Moyse Bayle reacted very unfavorably to the change of Marseilles' name and to rumors that Fréron planned to block the entrance to the Old Port, thus destroying Marseilles' commerce. Granet wrote a letter of condolence to his brother which was "circulated from house to house," and Bayle drafted an address to Barère reproving Barras and Fréron. The two representatives also had powerful enemies at the Convention and in the Committee of Public Safety. Robespierre seems to have been preparing the groundwork for their imminent disgrace as Dantonists. On January 23, 1794, the Convention recalled them to Paris. Barras has left an account, highly colored no doubt, of his reception by the Committee of Public Safety:

On seeing me enter, the members of the Committee remained seated in silence, their eyes riveted on their portfolios. . . . Remaining standing, and without any of them inviting me to take a seat, I gave them a few particulars regarding the condition in which had left the south; not a mark either of concurrence in, or contradiction of my report was vouchsafed me, not a question was asked of me. . . . When I had finished speaking . . . Billaud . . . said to me, "That will suffice, citizen representative . . . you may depart." [46]

He felt only too glad to comply.

With support from high places in Paris, the Club had defied the representatives openly in their last weeks in the city. When a secretary at a meeting of the Club read Bayle's letter to Barère, "transports of joy" burst forth; a copy was

[46] Barras, *Memoirs*, pp. 176–177.

printed for every member and placards were sent to all affiliates. During the trial in Paris of Maillet and Giraud (February 5–February 26), the Society openly supported these "two martyrs of liberty" and a great many members testified in their behalf; on February 26, the Tribunal unanimously acquitted them. "Our triumph is a prelude to that of our dear Marseilles and of all the oppressed patriots," wrote Maillet and Giraud.[47] On the day of their acquittal the Jacobins in Paris congratulated them on their freedom. When they returned to Marseilles the next month, a huge crowd greeted them and carried them in triumph to the Society.[48]

On December 29, 1793, the Convention appointed Maignet to be the new representative in the Bouches-du-Rhône and the Vaucluse. Maignet, an honest, zealous Montagnard, pleased the members. On March 1, after receiving numerous petitions and attestations from the Club, he nullified the ordinance of January 20 ordering the arrest of Isoard and other patriots. On March 3, again on the advice of the Society, he appointed a new Municipality filled with Jacobins. Finally, on March 13, he ordered that all the patriots disarmed by Fréron be rearmed—so long as they were members of the Club. Thereafter, Maignet regularly utilized the Club to perform useful projects for the state. Only in the last month of his administration did he begin to reject its demands and incur its criticism.[49]

There is practically no evidence on the Club's activities be-

---

[47] AD, B-du-Rh, L 2076, "Lettre de Moyse Bayle à son collègue Barère" (Marseille, 1794); AM, I₂, an untitled publication of Feb. 6, 1794; AN, W 329; for the letter of Maillet and Giraud see AD, Basses-Alpes, L 856/2, "Aux Citoyens composant la société populaire et républicaine de Marseille" (Marseille, 1794).

[48] AD, B-du-Rh, L 2076, Extraits, Tribune populaire.

[49] AN, AF II 91; AN, W 86.

tween the months of March and July, 1794. Scattered pieces indicate that it approved of the execution of the Hébertist and Dantonist factions, that it continued to feud with Fréron, and that it sought to implement the worship of Reason and Robespierre's republic of virtue in Marseilles; otherwise nothing of startling consequence appears to have occurred. The fall of Robespierre, however, set in motion a chain of events which brought about the downfall of the Jacobins in the Club and, in one sense, ended in final victory for the party of Fréron.

The Society reacted prudently to the news of 9 and 10 *thermidor* (July 27–28, 1794), concerning the fall of Robespierre. The first report came in the session of August 4. On hearing the news, a member rose to "thank the divinity" that the plot was foiled and to propose a congratulatory address to the National Convention. Maignet described the unmasking of the conspirators as a "day of triumph for the republic," and Jeanbon St.-André, who was then at the Club, also condemned the "atrocious . . . conspiracy."[50] On August 5 the Club sent an address praising the people of Paris for saving the country from the "new Catilines." At the same time it notified the affiliates that the "execrable Robespierre," Couthon, and St.-Just had perished.[51]

The Club's enthusiasm for the events of 9 *thermidor*, if it was ever more than feigned, did not endure very long. The leaders must have noted grimly the important role played in them by Fréron and Barras. The suspension of activity by the Revolutionary Tribunal confirmed their suspicions. On Au-

[50] AD, B-du-Rh, L 2076, scattered pieces.
[51] BN, Lb[41] 1187, "Adresse des Marseillais à la Convention nationale sur la conspiration de Robespierre" (Marseille, 1794). AD, B-du-Rh, L 2076, "La Société populaire de Marseille à celle de . . ." (Marseille, 1794).

gust 11, 1794, the Society voted to send Carle, Magnan, and Laliand[52] to Paris to "ascertain why the conspirators remained unpunished, and to demand the punishment of the guilty." With Réquier accompanying them, the trio arrived in the capital on August 21. Their first step was to visit Loys, who took them to the Jacobins. From Paris the deputies warned of the intrigues of the "moderates" who wished the destruction of the popular societies, especially that of Marseilles. In this crisis the Society gave vigorous support to the mother club in Paris. On September 11, several citizens of Marseilles appeared at the Paris Jacobins to pledge the "inviolable attachment" of the Society. When Jean-Pierre Audouin, a Montagnard deputy, "raised a cry of alarm" in his *Journal universel* against the release of prisoners, the Society in Marseilles applauded his editorial and recommended to the affiliates that they purchase this patriotic journal. Isoard, Maillet the younger, Giraud, and Chompré drafted an address asking the Convention to retain the Revolutionary Government in all its aspects. The Society had begun to wonder, it stated, "if the Mountain was no more."[53]

Latent sympathy for the martyred Robespierre burst into the open after the explosion of a powder factory in Grenelle. On September 7 Giraud announced the news of this tragedy and the death of "1,000–1,200" patriots by "sabotage" (actually the number was 400). The next day the Club attacked the "royalists and their inseparable friends, the moderates" in

[52] Jean-Joseph Magnan, a shoemaker, was born at Valensole in the Basses-Alpes. He belonged to the Club from 1790 to 1794. Jean-Guillaume Laliand, born at Nîmes in 1738, was a landed proprietor, municipal commissioner, and secretary of the Club in 1794.
See AN, W 86; *Moniteur*, XXI, no. 358, 738.
[53] AN, W 86, "La Société populaire de Marseille, à la Convention nationale" (Marseille, 1794).

an oration to the National Convention and the affiliates. It pledged the unity of the patriotic societies to combat this menace, and demanded "an authentic apology" to "the dead Robespierre." The Convention had been inexorable toward "its innocent colleagues"; now it must quash the caluminiators.[54]

In Paris, the attempted assassination of the reactionary deputy Tallien turned the political tide in favor of the Thermidorians. On September 10, in a tirade at the Convention, another deputy, Merlin de Thionville, denounced the Jacobins and the clubs as "nests of brigands." Fréron, in his *L'Orateur du peuple* on September 22, cried out against "the vast conspiracy" engineered by "the deputies of the Bouches-du-Rhône" (Granet and Bayle), the "leaders of the Jacobins," and "the intriguers of the Popular Society of Marseilles." He blamed the wounding of Tallien on "brigands" from Marseilles. The Society retaliated immediately by protesting de Thionville's speech. Only the agents of Pitt, the royalists, and the moderates could gain, it charged, from the closure of the societies.[55]

A close resemblance exists between the events of December, 1793, and those of September, 1794.[56] In both cases conflicts between the Society and national representatives led to disturbances and the arrest of the Club's leaders. On the first occasion, however, the Club found strong support in Paris. In September the Thermidorians controlled the Convention. There was another difference also. Earlier, in December, the

[54] AN, W 86; AD, Var, series L, supplement, St.-Zacharie.
[55] AN, AF II 90, no. 27; *ibid.*, W 86.
[56] This resemblance was noted by some deputies from Marseilles at the Paris Jacobins; *Moniteur*, XXI, no. 360, 755.

Society stood united against the representatives. In September a schism bifurcated the Jacobins of Marseilles into Montagnards and moderates. The latter congregated around the leaders of section eleven. This section had turned against the Federalists at the last minute, on the night of August 23, 1793, and entered the city alongside the army of Cartaux. Its belated conversion had earned it praise and special favors from the National Convention in 1793–1794. These favors rankled with those patriots whom the sectionnaires had arrested and driven from Marseilles. In August, 1794, when members of section eleven circulated a petition in favor of those remaining in prison in Marseilles they were denounced and excluded from the Club.[57]

The final defeat of the Club of the Rue Thubaneau was engineered by the two representatives-on-mission, Pierre-Jean-Baptiste Auguis and Jean-Jacques-Joseph Serres, who had been sent by the Convention into the Bouches-du-Rhône on August 26, 1794. The first encounter between the Club and these moderates on September 6 did not augur well for the future. Ten Club members, "armed with pistols and sabers," investigating the closure of the popular society at Aix, found Auguis and Serres unwilling to acquiesce in their demands. On September 12, in Marseilles, the representatives arrested a certain Reynier,[58] secretary of the revolutionary commission, and ordered him taken to Paris. On receiving this news, the Club's president, Maillet the younger, convoked an extraordinary meeting at 6:00 P.M. Speakers urged those attend-

[57] *Ibid.*, XX, no. 197, 139–142. AN, W 86.

[58] Reynier had written an incriminating letter to the national agent of Chabeuil, dated August 26, complaining of the release of 200 to 300 criminals at Marseilles and predicting new September massacres led by the Club.

ing to remain "united and energetic"; they had triumphed in the time of Fréron against longer odds. Two days later 150 clubbists, in disguise, ambushed the guards taking Reynier to Paris and freed him. When Auguis and Serres dismissed the commandant of Marseilles, Voulland, the Society invited him to remain. On September 13, when the representatives appeared in the Club, they were insulted and forced to retire. "Never have our ears heard such vociferations," they complained.[59]

Each side appealed to Paris for support. On September 14, 1794, the Club lamented to the Jacobins the "perfidious moderatism" in Marseilles; and when some deputies from Marseilles appeared in Paris on September 19, the president of the Jacobins there embraced them and praised their patriotism. The letters of Auguis and Serres to the Convention are reminiscent of those sent by Fréron. "It is not the masses,'" they wrote, "who are gangrened beyond hope; it is those who pretend to be patriots par excellence . . . this society [the Club] would be excellent without about fifteen members." [60] In its session of September 21, on the motion of Barras, the Convention approved the conduct of Auguis and Serres. One speaker accused the Club of plotting a new September massacre and denounced the "twelve to fifteen men who dominate there." Merlin de Thionville warned darkly that the Paris Jacobins had formed a union with the Club of Marseilles "to sustain their weakening and execrable authority." The

[59] G. Martinet, "Les Débuts de la réaction thermidorienne à Marseille: L'Emeute du 5 vendémiaire an III" *Actes, XC^e Congrès national des sociétés savantes*, II (Nice, 1965), 150–154; BN, Lc[11] 635 (72); *Tribune populaire*, sessions of Sept. 8–14, 1794; *Moniteur*, XXII, no. 3, 27–28, no. 4, 31–33; AN, W 86.

[60] AN, W 86; *Moniteur*, XXII, no. 3, 27, no. 5, 43.

same day the Convention passed a decree ordering Auguis and Serres to close the Club and place seals on its papers.[61]

The decree arrived in Marseilles on September 25, 1794; Auguis and Serres immediately ordered the arrest of thirty-five members of the Club. Martinet has vividly described the events which followed:

On 5 *vendémiaire* (September 26) at 1:00 A.M., sixty soldiers encircle the house of Carle, president of the Club. The latter climbs on the roof, harangues the soldiers, and throws himself into the street. Giraud, arrested at 8:00 A.M., cries, "I will always be a Montagnard; long live the Mountain and the Jacobins." Maillet the younger succeeds in fleeing, he will be arrested on 10 *vendémiaire* [October 1] by the municipality of Pennes-Mirabeau.

At the news of the arrest of the leaders of the Club, a riot broke out in the city. The representatives used troops to quell it and arrested 96 persons. In all, they implicated 244 people in this affair. On October 13 they sent 28 Club members to be tried by the Revolutionary Tribunal.[62] In the meantime they had purified the Society.

A regenerated Society of Marseilles opened its doors once again on October 2, 1794. The moderates of section eleven who had been excluded in August now filled its ranks. Auguis and Serres spoke at the first session. The new Society responded by expressing its horror "against the criminals who had led it astray and subjugated it" and by thanking the Convention for "throttling the criminal and Federalist factions." To its affiliates it announced its purification and depicted its martyred leaders as assassins. In subsequent addresses to the

---

[61] *Moniteur*, XXII, no. 4, 32–33.   [62] Martinet, pp. 154–166.

Convention it demanded their judgment and death.[63] Despite gradually decreasing attendance, the bastard regenerated Society of Marseilles lived on for another year; but the Club of the Rue Thubaneau, "the colossus of the Midi," was dead.

[63] *Moniteur*, XXII, no. 18, 174, no. 22, 212; AD, Basses-Alpes, L 856/2, "La Société populaire régénérée de Marseille á toutes les sociétés populaires de la République" (Marseille, 1794).

6

Personnel

For a full century after 1789 public opinion judged the Jacobins guilty, without benefit of trial, of being criminals and social misfits. The reproaches and innuendoes of Revolutionary enemies of the societies and their members were accepted at face value. Counterrevolutionaries and royalists charged that only brigands and homeless vagabonds joined the clubs. Such nineteenth-century historians as Taine depicted the Jacobins as "frenzied men" of "rapine and blood," "terrible apparitions" whose "abominable existence" soiled French history. Among some segments of the population these attitudes persist. Overall, however, those misconceptions have fallen into desuetude as a result of the analytical social and economic studies that have been made of club members. Unfortunately, no one has ever successfully examined the personnel of the Jacobin Club of Marseille.[1]

---

[1] The absence of archival data has been the principal cause of this neglect. When the writer commenced his research in 1968, the only readily available, known enumeration of members of the Club of Marseilles was a list dating from December, 1794, compiled by order of the Revolutionary Government in Paris (AD, B-du-Rh, L 2073). Though valuable, it is far less than a definitive tabulation since it was made at a time of declining attendance, after the purge of September, 1794. In addition, it provides very little information on the Jacobins

Unlike many other cities, Marseilles had only one Jacobin society in 1790–1795; but its membership did not remain static. For analytical purposes its lifespan may be partitioned into three segments: April 11, 1790–December 31, 1791; January 1, 1792–June 4, 1793; and August 25, 1793–December 31, 1794. The first period covers the birth and infancy of the Society; the second, terminated by the Federalist uprising and the closure of the Club, is marked by burgeoning republicanism and an ideological shift to the left; the third delimits the Club of the post-Federalist rebellion. The chief source of comparison with the personnel of revolutionary clubs elsewhere is Crane Brinton's book on the Jacobins, published over forty years ago. Contemporary scholars criticize Brinton's methodology. It is also true that he based his conclusions on

---

prior to the Federalist rebellion. About two-thirds of the 1,245 individuals cited joined the Club after August, 1793.

To supplement this list, I examined contemporary gazettes and the surviving *procès-verbaux*. The extracts of the sessions of June–August, 1790, that I discovered in uncatalogued police records of the Municipal Archives of Marseilles provided the names and professions of over four hundred members. A few handwritten petitions can be found in AM, I₂, cartons 1790, 1791, and 1792, and AN, series C; certain published petitions exist, such as the "Adresse à l'assemblée nationale par trois cents cinquante-sept citoyens actifs" (Marseille, 1791) in BM, 4717, and BM, Poitiers, S 22. But it was often impossible to make a positive identification of those who signed. A decree of the representative-on-mission, Maignet, dated March 23, 1794, and conserved in the National Archives (AN, AF II, 91), led me to the best roster of names. Maignet ordered the rearmament of all members of the Society and commanded the surveillance committtee to compile a register. This I unearthed in series H, military records, in the Municipal Archives of Marseilles. The 3,200 Marseillais listed were unquestionably members of the Club. The validity of this roster is confirmed by many notes written by the Society's examining committee (AM, 10 H 10).

a very limited sample of clubs. Nevertheless, his book remains the best socio-economic study of the Jacobin movement as a whole.

For the years 1789–1795, Brinton estimated that the Jacobins formed approximately 4.2 per cent of the population of France.[2] It seems possible that this is an underestimation; in Provence, at any rate, the membership of the popular societies ran at a much higher rate. Henri Labroue suggests that the club of Toulon had "several thousand" members in May, 1793. A register of April, 1793, listed 1,200 Antipolitiques at Aix. In the smaller clubs of eastern Provence the membership often comprised almost the entire male population. In 1792, St.-Zacharie had 195 clubbists out of 1,500 inhabitants (13 per cent); the society of la Garde Freinet, a commune with 1,500 residents, printed membership cards for 300 (20 per cent); and the club of Plascassier had a membership of 87 in a town of 226 (an amazing 39 per cent).[3]

Applying Brinton's approximation to Marseilles, one would expect to find 4,600 card-carrying clubbists in 1790–1795. The testimony of contemporaries indicates that the membership was actually much higher. In August, 1790, barely four months after the Society's founding, Joseph-Alphonse Esménard, one of its foes, spoke of 1,800 members. Extracts of meetings in the spring of 1791 indicate that more than 2,000 members regularly thronged the assembly hall. One year later, in April, 1792, unprecedented overcrowding caused the Club, as we have seen, to consider a new meeting place. On the eve of the Federalist rebellion (May, 1793), Maillet the younger estimated that there were three thousand members;

[2] Brinton, pp. 40–41.
[3] Labroue, p. 29; Ponteil, X, 206–207; Agulhon, I, 507–508.

and after the uprising Fréron, archenemy of the Society's leaders, often complained of the great size of the meetings, estimated at between 2,000 and 2,500 souls.[4]

These statements are startling when one considers the great turnover of personnel in the Society. During each purifcation a mass exit and inflow of members took place. On the basis of existing records it is impossible to determine precisely how many men were members of the Society. Exactly 4,902 (4.4 per cent of the total population) can be positively identified, but the total for the whole period 1790–1794 almost certainly exceeded 6,000.[5] The membership rolls of the Society reflected its political power. Its enrollment probably equaled that of any club in France.

Detractors of the Club have consistently branded its members aliens and brigands. "It is they," wrote an administrator of the department of the Bouches-du-Rhône in September, 1791, "who form 99 per cent . . . of the Club of the Friends of the Constitution of Marseilles." [6] On the basis of a scurrilous revolutionary pamphlet, the historian Taine depicted Marseilles as a "rendezvous for nomadic interlopers, vagabonds, persons without fixed callings, the lawless, bullies, and blackguards, who, like uprooted, decaying seaweed, drift from coast to coast, the entire circle of the Mediterranean Sea; a

[4] On Esménard see BM, 4717, "Adresse aux citoyens de Marseille." For information on meetings in the spring of 1791 see AM, 4D₁, To the deputies of Marseilles at the National Assembly, Mar. 16, 1791; CC, I₇₀, "Extrait des registres des amis de la constitution, séance du 16 mai 1791" (Marseille, 1791). On the petition of April, 1792, see AM, I₂, carton 1792; and for Maillet's assessment AN, AF II 90, "A mes juges." On Fréron see Poupé, *Lettres*, pp. 76–77.

[5] I identified 3,708 Jacobins in the Terror. For 1790–1791 and 1792–June, 1793, verifiable members numbered 1,292 and 1,222 respectively.

[6] AD, B-du-Rh, L 123.

veritable sink filled with the dregs of twenty corrupt and semi-barbarous civilizations . . . Marseilles belongs to the low class, 40,000 needy adventurers of which the Club is the leader." [7]

Statistical evidence contradicts these statements. The Club's membership was "homegrown." Throughout the Revolution the overwhelming majority of clubbists were sons of the four departments of old Provence: the Bouches-du-Rhône, Basses-Alpes, Vaucluse, and Var. In 1790–1791, a substantial 46 per cent were natives of Marseilles. While the ratio of Marceillais declined between 1791 and 1794, it never fell below 30 per cent. The proportion of non-French was infinitesimal, and many of the non-Provençal members had moved to Marseilles long before 1789. [8]

Political activism is not limited to outside agitators, nor is it the prerogative of youth. The Jacobins of France were not wild young radicals. Utilizing the registers of ten clubs, Brinton determined that the representative member had the surprising age of 41.8 years. [9] The picture is similar in Marseilles. Average age was at its highest in 1792–1793, at 43.0 years. It fell to 41.6 in 1790–1791 and 41.4 in the Terror. The Marseillais were middle-aged like the Jacobins elsewhere.

During the Revolution, as today, Marseilles was a congeries of small, closely-knit neighborhoods, fiercely particularistic

[7] H. Taine, *The Origins of Contemporary France*, trans. John Durand (New York, 1876), II, 113.

[8] I was able to trace the geographical origins of 491 members in 1790–1791, 560 in 1792–June, 1793, and 1,290, in August, 1793–December, 1794. Of these, the proportion accounted for by the four departments of Provence was 70.46 per cent for the first period, 66.78 per cent for the second, and 57.99 per cent for the third. The proportion of non-French never exceeded 4 per cent.

[9] Brinton, p. 56.

and suspicious of intruders. There is no evidence to indicate, however, that the Club members came from any particular section. They resided in all twenty-five districts of the city. In the pre-Federalist years, the bulk lived in sections one to twelve. During the Federalist rebellion all former members were ordered to turn in their cards. Only a few lists have apparently survived; in section seven, for example, fifty-five clubbists renounced Jacobinism, and in section twelve, thirty-seven. One wonders what percentage of the total membership these lists represented.[10] After the re-establishment of the Club in August, 1793, sections nine, eleven, thirteen, and fifteen provided the greater part of the Club's membership. It is interesting to note that sections nine and thirteen joined section eleven on August 23, 1793, on the eve of the army's entry into Marseilles, in taking up arms against the Federalists.

Bonds of consanguinity rather than simple patriotism linked the Jacobins of Marseilles. François and Augustin Maillet are but the best-known of dozens of pairs of brothers in the Club. Fathers frequently nominated their sons for admission. The census of 1793 indicates cluster patterns of habitation. For example, five clubbists and their families lived in house number eleven, block sixteen, section twenty-three in 1793. About eighty per cent of the members were husbands and heads of households. With their households dwelt a variety of dependents and relatives. Some, masters of their trades, supported employees and apprentices. A substantial number had domestic servants. Indeed, the overall impression of the Club's members derived from the census of 1793 is not one of servility. The Jacobins were customarily principal lodgers or owners of the buildings in which they lived.[11]

[10] These lists were provided by John B. Cameron.
[11] AM, 2F 6–50.

Vocational data survive on 4,334 members,[12] but to catalog them is an enormously complex and frustrating assignment. Drawing a distinction between the middle class and working class is notoriously difficult at any time. But the problem is compounded in Marseilles by the ambiguities and vagaries of eighteenth-century documents. A club member identified vaguely as a *marin* (sailor) on one register might, in fact, be an important captain. The use of different occupational descriptions, such as *chapelier* and *fabricant de chapeaux* for two hatmakers, often implied subtle differentiations in status. Moreover, being a *négociant* (wholesale merchant, or more generally businessman) did not always entail success and prosperity.

Disregarding success or failure in an occupation, Brinton divided club members by profession into bourgeois, working class, and peasantry. He labeled priests, professional people, artists, businessmen, shopkeepers, clerks, and military officers as bourgeois. Artisans and common soldiers were working class. The peasantry included owners, tenants, and laborers. For the two periods into which he divided his data, 1789–1792 and 1792–1795, his totals displayed a solid bourgeois pre-eminence:

	1789–1792	1792–1795
bourgeoisie	66%	57%
working class	26%	32%
peasantry	8%	11%

Brinton further subdivided the dominant bourgeoisie as follows:

[12] I determined the vocations of 1,080 members for 1790–1791, 894 for 1792–1793, and 3,599 for the Terror.

	1789–1792	1792–1795
shopkeepers	10%	17%
businessmen	9%	8%
professional	24%	18%

In his opinion a slight democratization occurred in the clubs after 1792. By the Terror, a majority came from the artisan and petty middle classes.[13]

Applying Brinton's methodology to the Jacobins of Marseilles, one obtains significantly different results:

	1790–1791	1792–1793	1793–1794
bourgeoisie	72%	63%	28%
working class	28%	37%	69%
peasantry	—	—	2%

Breaking down the bourgeoisie on Brinton's lines we discover:

	1790–1791	1792–1793	1793–1794
shopkeepers	14%	14%	12%
businessmen	17%	9%	0.6%
professional	8%	6%	2%

The socio-economic base, narrowly bourgeois in the beginning, gradually widened up to 1793. Then, after the Federalist rebellion, an abrupt democratization took place, possibly under the orders of the representatives-on-mission in Marseilles, and the relative percentages of bourgeois and working class underwent a complete reversal. The percentage of businessmen plummeted, and that of professional people also declined. Since Marseilles' environs are not well-suited to agriculture, the peasantry provided fewer members through-

[13] Brinton, pp. 50–51.

out than in Brinton's clubs; until the post-Federalist era there was no trace of farm owners or laborers, and even then they barely exceeded 2 per cent of the total.

The Federalist rebellion thus looms as the crucial turning point in the Club's history. Indeed, one is tempted to say that two radically different clubs existed in the city during the Revolution. Unlike the egalitarian Society of 1793–1794, the Patriotic Assembly of 1790 was overwhelmingly middle class. At least 138 members in its first year, or one-eighth of the total, were wholesale merchants. If one adds those members who were bankers, ship builders, captains, and brokers, then one-sixth belonged to the commercial and financial elite of Marseilles. Many of these individuals perished on the guillotine during the Terror.

The other elite classes also declined in significance between 1790 and 1794. In the year and a half after the Society's foundation nearly one-tenth of the known members belonged to the cultural and liberal professions. The number of lawyers, to cite only one profession, fell from twenty-five in the early period to four in 1793–1794. The Club also admitted a large number of property owners and bourgeois in 1790–1791, some of whom were as prosperous as the richest wholesale merchants. They, too, nearly disappeared from the Club in the course of the Revolution. A minimum of forty-nine clergymen enrolled in the Society during its first year. By-and-large, they took the oath to the civil constitution of the clergy in 1791, but the vast majority ceased to attend after the Federalist upheaval.

The basic components of the *sans-culottes* in Paris were the *boutiquiers* (shopkeepers) and artisans. These two groups likewise represented an important part of the Club's rank-and-file. In her book, *La Bourgeoisie parisienne de 1815 à*

1848 (Paris, 1961), Adeline Daumard defines a *boutiquier* as anyone who owned or rented a shop, including many varieties of merchants and master artisans. In contrast to the changes noted in the proportions of wealthy merchants and liberal professions, merchants and masters made up about twenty per cent of the Society's membership throughout the Revolution. The percentage may have been higher, for in the records of Revolutionary Marseilles it is very difficult to distinguish master artisans from journeymen and apprentices. Indeed, under the reign of equality in the Terror, the title of master craftsman lost favor and disappeared entirely. The Jacobin masters were often substantial property owners. Pierre Hermitte, master mason, owned property assessed in 1793 at 7,000 livres, ten times that of the average property owner.[14]

Nearly all the workingmen in the Club were specialized artisans rather than day laborers or proletarians. There were in fact no laborers in the Society prior to the Federalist rebellion and only a handful thereafter. The proportion of artisans in the Club rose from twenty-five to thirty-four per cent between 1790 and 1793, and then leaped up sharply to sixty per cent in 1794. Shoemaking was the most important single profession. An overabundance of shoemakers caused a depression in the industry on the eve of 1789; nevertheless, the presence of over five hundred shoemakers in the Society during the Terror is a truly astounding figure.

In a city famous for its fish soup it is surprising that only two members were fishermen. Both joined during the post-Federalist years. The number of salaried employees and functionaries increased steadily between 1790 and 1794. The Society's monopoly over local politics during the Terror led to the employment of many clubbists in the civil administrations.

[14] AM, G 102–103.

The militant Henri Chabaud, to cite only one example, began the Revolution as a hatmaker and by 1795 served as a judge of the district tribunal. Twenty-eight Club members (all but one of whom joined after 1793) were employed in domestic service. Most were concierges; apparently no mere household domestic ever joined the Club.

A social and economic classification of personnel would be more valid if adequate tax records were available. In determining the wealth of the French Jacobins, Brinton used data on such taxes as the *vingtième, capitation, taille,* and *vingtième d'industrie;* but the Marseillais paid none of these. Only one reliable tax record survives for the years 1790–1794, a *matrice foncière* (real estate register) of 1793.[15] It provides at best only a poor approximation of the wealth of the Society's members. First, it was a land tax and did not list personal property or income. Second, substantial changes might have already occurred in the patterns of property ownership by 1793. Third, identifying those listed is difficult. Finally, it made no mention of property owned outside the canton of Marseilles.

Leaving aside assessments on collectivities, the *matrice foncière* listed 9,252 property owners, of whom only 402 can positively be identified as Jacobins. A relatively small percentage of these joined in the post-Federalist period.[16] The inescapable inference is that those who became members during the Terror were less wealthy than those who joined in either of the earlier periods. This conclusion is borne out by the stairstep decrease in average property assessments: 2,178

---

[15] *Ibid.*

[16] I identified 229 property owners who were members in 1790–1791 (17.7%) of the Club's membership), 161 (13.2%) in 1792–1793, and 227 (6.0%) in 1793–1794.

livres for 1790–1791, 1,631 livres for 1792–1793, and 1,001
livres for 1793–1794.

Substantial alterations thus took place in the economic and
occupational status of the rank-and-file clubbists. The founder
of 1790 belonged to a social stratum that was distinctly superior to that of the member of 1793–1794. The former came
from the commercial, professional, and industrial upper middle class, while the latter was typically an artisan or petty
merchant. The aristocracy and the poor never frequented the
Club in large numbers. The change was gradual until the
post-Federalist era when a decisive broadening of the Society's social base occurred.

The Club of the Rue Thubaneau had an exceptionally large
membership. Yet, a relatively small core of militants dominated its proceedings throughout the Revolution. They regularly attended the sessions, signed the petitions, monopolized
the rostrum, and staffed the committees and commissions.
Comparisons of these leaders with the rank-and-file yield many
similarities and some marked differences. The militant, like
his more passive brother, was typically a middle-aged native
of Marseilles or the surrounding region. During the period
1790–1794 his economic and social status declined significantly, but in all periods he claimed a more elevated social
position than the average member.

In 1790–1791, the Club drew its leaders from among the
most wealthy and prestigious citizens of Marseilles. Of the
nearly ninety different members who held office during this
time, approximately half were from the world of commerce
and finance.[17] M. le Bailli de Foresta, president in July–August,

---

[17] To avoid an arbitrary definition of "militants," I analyzed only
regularly elected officers of the Club. At least ninety men held office
between April, 1790, and December 31, 1792. I discovered the pro-

1790, was tax collector and procurator of the Order of Malta and owned property valued at 18,840 livres in 1793. Wealthy bourgeois such as Cabrol de Moncaussou and Pierre-Robert Rivar also served as president during the summer of 1790. Etienne Martin, Etienne Martin *fils* d'André, Jean-Louis Millot, François Peyre-Ferry, Jean-Baptiste Morery, and Jacques Borély were but a few of the rich wholesale merchants who were elected to positions in the Club in 1790. With their oratorical talents and legal skills, lawyers and professional people such as Barbaroux, Brémond-Jullien, Joseph Lavabre and Etienne-Jean Lejourdan filled many official posts. Only a few rich artisans held office in 1790–1791; among these were Laurent Granet (master cooper) and Jean-Joseph Astier (soap manufacturer).

As the Revolution moved to the left, most of the early leaders fell out of step with their more militant brothers. Indeed, some emigrated and others died on the guillotine during the Terror.[18] By late 1791 the Montagnards who later dominated the Society had already achieved prominence. Their definitive triumph occurred between January 4 and January 23, 1793. The defeat of the moderates at this time coincided with virulent and mounting attacks on the rich and contrib-

---

fessions of seventy-two. The results clearly illustrate the upper middle class character of the early Society. There were 17 wholesale merchants, 9 bourgeois, 6 lawyers, 4 masters of fine arts, 3 priests, and 3 doctors. The remaining thirty were scattered among twenty-three separate professions.

[18] Among prominent founders executed during the Terror were: Cabrol de Moncaussou, Lavabre, Leroi D'Ambleville, Jean-Joseph-Casimir Cavalier (priest), and Pierre Laugier. Laugier, an examiner of commercial records, was vice-president on at least four occasions in 1790–1791 and president as late as the month of February, 1793. He was the first Federalist executed after the re-establishment of the Society.

uted to the revolution of the Federalists. It is significant that no turnover took place in the leadership of the Club after 1793. The same individuals who dominated prior to the rebellion of the sections also directed its affairs and molded its philosophy during the Terror.

The officers of 1793–1794 remained overwhelmingly middle class in the traditional sense, but they belonged to a relatively lower social stratum than the founders. Only a few "millionaire Jacobins," such as François Peyre-Ferry and the shipowner Jean-Pierre Amy, still occupied important positions, while the role of the petty merchants and clerks greatly increased. The number of workers in positions of leadership remained insignificant. The nucleus of the Society in this period was a small group of teachers, ex-professors, and former priests. François and Augustin Maillet, Etienne Chompré, Charles Guinot, and Antoine Réquier had all worked as schoolmasters and instructors before 1789. The two militant Oratorians, Isoard and Joseph Giraud, also had teaching experience. Their educational competence, their abilities as speakers and writers, and their broad exposure to the ideas of the *philosophes* made them natural leaders. The arrest and imprisonment of these talented Jacobins in September, 1794, meant the end of the political power of the Club.[19]

[19] Of eighty-six officers in 1792–June, 1793, occupations were discovered for sixty-four. Eight were wholesale merchants, three bourgeois, and ten lawyers. The number of artisans remained insignificant, but the combined total of petty merchants and clerks increased to fifteen. If one includes the three priests of the Oratory, then ten teachers or former teachers held office.

Data survive on the occupations of forty-four officers after the Federalist rebellion. There were no bourgeois, and the number of lawyers and wholesale merchants had declined to three each. There were five teachers, four former priests or monks, seven petty merchants, and four clerks. Nine officers could be classified as artisans.

7
Ideology

The Jacobin clubs developed a remarkably complex body of ideas and beliefs. Orthodoxy was represented by the Society of the Rue St.-Honoré in Paris, but doctrine proved sufficiently malleable to allow local variations. The extent of these deviations depended on the location of the club and the period of the Revolution. It is self-evident that maritime cities such as Marseilles had significantly different interests from cities of the interior like Lyons. It is also true that the provincial clubs enjoyed greater independence before 1793 than they did later.

Nearly all the societies of France displayed regional chauvinism in varying degrees, but none equaled the Marseillais in arrogance and self-exaltation. The highest compliment given by the Club to another society was that its members were "worthy of being Marseillais." In their own eyes, the Club of the Rue Thubaneau was the paladin of liberty. They exalted its grandeur in speeches, letters, songs, and verse. "Already, brave Marseillais," bragged Maillet the elder in 1790, "France and the whole of Europe has bestowed on you its glorious palms." [1] A *Chanson nouvelle* of July, 1792, apostrophized:

---

[1] CC, I 70, "Adresse au peuple Marseillais" (Marseille, 1790).

Redoubtable Club of Marseilles;
Enemy of intrigues
You will foil forever
The plots of our enemies.[2]

Perhaps the most explicit portrayal of the spirit of the Club members occurs in a personal letter written by Henri Chabaud to Blanc-Gilly. In order to recoup his popularity in the Club, Chabaud advised Blanc-Gilly to "announce the plots of the wicked, even speak of your opponents, but always depict yourself as an intrepid man. Crush your enemies. Such is the spirit of the Marseillais." [3]

Satellite societies catered to the vanity of the Marseillais. They praised the Club as the "eldest son" of the Jacobins, the "savior of the Midi" and of France, and they begged to march alongside the "heroes of the Revolution." "Marseillais, who are the Mountain of the Midi!" wrote the Republican Society of Digne (Basses-Alpes) in 1793, "everything indicates that the time has come when the people have tired of treason. It is for you to give us the signal of awakening. Even Paris waits for it." [4] The praise of Parisian Jacobins also bolstered the ego of the members. Carra owed his popularity in Marseilles to editorials such as the following, published on October 22, 1790:

Today while the capital and the provinces content themselves with astonishment at the imperturbable audacity of the ministers . . . Marseilles alone . . . takes a posture suitable to the descendants of the Greeks and the Romans, to the free French . . . the globe does not contain on its entire surface a race of men more

[2] BM, O. 11136.   [3] AN, F7 4603.
[4] AD, Var, L 856/2, The Republicans of Digne to Marseilles, Apr. 7, 1793.

handsome, more noble, more sensible, and more valiant than our brethren at Marseilles.[5]

In speaking of themselves, the Marseillais usually boasted of their pre-Revolutionary past. Steadfast enmity to tyranny exemplified this history. The Phocaeans had bequeathed liberty as a patrimony, and history had "always proven" the Marseillais worthy of their ancestors. Their forefathers had withstood the furies of "the Caesars, the Neros, and the Caligulas," and the oppression of the kings of France; the Club would defy the modern-day tyrants. An address to the National Assembly on March 20, 1791, concluded:

The Phocaeans, our fathers, on approaching these coasts, cast a mass of iron into the water, vowing to return to their fatherland and submit to the yoke of despotism only when this mass floated to the surface. It is still in our gulf, and we ourselves vow to succumb to servitude only when it floats on the waters.[6]

The "glorious facts of Marseilles' Revolutionary patriotism" boosted the Society's pretensions. As early as 1790, Alexandre Renaud bragged that the Marseillais seemed destined "to provide a patriotic example for other cities."[7] Members never tired of enumerating the achievements that had "rendered the city illustrious." Had not Marseilles in 1789 been the "first" to clutch liberty to her bosom and to organize a national guard? In 1790, did it not sweep away the "infamous league" of Bournissac, D'André, and Lieutaud and overturn the "menacing citadels"? Was it not true that Marseilles' army had crushed the aristocrats of Aix, Arles, and Avignon and overthrown the tyrant in 1792? Did anyone deny that the Club had inspired

[5] *Annales patriotiques*, Oct. 22, 1790, pp. 468–469.

[6] *Procès-verbaux de l'Assemblée Nationale*, vol. XX, Mar. 20, 1791.

[7] BM, 4717, "Souscription pour l'érection d'un monument patriotique" (Marseille, 1790).

the Midi to repel the thrusts of the Piedmontese and the Spanish? Surely the Marseillais were "the saviors of France."

Between August 10, 1792, and the Federalist rebellion, the arrogance of the clubbists knew no bounds. On October 25, 1792, the Society had a medal struck in honor of "our brave brethren, the destroyers of despotism." On one side Marseilles was depicted as a woman in Greek costume holding the figure of a goddess representing the Republic. The legend read, "She appeared August 10, 1792, at the command of the Marseillais." [8] The Club also became more arbitrary in its relations with outsiders. On January 23, 1793, it justified an address to the Convention with these words: "Although it is only a fraction of France, Representatives, Marseilles has every right to give its views; it is the center of public opinion in the Midi which it has saved by its citizenship." [9]

The Federalist rebellion tarnished the image of the Club. The sections closed the Society; the city rebelled against the Mountain; and Marseilles' army was defeated in battle. The Society re-emerged on the defensive. To salvage their pride, the members contended that the great mass of Marseillais had remained loyal to the Convention and had only been led astray by "bad citizens" posing as patriots. "Marseilles has never rebelled against the Fatherland," wrote Charles Guinot in May, 1794, "it has only been deceived." [10] By the summer of 1794, the Club had recovered much of its bluster and swagger. Its addresses to the Convention reflected the old pride in being Marseillais. [11]

[8] *JdD*, Oct. 25, 1792, p. 411.

[9] BM, 5314–5315, "Adresse de la Société des Amis de la Constitution" (Marseille, 1793).

[10] AD, Basses-Alpes, L 856/2, "Extrait du Journal Universel" (Marseille, 1794).

[11] See Aulard, *Jacobins*, V, 351.

Since the time of Edmund Burke, some historians have maintained that Jacobinism was, in essence, a religious movement. In the United States this analogy was popularized by Crane Brinton. Brinton contended that Jacobinism possessed all the elements commonly associated with religion: ritual, a cosmology, an ethical code, a teleology, and a church. In his opinion it was "one of the first and one of the most important of the efforts made in modern times to supplant Christianity, to root it out and replace it." Brinton's description of Jacobinism as a "secular religion" has been criticized by a host of other historians. Peter Gay argued that the so-called religious activities of the Jacobins "reflect no more than the depths of poor taste reached by obscure and uneducated men" and the "widespread use of religious connotations proves no more than the ease with which the revolutionaries used familiar metaphors." [12]

While Brinton's analysis is surely too simplistic, it is also true that Gay goes too far in his renunciation of the religious nature of Jacobinism. At bottom, the debate is a question of semantics or, as Brinton said, "taxonomy". If Jacobinism was not a "secular religion," then it was certainly an "ideological creed," a "political faith," or an "exclusive doctrine." No one denies that the Jacobins were zealous, doctrinaire, and visionary. And, while they lacked the hindsight of twentieth-century historians, it is significant that those who joined the clubs described their movement as a religion. As a speaker at the Club of Marseilles said in 1791:

What idea is as sublime as the institution of patriotic assemblies? They are for me a second religion. . . . Are they not essentially

[12] For Brinton's quote see "Comment on Gay," *American Historical Review*, LXVI (April, 1961), 677–681. On Gay see the same issue of the *AHR*, "Rhetoric and Politics in the French Revolution," 664–676.

bound to religion, since patriotism is religion's soul and sustenance? Yes, Gentlemen, your assembly in this temple of Civil Liberty is a true dependency of religion.[13]

The rhetoric of the Marseillais, like that of other Jacobins, was full of religious terms and phrases. The members referred to their assembly hall as a "temple of liberty." It fulfilled all the functions formerly performed by churches and chapels. It was the "asylum of the poor, the support of the persecuted, the tribune of the defender of the rights of humanity . . . , the school of doctrine and of morals."[14] The Jacobins of Marseilles also emulated their brothers in developing a vast apparatus of ritual. Responsive readings and professions of faith became increasingly common with the Revolution's passage. Members also erected altars to the fatherland, organized patriotic processions, planted sacred trees of liberty, took oaths, and sang hymns in the sessions.

Like many ideological and religious movements Jacobinism venerated its martyrs and idols. Busts and inscriptions commemorated long-dead heroes; for the newly martyred, solemn obsequies were held. The Club reserved special esteem for Brutus, "the destroyer of the tyrant," and after 1793 for Marat and Lepelletier. But it had its own local martyrs as well. During the Terror the Society planned a pyramid to commemorate those executed during the Federalist rebellion.[15] When the youthful Toussaint Pascal died in 1791, speakers compared his life with the words of Solomon: "The zeal for your abode, oh my God, devours me. . . . The zeal for the new constitution . . . for the rights of man and of the citizen consumed Tous-

[13] BM, 4717, "Discours de M. Blanc-Gilly le dernier jour de la présidence."

[14] *JdD*, Mar. 8, 1792, pp. 5–6.

[15] AM, 4 D₇, To the president of the popular society, Oct. 6, 1793.

saint Pascal." [16] In ceremonies after Mirabeau's death Chompré beatified the Great Tribune as the "spirit of Jesus Christ in a mortal state." Like Christ, Mirabeau had come to earth and walked among his disciples "preaching obedience to the nation, to the law, and to the king." [17]

In the best religious and totalitarian tradition, the Jacobins of Marseilles exhibited extreme intolerance for other political groups. In order to be one of the elite, in order to be truly patriotic, it was necessary to accept their creed. "The true friends of the revolution do not thing that there are two ways to arrive at prosperity and public tranquility." [18] The Society solemnly burned all publications that it considered heretical. As faithful converts, the members heaped special scorn upon revisionists. When the Club purged Etienne Martin at the end of 1791, it destroyed all his portraits, engravings, and honorary inscriptions. After the incriminating papers of Mirabeau were discovered in Paris the Marseillais solemnly veiled his statue. When the Abbé Raynal retracted the principles expressed in his *Histoire philosophique et politique des établissements et du commerce des Européens dans les deux Indes* (May 31, 1791), the Club organized a procession to conduct his bust to the mental asylum.[19]

The members of the Society were avid proselytizers. In-

[16] Pascal, the son of a pharmacist, was one of the most important early revolutionaries in Marseilles. Arrested after the riot of August 19, 1789, he became a municipal officer in 1790. See BM, 4717, "Aux mânes de Toussaint Pascal" (Marseille, 1791).

[17] BM, 4717, "Eloge d'Honoré-Gabriel-Riquetti Mirabeau" (Marseille, 1791).

[18] *Ibid.*, "Lettre de M. Martin, député à l'Assemblée Nationale aux amis de la Constitution de Marseille, suivie de la réponse à ladite lettre" (Marseille, 1792).

[19] On Mirabeau see *JdD*, Dec. 15, 1792, p. 500. On Raynal see Aulard, *Jacobins*, II, 510.

deed, the Club often referred to its commissioners as "missionaries of liberty." These evangelists spread Jacobin doctrine and established new "temples of liberty." "Let the societies be formed in all parts," said an honorary member in 1790, "let them resemble temples elevated to the Fatherland where each citizen comes to bring the offering of his services." [20] Since the temples of liberty were the strongest pillars of the Revolution, the infidels—the aristocrats, moderates, fanatics, etc.—naturally hoped to destroy them. The Jacobins of Marseilles vowed to die for their beliefs. Popular societies were inviolable and eternal. If ever the "criminals attempt to close the society of Marseilles," said Beissière in September, 1794, "let them perish . . . or bury us under the walls of the Mountain." [21]

To become a Jacobin convert, one had to conform, in theory, to a rigid ethical code, the tenor of which was almost puritanical. The true patriot was a man of sobriety and high purpose. Cherishing the nation above all, he was courageous, contemptuous of death, and indifferent to calumny and physical persecution. "Neither hatred, nor passion, nor rancor, nor any other irascible passion" should have access to his heart.[22] Few jokes lightened the mood of meetings; only humorless platitudes directed against the aristocrats.

Patriotism was not a contemplative virtue. A good club member had to be constantly vigilant. The Revolution was a time of mortal combat between "reason and prejudices, truth

[20] BM, 4717, "Discours prononcé . . . par M. Maximin Isnard, . . . et réimprimé d'après une délibération prise dans l'assemblée patriotique de Marseille" (Marseille, 1790).

[21] AN, W 86.

[22] BM, 4717, "M Vieilh, . . . sur le développement du mot patriotique"; CC, I₇₀, "Mémoire justificatif des citoyens Augustin Maillet, président, et Joseph Giraud, accusateur public" (Paris, 1794).

and error, justice and inequity, and liberty and slavery." If the Jacobins ever slept, they could "expect to wake up slaves." "Watch more and more," the Club's correspondence committee warned the Society of Mazargues in June, 1794, "thwart everything that can blacken the republic." [23] While the Society remained steadfastly hostile to counterrevolutionaries, the feeling toward fellow patriots was one of brotherhood. Duty bound every Jacobin to "love free men without distinction." The union of all "free" and "virtuous" citizens was the firmest base of liberty.[24] "If the free man is a perfect image of the divinity," argued a member in April, 1794, "is it not honoring the divinity to cherish free men?" [25]

A selfish person could not be a good patriot. The Jacobin had to be free of the spirit of pride and domination. His oath to the Society required him to aid the poor and to work for the public good with all his might, even if that entailed loss of fortune or domestic repose. Generosity was, perhaps, the moral requirement that the Marseillais most nearly fulfilled. Examples of their acts of self-sacrifice could fill many pages.

The virtue praised most highly was probity. In public affairs, "the least deviation" from honesty was a crime. No doubt many members of the Club like Louis Barthélemy, and perhaps Isoard, lined their pockets with Revolutionary booty. But theoretically they repulsed such temptation. When some suspects "offered" 30,000 livres to Alexandre Ricord during the Terror, he turned it over to the Society, boasting, "Before the Revolution I possessed little, now I own nothing but the esteem and confidence of true Republicans." [26] Emphasis on

[23] AM, I₂, carton 1794.

[24] BN, Lb⁴⁰ 996; AN, W 86, "Profession de foi."

[25] AD, B-du-Rh, L 2076, *Tribune populaire*, Apr. 20, 1794.

[26] AM, I₂, carton 1794, "Extraits des délibérations de la Société populaire de Sans Nom, séance du 8 pluviôse an II" (Marseille, 1794).

moral excellence reached its peak during Robespierre's Republic of Virtue. The decrees of the mother society in Paris and the letters of the Montagnard representatives of the Bouches-du-Rhône deeply influenced the Club. In a letter read in the session of June 1, 1794, Moyse Bayle and Granet described the true patriot as a man who "has endured every kind of privation, who has seen his fortune decline and never attempted to recoup it, who has not coveted office, but if fulfilling one, has never turned a penny to his profit, a man who has always been the constant enemy of oppression; this man alone is a good patriot." [27]

In 1790 the Club members found no conflict between patriotism and the principles of organized religion. In speeches they invoked God's protection on the Revolution and declared religion and patriotism to be inseparable.[28] A significant percentage of the Club's founders were clergymen, and Christian symbols, phrases, and parallels abounded in addresses and essays. The Society often patronized Catholic religious ceremonies. It sponsored a Te Deum at the Cathedral on July 23, 1790, for example, to celebrate the first anniversary of the Assembly at the Arquier Tavern and also to give thanks to the Supreme Being for an abundant harvest. The Journal de Provence reported that "this religious fête was brilliant, both in the number of spectators who attended it, and in its execution that left nothing to be desired." [29]

Despite these manifestations of orthodox Catholicism, the Club was, from the beginning, antihierarchical and Gallican. Its members professed respect for primitive Christianity and

[27] AD, B-du-Rh, L 2076.

[28] BM, 4717, "Discours sur la confédération nationale" (Marseille, 1790).

[29] *Journal de Provence*, July 27, 1790, pp. 302–303.

the "true teachings" of Christ rather than the organized church. In "the first age of the world," they argued, reason and religion had collaborated to build a great civic state, free from passions and prejudices. The Catholic hierarchy had subverted this blessed state. Bishops and popes pursued their own interests rather than the glory of man or God.[30]

Among the "murderous" high clergy, the Club singled out the former archbishop of Aix for special hatred. In December, 1790, it sent a long petition to the National Assembly demand-his dismissal for inciting civil war in Provence. As for the pope, he was the ally of the tyrants of Europe. His agents hid "daggers" under the veil of "holy religion" to stab the inno-cent patriots.[31] The Club emphasized the "atrocities" of the papal government in its propaganda, and published antipapal tracts and songs:

> The time when frightened citizens
> Dreaded the deviations of the Italian canon
> That unhappy time, for us, when enslaved Europe
> Approved and shared the errors of Italy.
> This time is no more.[32]

Not surprisingly, the Society became a firm supporter of the civil constitution of the clergy. It held a magnificent cere-mony on May 16, 1791, to commemorate the installation of the new constitutional bishop of the Bouches-du-Rhône, Toussaint Roux. Over 2,000 Jacobins listened to Roux declare

[30] CC, I₇₀, "Discours de M. le Président et discours en réponse de M. L'Evêque. Extrait des registres des amis de la constitution, séance du 16 mai 1791" (Marseille, 1791).

[31] On the archbishop see BM, 4717, "Testament et dernier soupir du haut clergé de France" (Marseille, 1790); on the Pope see CC, I₇₀, "Adresse au peuple Marseillais."

[32] AM, I₂, session of July 8, 1790.

that patriotism and religion should march together. Following his discourse, those priests who were members of the Club rose one by one to pay homage to the constitution.[33] In succeeding years the Society defended these ecclesiastics and the constitution they had vowed to follow. The friendly relationship endured until the spring of 1793, when many of the constitutional priests compromised themselves in the Federalist revolt.

If the Club members befriended the constitutional priests, they declared war on those they called the *réfractaires* and *fanatiques*. The non-juring priests ranked second only to the aristocrats as the most dangerous counterrevolutionaries. Their "incendiary" writings inflamed the populace, and they employed the confession "to seduce and win the sex always so weak and alarmed over its conscience." Their immediate goal, the Marseillais believed, was to destroy the Club and massacre its members. Thus on April 16, 1792, the unexpected appearance at the session of a considerable number of Catholic petitioners, ringing bells and carrying crosses and wooden effigies, threw the clubbists into near panic.[34] In its propaganda, the Society took massive countermeasures to discredit non-juring priests. In the first number of the *Manuel du laboureur et de l'artisan*, Jacques Monbrion warned the peasants of Provence to be wary of their tactics:

They [the fanatics] approach you with angelic softness; heaven is in their eyes, hell is in their hearts. . . . They try to persuade you that God presides over their impious maneuvers. Do you trust these words? Ah! Reflect first on the unnumbered assassinations that the fanatics have committed in every country where

[33] CC, I₇₀, "Discours de M. le Président et . . . de M. l'Evêque."
[34] *JdD*, Apr. 19, 1792, p. 79.

they reign. Transport yourself a minute to the atrocious scenes of St.-Barthelemew and the Sicilian Vespers.[35]

By 1792, the spokesmen of the Club had passed beyond mere hostility toward the Church hierarchy and the nonjuring priests and begun to attack Catholicism as such. In April, 1792, when the Society learned that some journeymen stonecutters had instituted a fund to pay for the celebration of masses, it expressed extreme displeasure at this revival of old abuses. In August, 1792, it prohibited priests from appearing at the Club in their robes.[36] During 1793–1794 a radical phase of de-christianization began. The Club's propagandists urged the expulsion of all priests from the Republic and vowed a war of "destitution and deportation" against them.[37] The clergymen who still belonged to the Society followed the example of their counterparts elsewhere in France. On November 17 and 18, 1793, Emmanuel de Beausset and Isoard renounced their vows and rendered homage to "reason and philosophy." On November 28 Beausset announced plans to marry. Henceforth, he desired only two titles, he said, those of man and citizen. "The first use that I make of both is to unite my fate to a companion. . . . O! Nature, that sacerdotal despotism had the audacity to shackle, I return at last under your authority." [38]

Throughout the Revolution the Club professed tolerance for minority sects. The *Manuel du laboureur* offered this advice in June, 1792:

[35] AM, Toulon, L 56, pp. 1–2. [36] *JdD*, Sep. 4, 1792, p. 324.
[37] AN, W 86, "Profession de foi"; AD, B-du-Rh, L 2076, "Discours prononcé par le citoyen Maillet aîné, vice-président de la société populaire de Marseille" (Marseille, 1794).
[38] AM, 1 D₄.

Good people refrain from the belief that those who are not of your religion do not have virtues like you; the Jew, the Protestant, the Mohammedan, and the Christian all adore the same God, but in different manners; the last believes himself best, but he is still obliged to tolerate the others.[39]

Where Jews and Protestants were concerned, the Club practiced these principles. It admitted the former as members, and protected the latter, who had been the victims of eighteenth-century persecutions. The lone Protestant minister in Marseilles was a member. When "fanatics" menaced his church in April, 1792, the Club dispatched a deputation to the Municipality to insure the free practice of religion. When a new Protestant chapel was erected in October, 1792, the Society sent a special delegation to attend the dedication service.[40]

That the Society should have practiced tolerance toward Protestants and Jews is scarcely surprising. Its members were children of the eighteenth-century, spiritual sons of the *philosophes*. The doctrines and metaphors of the Enlightenment punctuate their works. They viewed themselves as soldier-philosophers "blending the intrepidity of true heroes and the profound knowledge of thinking and calculating beings." With an optimistic belief in the future went trust in the efficacy of nature; the *Manuel du laboureur* took as its motto a quotation from antiquity: "Men are truly virtuous only when they draw close to nature." [41]

The most obvious manifestation of the Jacobins' beliefs was the worship of Reason. The "spark" of Reason had originated

[39] AM, Toulon, L 56, undated (no. 7).

[40] V-L. Bourilly, "Les Protestants à Marseille au XVIIIᵉ siècle," *Bulletin de la Société historique du protestantisme français* (1910), pp. 425–431, 513–533; *JdD*, Apr. 19, Oct. 27, 1792, pp. 81, 416.

[41] Undated (no. 1), p. 1.

among the English, passed to the Americans and the Batavians, and finally flamed into the sublime Revolution.[42] It was the despair of despots. "The thunder of Reason," wrote Monbrion in 1791, "rumbles in the atmosphere, and brings fear into the soul of the tyrants." [43] During the Terror, the Society left "superstitious religion" to "imbeciles." No catechism was needed save Reason and good sense:

> Is an intermediary necessary
> Between man and his creator?
> No, Reason that enlightens us
> Engraves the law in our hearts.
> Gift of eternal wisdom,
> It is the only faithful guide
> That our steps must follow;
> Blind faith is only a vain dream
> The priest is the echo of the lie,
> But Reason does not deceive.[44]

Like all enlightened men, the leaders of the Club believed in the supreme value of education. Man had only to propagate "the light," and he would be free. If the enemies of the Club succeeded in their schemes, it was because this rule was not being followed. "Citizens," said a speaker during the Terror, "our errors are born from ignorance; the wicked have made them instruments of crime and have covered France with misfortunes and misery. . . . It is necessary, citizens, to make ignorance disappear by instruction." [45]

---

[42] See BM, 4717, "Discours prononcés à l'assemblée de la société des amis de la constitution, par Messieurs Corail . . . Rebecq . . . et Albouis" (Marseille, 1792).

[43] *Ibid.*, "Crimes du lèse-nation" (Marseille, 1791).

[44] BM, 2401, "Ode à la Raison" (Marseille, 1794).

[45] AD, B-du-Rh, L 2076.

The leading figures in the Society read the *philosophes*. They quoted Mably, Montesquieu, Helvétius, and Voltaire, but they had a particular reverence for the *Social Contract* and for Jean-Jacques Rousseau, "the benefactor of the human race"; he had been the first Jacobin, "the first defender of liberty and equality." [46] They continually drew analogies between antiquity and the events of the Revolution. They idolized Republican Rome and Athens. Brutus the assassin was lionized; Caesar was denounced. In republican tracts, they compared the inviolability of kings to the divinity of the Roman emperors. And their own valor the Marseillais likened to that of the Spartans.

Central to the political doctrines of the Jacobins of Marseilles was their concept of "the people," a term used incessantly but never defined with clarity. In one sense "the people" represented everyone in France except the privileged, that is, the nearly 25,000,000 members of the Third Estate. Sometimes, however, the term was used to denote just the small people, that is, the laboring classes or the peasants. Most scholars agree that the Jacobins distinguished themselves from the people; they were its spokesmen and instructors. Broadly speaking, the Marseillais conformed to this general principle. "Our profession of faith, our most sacred oath," said a member in 1790, "is to aid the People, to watch over its rights." [47] This precept applied throughout the Revolution; it is the duty of a Jacobin, emphasized the "profession of faith" of September, 1794, "to enlighten the people." [48]

[46] See BM, 4717, "Extrait des délibérations de l'assemblée patriotique, séance du 31 décembre, au soir" (Marseille, 1791); *JdD*, Mar. 7, 1793, p. 641.

[47] BM, 5220, "Adresse d'un membre de l'assemblée patriotique aux citoyens de Marseille" (Marseille, 1790).

[48] AN, W 86.

The basic premise of the political philosophy of the Marseillais, like that of the *sans-culottes* of Paris, was the idea
that "sovereignty resides in the people"; from this principle
all others derived. Their definition of popular sovereignty was
founded on article three of the Rights of Man. The *Manuel
du laboureur* attempted to explain the principle simply: "The
nation alone is sovereign; from it alone derive the prerogatives
accorded to the Executive Power and to all the constituted
authorities; it can change at its will that which it has created." [49]

From the general doctrine of popular sovereignty any number of specific arguments could be derived. In 1791–1792, for
instance, the Club invoked this principle to deny the sovereign
rights of the king. Barbaroux's address to the Legislative Assembly denied the king's right to be called "sire" or "majesty":
"This title belongs only to the twenty-five million men who
form the French nation, because in these twenty-five million
resides the sovereign power, since they alone have created the
constitution and the King." [50] The Society also used it to question the legality of unpleasant decrees of national or local authorities. Any law or ordinance contrary to the rights of the
people was ipso facto null and void. In justifying the illegal
activities of the electoral assembly of the Bouches-du-Rhône
in 1792, Pierre Micoulin cited Cicero: "An unjust law, under
whatever name one gives it, should no longer pass for a
law." [51]

Like the sections in Paris, the Society of Marseilles expanded the idea of popular sovereignty into a full-blown concept of direct democracy. Words like censure, control, and

[49] Undated (no. 6), p. 45. See also Albert Soboul, *Les Sans-culottes
parisiens* (Paris, 1968), p. 101.
[50] Lourde, II, 55–56.   [51] AD, B-du-Rh, L 278.

recall became common parlance. When Narbonne, minister of war, dismissed Puget-Barbentane, commander of the troops at Aix, in February, 1792, "only because he was Jacobin," the Club wrote angrily to the king demanding his reinstatement: "You will perhaps be astonished at our language. You would not be if you recognized that the people are sovereign and you only a subject." [52]

The Marseillais continually prompted their rural disciples to be vigilant, for the most dangerous enemies were often "hypocritical officials." "Never avert your eyes," they warned the Society of Peyrigord; "spy upon the public conduct and even the private life of the officials in order that they cannot prevaricate in their sacred functions." [53] By 1793 the Club was vehemently denying the inviolability of legislators. This "absurd right," an "outrage to justice and reason," spared the enemies of the Revolution from the people's vengeance during their terms of office; officials who betrayed the people deserved "the blade of the guillotine."

The doctrine of popular sovereignty slowly evolved into a defense of violence and Revolutionary justice; by the summer of 1792, as we have seen, the Society was defending popular terrorism. In the course of this evolution, it produced what was perhaps the most important offshoot of popular sovereignty, the concept of "resistance to oppression." The Club repeatedly emphasized this idea in calling for a march on Paris in 1792. Every citizen had the inherent privilege of arming himself against "illegal and tyrannical constraint." If the nation wanted to correct the abuses that had slipped into the Constitution, it had only to rise up; "all the executive powers of the universe could not prevent it." [54]

[52] *JdD*, Mar. 24, 1792, p. 35.   [53] AD, B-du-Rh, L 2070.
[54] *Manuel du laboureur*, undated (no. 6), p. 46.

The complete application of popular sovereignty could only result in liberty. In defining liberty the Jacobins of Marseilles rarely deviated from the orthodoxy of articles four and five of the Rights of Man. Liberty consisted essentially of the right to do everything which the laws did not prohibit and which did not harm one's neighbor. A corollary of liberty, therefore, was respect for the law. In modern-day terms the members of the Society considered themselves proponents of law and order and, correspondingly, enemies of anarchy and violence. One who transgressed the law defiled liberty.

To justify their own illegal activities, the theorists of the Club developed a supplementary doctrine of "suspension or abuse of the laws." Like all good principles, law and order could be perverted and abused. When the enemies of the constitution flouted the laws, the people took back its "sceptre" and unsheathed its "redoubtable sword." As the best means of defending liberty, the people joined, propagated, and defended popular societies. "Consider a little," said an address of the Club in 1790, "what the suspension of the Patriotic Assembly would cost liberty." [55]

United against liberty was a nefarious international counter-revolutionary league. Such a coalition naturally developed, argued the Jacobins, when a people sought freedom; England experienced twenty years of war "to acquire that half-liberty that it glorifies," and when the "courageous Philadelphes" attempted to throw off the yoke of despotism the counterrevolutionaries ignited an international war to stop them. At the head of the coalition against liberty sat the kings of Europe, an "infernal race" of "reborn Neros." In the early years of the Revolution, the chief tyrant was the Emperor Leopold. The Marseillais considered him a man of unequalled perfidy and

[55] BM, 4717, "La Vérité ou seconde adresse" (Marseille, 1790).

rejoiced at his death in 1792. In the beginning they regarded the English as friends of the Revolution and, being well-versed in English history, constantly cited it as a guide. In ceremonies at the end of 1791, the Club solemnly unfurled the Union Jack in the assembly hall and sang odes in its honor.[56]

Because of Marseilles' maritime interests, the English eventually replaced the Austrians as the principal enemy. As early as February 8, 1793, a member made a motion to remove the English flag from the assembly hall. By August, 1794, the "English brothers" had become the "insolent English." [57] The Club especially detested "the infamous Pitt" and imagined his spies to be everywhere. When the representative of the Convention, Gasparin, died (of natural causes) at Avignon in 1793, the Marseillais reported in a letter to the Convention that he had been poisoned by the agents of the English minister.[58] The principal goal of Pitt and his allies, as the Jacobins saw it, was to undermine the popular societies: "Pitt, yes Pitt, would pay dearly not for their destruction (to destroy them is impossible), but just for their isolation. His agents swarm the length and breadth of the Republic. . . . They would like to sever the ties of affiliation." [59]

In 1790 and 1791 the Marseillais claimed to follow the principles of universal peace formulated by the Abbé of Saint-Pierre. Wars belonged to the past since they were only the "quarrels of kings." However, the fear of the émigrés and

[56] *Ibid.*, 4717, "Adresse aux Parisiens" (Marseille, 1791), and "Alliance des drapeaux constitutionnels de France et d'Angleterre" (Marseille, 1791).

[57] *JdD*, Feb. 12, 1793, p. 600; AN, W 86, session of Aug. 24, 1794.

[58] AN, C 285, "Adresse à la Convention nationale" (Marseille, 1793).

[59] AN, W 86, "La Société populaire de Marseille à la Convention nationale" (Marseille, 1794).

foreign princes eroded these beliefs, and an evangelical conviction grew up that peace could not be attained until liberty and equality took root in other nations. By early 1792 the Club was arguing for a declaration of war. When the conflict came, it emphasized that France had declared war on the kings of Austria and not on the Austrian people. Later, it checked to see if the crews of captured English ships had been treated humanely. On one occasion the humanity of the crew of the corsair *Saint-Pierre* was so praiseworthy that a resolution was sent to Carra in Paris for publication. The crew's behavior "proved beyond question that the French have declared war only against tyrants and their satellites, and that they will always remain fraternally united with the peoples." [60]

Within France the most important political allies of the foreign tyrants, at least prior to 1792, were the government ministers. As we have seen, the Club attacked them with unflagging zeal. Equally virulent anathemas were levelled at Marie Antoinette. When in March, 1792, false news of her death arrived, the Club made plans for a bonfire on mount Notre-Dame-de-la-Garde. The *Journal* justified this on the grounds that a country which had been ravaged by a plague ought to give thanks for its end to the Supreme Being.[61]

Behind the Austrian committee and the ministers came the Feuillants, moderates, émigrés, and counterrevolutionaries, known collectively as "aristocrats." The Society applied this name arbitrarily to all types of enemies; the aristocrat was a vicious creature "with the claws of a harpy, the tongue of a bloodsucker, the heart of a vulture, and the cruelty of a tiger." "Like vampires," the aristocrats savored the blood of patriots. They were responsible for poor harvests and eco-

[60] *JdD*, Feb. 19, 1793, p. 612.   [61] *Ibid.*, Mar. 29, 1792, p. 43.

nomic crises; they also insinuated themselves into office and into popular societies. The "proscriptions of Sulla and the Saint-Bartholomew's day massacre would be as nothing if the aristocrats ever triumphed." [62]

In an article published in 1942, the Marxist historian Alfred-Chabaud said of Revolutionary Marseilles:

The proletariat acted as if it was conscious of the class struggle, as if it knew that it would obtain nothing except through violence; but it is only in the Club of Marseilles that *socialist revolutionary* propaganda was elaborated. It was circulated in 1792 and in the first months of 1793.[63]

The accusations made by the Society's contemporary antagonists, who saw its members as the enemies of the rich, of property, and of commerce, seem to confirm Alfred-Chabaud. Their attitude is well illustrated by an inflammatory attack dating from the Thermidorian Reaction entitled *Adresse de la société populaire des Wisigoths et des Vandals séante à Marseille, à la société populaire des Ostrogoths et des Welches séante à XXX*. This fictionalized account of a meeting of the Club ended with the members going en masse to burn the homes of the rich and seize their belongings.[64] The charges are interesting because they conflict with traditional interpretations of Jacobin ideology. Historians have described Jacobinism as being essentially bourgeois in character. Obviously, the economic and social attitudes of the members of the Marseilles Society warrant examination.

The Club interpreted article one of the Declaration of the Rights of Man literally. Every man was equal before the law.

[62] BM, 4717, "Confession Pascale des Sieurs Bournissac, Thulis, Durand, La Flèche . . . et autre sang-sues" (Marseille, 1790); AN, AF II, 185," "Catéchisme du peuple."
[63] "Essai . . . ," p. 118.   [64] BM, 1996.

No one had the right to own slaves or to be privileged because of his birth. All citizens must pay taxes in proportion to their wealth; the same laws judged everyone, and every male had the right to vote and hold office. Here, however, equality ceased. It did not extend to personal distinctions, nor to private property.

The ideal of the Marseillais was not a twentieth-century collectivist state, but, as was the case with Jacobins elsewhere, a Jeffersonian paradise of small property owners. In executing a law relating to the sale of national lands in 1793, for example, the Club recommended that the land be auctioned in small pieces so that those with only modest means could share in its acquisition.[65] Throughout the Revolution they stoutly defended the good citizen's right to hold property, and they sought to curtail arbitrary expropriations. In a letter to the antipolitiques on November 9, 1792, for example, they made an impassioned plea for the sanctity of private property:

We invite you to propagate it in your Society and especially among your neighbors of the countryside, where many less enlightened men are easily induced into the error of believing that goods are common property. The property of another does not excite our cupidity; to tell the truth, Republicans ought to have none.[66]

Anselme, the mythical country wise man of the *Manuel du laboureur et de l'artisan*, admonished the country people of his region in this fashion: "Every time that someone tells you: YOU SHOULD HAVE HALF THE PROPERTY OF YOUR NEIGHBOR; shun that man! He is a veritable enemy of the constitution; he wants you to misinterpret equality so that he can slander the Declaration of the Rights of Man."[67]

[65] *JdD*, Mar. 12, 1793, p. 647.   [66] AD, B-du-Rh, L 2038.
[67] No. 6, p. 44.

In the first years of the Revolution the Club adhered rigidly to the laissez-faire principle in labor relations, opposing any type of guild or laboring association and believing that every man should be "free to exercise his talents according to his tastes and particular abilities." Accordingly, it applauded the decree of February 17, 1791, which abolished guilds and corporations.[68] The Club also observed strict neutrality in labor disputes. When two workers made a complaint against their employer at a meeting of the Society on June 13, 1790, the assembly refused to consider it. In 1791 a delegation of journeymen bakers implored the Club to regulate the power of master bakers and to help them in establishing a sort of health insurance scheme; there is no evidence that the members acted on this matter.[69]

While this may have been the Society's position on labor disputes, it unfailingly acted to protect the indigent from exploitation by hoarders and speculators, "a cursed caste" who found wealth in public misfortune. By 1792–1793, calls for the punishment of speculators came continually. On March 11, 1793, the Society printed the letter of a *sansculotte* and sent copies the length and breadth of France. It demanded legislation on this matter:

Do you wish to sever a head no less criminal than that of the last of the tyrants? . . . Enact severe laws against hoarding; proclaim this great truth, that no individual has the right to say to another, "I have the bread and you will die of hunger. I have garments and you will not be clothed. I have leather and you will go barefooted."[70]

[68] BM, 4717, "Adresse de l'assemblée patriotique à ses con-citoyens" (Marseille, 1791).
[69] AM, I₂, cartons 1790, 1791.
[70] AD, B-du-Rh, L 2071. *JdD*, Mar. 14, 1793, p. 652.

During 1792, the Society conceived many plans to reduce the price of food and clothing. On February 18, for example, Jean-François Méry obtained the approval of the Municipality to form a public, non-profit corporation to bake bread in the ovens of Forts St.-Jean and St.-Nicolas. Consumers would profit by obtaining cheaper and better quality loaves.[71] Two months later, the Club acted to lower the price of meat after a complaint from the Municipality that the meat cutters sold beef and pork above fixed prices. On April 18 over fifty-five men and women pledged contributions totalling 29,118 livres for the purchase of animals to be butchered and sold at cost to the citizens. The Society formed a committee of fifteen to oversee this fund.[72]

During the Terror the Club became even more zealous in watching over popular interests. On October 31, 1793, for example, it passed a resolution denouncing frauds in the sale of fruits and fish and calling for the posting of national guardsmen on all the routes to Marseilles to guarantee the free entry of provisions. In the same week the Society sent commissioners to the Municipality to urge a search of the residences of suspected hoarders and the seizure of merchants seeking to evade the law.[73] It applied constant pressure on the authorities. Typical of its actions was a reminder it gave the Municipal Council on February 9, 1794: "The people through the Popular Society has made diverse deputations to you. It

[71] Méry, an entrepreneur, was born in Marseilles about 1744. He served for a time on the Federalist Popular Tribunal. See BM, 4717, "Plan économique pour diminuer le prix du pain . . . présenté à l'assemblée patriotique" (Marseille, 1792).

[72] *JdD*, Apr. 21 and 24, 1792, pp. 83–88.

[73] AM, I₂, carton 1794, Extract of the session of the popular society of Marseilles, Oct. 31, 1793; *Journal républicain*, Oct. 30, 1793, pp. 98–99.

says again, I have need of bread; I will content myself with little. I only ask that the distribution be equal." [74]

To the Club members of Marseilles, no less than to the *sans-culottes* of Paris, the great enemy was the aristocrat. The aristocrat was more a political than an economic entity, but the Marseillais still evinced a strong hatred of the so-called "aristocracy of riches." Like other Jacobins they rarely condemned the rich just for being rich, but rather for being the "evil rich," "the selfish rich," or the "rich enemy of equality." Theoretically, it was difficult for a rich man to be a good patriot, but in fact many clubbists at least prior to the Terror, were the possessors of "honest fortunes." If he remained a supporter of the constitution, the rich man had nothing to fear. "The names of Lucullus, of Crassus, of Appius," said a member in 1792, "have inspired only contempt; those of the Gracchae, of Decius, of Curtius . . . will pass down to the most distant posterity." [75]

Distrust of the rich was matched by lavish praise for the popular classes, which became a main theme of Jacobin propaganda after 1792. Both the *Journal des départements méridionaux* and the *Manuel du laboureur* consecrated their pages to the instruction of the working class. "Honest and laborious artisans," said the *Journal* in its first prospectus, "estimable cultivators, interesting workers; you who form the most useful, the most respectable and the most virtuous part of the Nation: it is your suffrages alone that we desire!"

Skirmishes with the "selfish rich" abound in the history of the Club. Elements of the wealthy merchant class had led the bourgeois guard of 1789, supported the provost Bournissac,

[74] AM, 1 D 12.

[75] BM, 4717, "Discours prononcés à . . . la société des amis de la constitution, par Messieurs Corail, Rebecq."

and leagued themselves with Lieutaud. "It is undoubtedly those companies of avid men possessing too much gold," said the *Annales patriotiques* in 1790, "who have caused the troubles of Marseilles." [76] In late 1791 a serious dispute developed between the Club and the wholesale merchants of the Chamber of Commerce. Following the news of a riot in Santo Domingo which had destroyed some of their property, the wealthy merchants addressed a supplicatory letter to the king complaining in vague terms of "the enemies of the prosperity of the state." The Club denounced this "unconstitutional step," in a petition to the Legislative Assembly on January 3, 1792. In the following weeks speakers in the Society accused many of the merchants of being hoarders. The latter retaliated with the well-worn charge that the clubbists sought to destroy the city's commerce, and organized a battalion of portworkers (whose living depended on commerce) to defend them against the "brigands" of the Society. On February 1, 1792, 200 portworkers actually marched on the Club; only the intervention of the Municipality averted a serious incident.[77]

From mid-1792 to 1794, tirades against the rich became much more frequent. Radicals like Isoard and Tourneau took the lead. As members of the central committee they formulated plans to extort money from the wealthy and bombarded affiliated clubs with propaganda against the rich. Some of their letters to the Basses-Alpes are still preserved. In an epistle of

[76] BM, Toulon, 19665, *Annales patriotiques de Marseille*, no. 7, p. 76.
[77] For the letter to the king consult BN, Lk² 369, "Au Roi" (Marseille, 1791). AN, D III 30, "Dénonciation à l'assemblée nationale, d'une lettre écrite au Roy, par quelques négociants de Marseille" (Marseille, 1791). On the portworkers see AN, F⁷ 4603, Chabaud to Blanc-Gilly, Feb. 12, 1792; *Journal de Provence*, Feb. 4 and 16, 1792, pp. 122–123, 161–162.

April, 1793, they advised the Society of Digne to institute forced taxation. "I am anxious to have the Basses-Alpes work in concert with the Marseillais," wrote Isoard, "the rich have arms and money." To the Club of Manosque, they sent warnings of the machinations of the bourgeoisie, counselling the Manosquains to follow the lead of the "cultivators of Aubagne even up to the point of killing the bourgeoisie, because they are the enemies of the patriots." They also urged the formation of an army of 800 dedicated *sans-culottes:* "Commissioners will come soon to tell you what you must do. We merely announce that it is necessary to exterminate the rest of our tyrants." [78]

As the next chapter shows, commissioners of the Club intervened constantly in the affairs of the clubs and communes of Provence on the side of the "poor cultivators" and against the "bourgeoisie." In April, 1792, they refused to approve a union of the "popular society" and the Friends of the Constitution in Nîmes: "Union is impractical, because one club is composed of rich, the other poor; one has bad principles, the other good." [79] In another instance two months later, commissioners dissolved the club at Cotignac in the Var which was "especially composed of bourgeoisie" and reaffirmed the position of the rival society which was drawn from the "ranks of the people." [80] Although the social composition of local factions was not so clear-cut as these examples indicate, it is significant nonetheless that the Marseillais identified their cause with that of the poor workers and peasants.

It is inaccurate in one sense to say, as Alfred-Chabaud did, that the Club had a socialist revolutionary philosophy. The Jacobins of the Rue Thubaneau always remained essentially

[78] AD, B-du-Rh, L 3037.   [79] *JdD*, Apr. 10, 1792, pp. 63–64.
[80] Agulhon, II, 511.

bourgeois in their attitudes toward private property and industry. Yet social consciousness did intensify noticeably between 1790 and 1793. Envy and dislike of the rich motivated the Society's members in their attacks on the Chamber of Commerce. Radicals of the Club, like Isoard in 1793, stimulated class hatred in the countryside. In short, the Jacobins of Marseilles were social revolutionaries if not revolutionary socialists.

8

Clubs, Communes, and Commissioners

Compared to twentieth-century political parties, the Jacobin movement was neither highly organized nor tightly disciplined. All the clubs more or less professed allegiance to the mother society in Paris, but geographical distance lessened its influence. Small clubs often looked for information and guidance not to Paris but to an intermediate point, the urban societies of their region. Jacobinism cannot be truly understood without some examination of regional networks and local patterns of interaction.

No one is certain how many Jacobin clubs sprung up in France between 1789 and 1795. Brinton estimated the number at 6,800.[1] After detailed research, Chobaut pinpointed 825 in the Vaucluse, Var, Bouches-du-Rhône, Basses-Alpes, Drôme, and Gard. If Brinton's approximation is accepted (and it may be high), then these six departments accounted for 12.1 per cent of the total number of popular societies in France.[2] Chobaut attributed the disproportionately high number to the

[1] Brinton, p. 38.
[2] Hyacinthe Chobaut, "Le Nombre des sociétés populaires du Sud-Est," *Annales historiques de la Révolution française*, III (1926), 450–455.

political temperament of the southerners, but there may be another explanation. In 1792–1793, in the first four of these departments, and in parts of the other two, the influence of the Club of the Rue Thubaneau reached a peak. It founded scores of new societies and regularly meddled in the affairs of the communes.

The political arm of the Club outside Marseilles was the commissioner. At the height of the Society's power, commissioners roamed an area stretching as far as Castres and Montpellier to the west, Lyons and Bourgoin to the north, and the Alpine frontier to the east. The diversity of their exploits equaled their geographical breadth. Escorted by armed national guardsmen from Marseilles and satellite communes, the Club's legates established societies, taxed the rich, made arrests, and dismissed elected officials. In many respects their activities foreshadowed those of the Revolutionary armies of the Terror.[3]

The practice of sending out commissioners dated from the earliest days of the Club. The first recorded commission journeyed from Marseilles to Nîmes on May 9, 1790. Gradually, the Society regularized and institutionalized its evangelism. In 1792–1793 scarcely a day passed when one or more legates did not leave Marseilles. After the Federalist rebellion, the rate diminished considerably but did not cease. As the Club gained ascendancy in local politics, officials began to vest its commissioners with legal authority. After the Legislative Assembly's decree declaring the fatherland in danger, in July, 1792, thirteen commissioners of the Society, armed with full powers by the Municipality and district administra-

[3] AD, Tarn, L 1531; AD, Hérault, L 5500; *Extraits pris sur les registres de la société populaire de Bourgoin*, ed. L. Fochier (Vienne, 1880), session of July 30, 1792.

tion of Marseilles, visited more than a dozen southern departments to raise a force of 6,000 men and rekindle the spirit of patriotism. Following the kidnapping of the Directory of the department in August, 1792, commissioners of the Club became ipso facto legates of the department.[4]

Initially, the Society assumed responsibility for the expenses of its missionaries. As their assignments multiplied, however, the financial burden became too onerous, and by 1792 it was expected that the club or commune that had asked for a commissioner would pay his costs. Three commissioners in the Vaucluse in 1792 charged 100 livres per day to arbitrate a dispute between two communes. Antoine Réquier, an emissary of the Club's secret committee at Auriol (Bouches-du-Rhône) in the fall of 1792, earned 10,000 livres for his efforts.[5] Some commissioners probably profited at the expense of those they were instructing. In the autumn of 1792 complaints poured into the Club of "pillage" and "thefts" by individuals calling themselves Marseillais. Whether all these "Marseillais" were, indeed, the Society's representatives is a matter of debate. At any rate the Club launched a full-scale investigation. After heated debates in November the members dismissed the charges, characterizing them as an aristocratic plot to discredit the Jacobins.[6]

The arrival of a Marseillais at a Provençal village was an event of considerable significance. The minutes of the popular society of Castellane (Basses-Alpes) of August 17, 1792, re-

[4] For the Nîmes mission see *L'Observateur marseillais*, May 18, 1790, pp. 6–8; on the thirteen commissioners of July, 1792, see BM, 4717, "Adresse des autorités administratives."

[5] AD, B-du-Rh, L 126, L 3104.

[6] *Ibid.*, L 129, Letter of Sep. 28, 1792; L 2080, The popular society of Martigues, session of Nov. 20, 1792; L 292, Letter of J. Estienne, Nov. 20, 1792; *JdD*, Nov. 29, 1792, pp. 474–477.

count the splendid reception given to some commissioners who had come to the Basses-Alpes to "revive patriotism." Representatives of the Castellane society conducted them to the tribune amidst thunderous applause. Cries of *"Vive les Marseillais, vive la société patriotique de Marseille"* rang out through the hall. Patriotic speeches were exchanged, and everyone vowed to defend the constitution "to the last drop of blood." After the session the throng sang hymns and danced in the streets.[7]

The commissioners' reports that have survived are vivid and colorful. On even the most trivial assignments, they tended to dramatize and boast of their exploits. Although the majority returned home unscathed, their letters leave an impression of never-ending peril. The elements conspired against them; still worse, one had always to fear the plots of the "aristocrats." A bulletin from Beere in January, 1793, recounts one such conspiracy foiled and the chase that followed:

A short distance from Berre we had quite an unfortunate adventure. A woman ran to us across a field crying, "Help! He wants to murder me." Hearing these cries, we descended from the carriage, drew our weapons, and pursued the fleeing accused. Citizen Bontemps who went ahead, shouted, "Stop, my friend, we do not want to hurt you"; deaf to this request, the fugitive entered a house and reappeared immediately with a gun; he took aim on Citizen Bontemps.

Fortunately, the intrepid Marseillais disarmed this dangerous assassin.[8]

While the commissioners of the Club of Marseilles operated in many departments of southern France, they were omnipresent in the Bouches-du-Rhône, Var, Basses-Alpes, and

7 AD, Basses-Alpes, L 851.   8 AD, B-du-Rh, L 126.

Vaucluse. The societies in these four departments were clearly subordinate to the Club of Marseilles. By focusing on each of the departments in turn, one can obtain a clearer picture of the very real power of the Society of the Rue Thubaneau.

Bouches-du-Rhône

The center of Marseilles' sphere of interest was its home department, the Bouches-du-Rhône. At least sixty-two societies in the department were affiliates of the Club. Chief among them was the Club of Antipolitiques in Aix, founded by the Abbé Rive on November 1, 1790. According to Ponteil, the Antipolitiques were largely peasants, small shopkeepers, and artisans. As early as January 6, 1791, Rive's club requested union and correspondence with Marseilles, but it did not obtain this prize until three months later.[9] From that time forward the Marseillais regarded themselves as protectors, instructors, and elder brothers of the Aixois. The unity between the two societies remained an article of faith throughout the Revolution. "Nothing can part the sacred bonds of our alliance," promised Blanc-Gilly in a speech at the Antipolitiques in 1791, "because it was formed under the auspices of a common cause." [10]

One of the ways in which the Marseillais dominated their brothers at Aix was by attending their meetings; a host of clubbists from Marseilles joined the nearby society. In their capacity as members of the Antipolitiques, the Jacobins of Marseilles drafted letters and addresses and generally influenced policy. "All goes well with the brave Antipoli-

[9] AD, B-du-Rh, L 2026, session of Jan. 13, 1791. *Annales patriotiques*, May 4, 1791, pp. 1370–1371.
[10] AD, B-du-Rh, L 2027.

tiques," wrote Chabaud to Blanc-Gilly in February, 1792, "as long as three Marseillais, Chompré, Moyse Bayle, and Pierre Baille are there." [11] In addition to having resident personnel in Aix, the Club also sent frequent commissions to instruct and discipline the Aixois. The Antipolitiques responded with an equal number of deputations to Marseilles; emissaries from Aix frequently sought advice or legal counsel from the Club.[12]

The Antipolitiques subscribed to Ricord's *Journal* and the *Manuel du laboureur* and read them aloud in their meetings. Only Carra's *Annales* exceeded the *Journal* in popularity. Correspondence between the two clubs ranged from trivial matters—the recommendation of a neighboring society for affiliation—to such serious problems as the pursuit and apprehension of suspects. Letters from Aix were usually respectful in tone and supplicatory in nature. Those from the Club, by contrast, were often condescending or peremptory. On November 30, 1792, for example, the Club reproved the Antipolitiques for participating in the exclusion of some "good patriots" from the Society of Grambois.[13]

The Jacobins of Aix worked jointly with the Club on missions into the surrounding countryside. In early June, 1791, representatives from Aix accompanied some Marseillais to Arles. On June 8, 1792, two Aixois joined commissioners from Marseilles in re-establishing order at Buis (Drôme).[14] As we have seen, the two societies also collaborated in the control and manipulation of elections. The Antipolitiques professed ardent allegiance to the Club of Marseilles and offered total assistance in combating the enemies of the Revolution. In February, 1792, for example, on hearing that some port-workers of Marseilles, deceived by the "bloodsuckers," had

[11] AN, F⁷ 4603.　　　[12] AD, B-du-Rh, L 2026–L 2028, L 2038.
[13] *Ibid.*, L 2025.　　　[14] *Ibid.*, L 2026–L 2027; AD, Drôme, L 774.

menaced the Club, they immediately proffered aid in case of future disturbances: "six thousand brave peasants of our Terroir are ready to leave at the first signal." [15]

The smaller societies of the Bouches-du-Rhône were likewise subordinate to Marseilles. Indeed, many of them were established and organized by commissioners of the Club. During the golden age of this activity, between 1791 and 1793, the Society founded patriotic clubs at Allauch, Aubagne, Auriol, Bouc, Gemenos, Grans, Mazargues, la Pennes, Rognac, Sénas, Trets, and elsewhere. (Only exhaustive, commune by commune research could determine the precise number of popular societies founded by the Marseillais in the Bouches-du-Rhône.) Many more societies established themselves because of a desire to emulate the "saviors of the empire." Newly formed clubs such as Eguilles (June 22, 1791), and Peynier (June 26, 1791) made their first order of business the dispatch of a letter or deputation seeking union with the Marseillais and their intercession in securing affiliation with the Jacobins. [16]

From the rural affiliates in the Bouches-du-Rhône, letters and delegations poured in to the Club. With each successive triumph of the Society the flattery became greater. Along with professions of devotion came vows to die by the side of the warriors of Marseilles and gifts for the revolutionary armies or the dependents of the volunteers. In March, 1793, alone, Cassis and la Ciotat contributed over 3,000 livres to Marseilles for patriotic causes. In return for flattery and allegiance the Club provided counsel, aid, and protection, and

[15] BM, 4717, "Extrait . . . des délibérations de la société des anti-politiques . . . 5 février 1792" (Marseille, 1792).

[16] AM, I₂, Letter of June 26, 1791; AD, B-du-Rh, L 2064, Minutes of the society of Eguilles.

regularly intervened on behalf of the affiliates with the elected authorities of the region; officialdom listened more readily to the requests of the Marseillais. Small societies and rural communes also begged for help in securing food supplies. These requests consumed so much time in the sessions that the Club decided in February, 1793, to discontinue public deliberations on the subject for fear of causing further price rises.[17]

When not serving as a barrister, the Club functioned as a court of last appeal for oppressed or feuding citizens. The Friends of the Constitution of Peynier, for example, appeared before the bar of the Society twice in April, 1792. Once they sought advice on the legality of destroying symbols of "pride and tyranny" on a local château. On another occasion, they pleaded with the Club to transfer the seat of their canton from Trets to Peynier.[18] Committees of the Club spent countless hours mediating disputes between clubs. When serious troubles erupted, the Society normally sent commissioners to conduct on-the-spot investigations. To justify intervention in affairs of their neighbors, the Club members cited the dictum laid down by Moyse Bayle when disturbances broke out at la Ciotat in 1791: "Marseillais, it is reserved to you to bring about the triumph of our sublime constitution and to defend the oppressed." [19]

From 1789 to 1794 the Bouches-du-Rhône suffered innumerable municipal disturbances. The most celebrated series of incidents prior to the Federalist rebellion was that involving the Chiffonnists and Monnaidiers of Arles, but vague and ill-defined patriotic and counterrevolutionary factions material-

[17] On Cassis and la Ciotat see AD, B-du-Rh, L 2071. On the question of food supplies see *JdD*, Feb. 14–21, 1793, pp. 608–616.
[18] *JdD*, Apr. 21, May 3, 1790, pp. 87, 105.
[19] AM, I₁ 73, Motion of M. Bayle.

ized in almost every township and hamlet. The so-called patriots almost invariably called themselves "poor artisans and cultivators" and their enemies "bourgeois." The dearth of records and the frequency and force of personal feuds in French villages make it difficult to judge the accuracy of these descriptions. What is certain is that the commissioners of Marseilles consistently and vigorously defended the cause of the patriots.

Municipal quarrels often began with the establishment of two rival clubs. Such was the case in Aubagne, today an industrial suburb of Marseilles but in 1789 only a sleepy Provençal village. There, in April, 1791, some citizens broke away from the original society of friends of the constitution and formed a club of Antipolitiques. According to contemporaries, the latter were artisans and peasants, and the former were bourgeois and aristocrats. A petition of the so-called bourgeoisie lends some credence to these descriptions since it contains the signatures of bourgeois, businessmen, surgeons, and doctors (i.e., the economic and social elite of Aubagne) but no peasants' names.[20]

The Club ordered a series of "pacifying commissions" to Aubagne in 1791 to resolve the factionalism. The commissioners, however, openly favored the Antipolitiques, who in turn vowed "to march anywhere to sustain the Club of Marseilles." Ultimately, a serious crisis flared up on the eve of the municipal elections of 1792. The "bourgeois-aristocratic" group had conceived plans for a large banquet to be held on February 12, 1792, in the château of the former bishop. The Club later charged that the 300 guests included "all the aristocrats and rebel priests" from the region. After the Directory of the district had declined to intervene, the frightened Anti-

[20] AD, B-du-Rh, L 292, Troubles at Aubagne.

politiques turned for help to the all-powerful Marseillais. The Club immediately dispatched two commissioners, escorted by a battalion of national guardsmen, "to go taste the wine of the aristocrats." The Marseillais dispersed the banqueters by brandishing sabers and firing their muskets. An occupation force remained in Aubagne until the new municipal elections. The power of the aristocrats had been broken.[21]

As the Society's political star rose, the submissive Directory of the department gave its commissioners legal authority. At Berre (twenty-seven kilometers southwest of Aix), entreaties by the "true patriots" against a "fatal league" led to protracted intervention by commissioners jointly representing the Club and the department. At least four groups of Club members, assisted by auxiliaries from the societies of Aix, Eguilles, Velaux, Rognac, and la Fare, visited Berre between September 1, 1792, and March 15, 1793. Empowered "to propagate republican spirit, maintain good order, and instill respect for persons and properties," the commissioners dissolved the Municipality, declared some individuals ineligible for public office, held new elections, and levied an indemnity of 8,800 livres on the "counterrevolutionaries." It is no wonder that the patriotic Berratins went twice to Marseilles in 1793 to thank the members of the Society "for all the trouble they had taken to bring peace to Berre." [22]

Once a commissioner left Marseilles, the Society found it difficult to monitor his activities. Numerous complaints survive concerning pillage and banditry by "gangsters" from Marseilles. Among those investigated in November, 1792,

[21] *Ibid.* See also AM, I₂, carton 1791, "Adresse de la société des amis de la constitution d'Aubagne à la société des amis de la constitution de . . . Marseille" (Marseille, 1791).

[22] AD, B-du-Rh, L 292, Troubles at Berre; *JdD*, Feb. 19, 1793, p. 612.

were some commissioners who terrorized the citizens of Auriol, a small commune twenty-seven kilometers east of Marseilles. There, a major outbreak of troubles had occurred in April, 1792, between a club of "friends of the constitution" (founded by Monbrion) and an "aristocratic" society of "friends of peace and order." In May and June commissioners endeavored several times to reconcile the two parties, but after new disorders in August the Society's secret committee gave five members unlimited powers to bring the counter-revolutionaries to heel. Two legal representatives from the departmental administration accompanied them. On September 14, 1792, with a battalion of Marseillais, they marched into Auriol and disarmed the citizens. In subsequent weeks, a mob hanged two suspects, and the seven commissioners levied a 40,000 livre indemnity from the "aristocrats." Simple extortion seems a better explanation for the Auriol levy than class conflict. The commissioners failed to account for the money they collected, and the individuals who paid the forced loan were by no means aristocrats. Joseph Guigou, a cultivator, "paid 600 livres after being threatened with the gallows." A peasant's wife, Thérèse Estienne, forfeited 400 livres on the grounds that she was a "f . . . . *aristocrate*." [23]

Eyguières and Salon (two communes fifty-five and forty-five kilometers northwest of Marseilles) were visited by four commissions between September, 1792, and March, 1793. In the Bouches-du-Rhône only the action taken in Arles exceeded these missions in scope and importance. In both communes the Society intervened against an alleged bourgeois aristocracy. The so-called bourgeois party of Salon controlled both the municipal government and the popular society. Three bourgeois, two doctors, a judge, a notary, and a pastry

[23] *JdD*, May 15–June 16, 1792, pp. 129–188. AD, B-du-Rh, L 3104.

merchant ranked among its principal chieftains. The popular party supposedly represented the poor peasants; but, in addition to two peasants, its leaders included a lawyer, a café owner and his stepson, and an innkeeper.[24]

The electoral assembly of the Bouches-du-Rhône meeting at Avignon in early September, 1792, to elect representatives to the Convention served as the catalyst in this long and complicated affair. At the urging of the Jacobins from Marseilles, it illegally ordered eight electors (with 1,200 men and five cannons) "to re-establish order and throttle conspiracies" in the department. The eight commissioners carried out their mandate zealously, disarming suspects, purging administrations, and calling new elections before bitter complaints from several communes led the department to recall them on September 22. The next day, before the news of this decree had reached the commissioners, irregulars from Eyguières and Salon ambushed one elector and two hundred volunteers from Arles in a gorge outside Eyguières. At least twenty Arlésiens were killed or wounded.[25]

When the news reached the Society, it excoriated the bourgeois of Eyguières and compelled the departmental administration to order six commissioners to investigate the tragedy; the Club named four of the six and formed a special committee to collect information and oversee developments. In their three weeks' sojourn at Eyguières the commissioners complained ceaselessly of interference by the popular society and the "aristocracy of riches" in Salon.[26] On October 16, 1792,

[24] AD, B-du-Rh, L 3105.

[25] AD, B-du-Rh, L 278, Electoral assembly. *Ibid.*, L 125–126, diverse letters. AN, F⁷ 3659³, Extract of the registers of the commune of Eyguières, Sep. 22, 1792.

[26] *JdD*, Sep. 29, Oct. 11, 1792, pp. 367–368, 387; AD, B-du-Rh, L 126, To the deputies at the National Convention, Oct. 20, 1792

the Club called for a new mission supported by national guardsmen to bring order to Eyguières and the next day named five of its members to lead the expedition. On October 19 they left Marseilles, with 600 men and two cannons. In a letter to the representatives of the Bouches-du-Rhône at the National Convention the department's administration explained:

It is the only means to re-establish calm in this region, to make the spirit of republicanism germinate, and to uncover and punish the authors of the disorders; it is the strongly pronounced wish of all the Marseillais, those heroes of the Revolution; it is the unanimous desire of the Club of Marseilles, that center of patriotism which has spread the love of liberty to all the Midi.[27]

Between October 19 and November 8, 1792, these commissioners fulfilled their assignment so assiduously that they earned a rebuke from the minister of the interior, Roland. At Eyguières they terrorized the populace, installed a new Municipality, and arrested four counterrevolutionaries. In Salon they exacerbated factional antagonisms.[28]

In November, the bourgeois party of Salon raised 1,500 livres for a deputation to Paris to defend its cause before Roland and sent 30 deputies to Marseilles to make a formal protest before the Club. On December 15, the Society demanded that the department recall the intriguers of Salon "once and for all . . . to the principles of justice and humanity." Still another commission left Marseilles headed by François-Paul Grimaud, Jean Bazin, and Sébastien Abeille. The Federalists later executed all three for their part in this

(and other letters); AN, F⁷ 3659³, Deliberation of the popular society of Salon, Oct. 15, 1792.

[27] AD, B-du-Rh, L 126.

[28] AN, F⁷ 3659³; *JdD*, Nov. 1–13, 1792, pp. 413–438.

affair. During their stay in Salon they "preached unceasingly against the rich and the bourgeoisie." "We must destroy them," Grimaud cried on one occasion, "we must not leave one of these bourgeois alive." [29]

The three commissioners entered Salon on December 21, 1792, accompanied by 400 soldiers and national guardsmen. In the following days they disqualified the newly elected bourgeois mayor, dissolved the bourgeois society, and disarmed many of the "most notorious bourgeois criminals." These measures provoked a new rebellion in Salon on February 16–17, 1793. The bourgeoisie seized the city hall, expelled the patriots, and attempted to arrest Isoard and Pierre Galibert, who had recently arrived to augment the commission. On February 19, bent on vengeance, the five commissioners re-entered Salon with 700 men. A reign of terror ensued. The Marseillais imprisoned those bourgeoisie who had not fled and declared the rest émigrés. During the night of February 21–22, approximately 100 men broke into the jail, seized Joseph Giraud, bourgeois, Roland, curé and Etienne Bédouin, bourgeois, and executed them. When tried later by the Federalists, the commissioners claimed that these murders occurred without their knowledge, but they did little to prevent them or to apprehend the guilty parties. On March 9, Etienne Rougier, another bourgeois, was dragged from the home of a friend and killed. Searches of domiciles began and forced loans were levied. Etienne Rey, a doctor, later testified that the commissioners planned to tax the inhabitants of Salon 250,000 livres, and that he had paid 20,000 "to save his life." [30]

[29] *JdD*, Nov. 29, 1792, pp. 484–485. AD, B-du-Rh, L 3105–3107, L 3044–3047.

[30] AD, B-du-Rh, L 3105–3107, L 3044–3047, L 127.

Basses-Alpes

In the Basses-Alpes the Club of Marseilles also had immense influence. Departmental officials sought its approval for their actions, pleaded for its intercession in securing grains, and begged for its support at the slightest movement of the Piedmontese. Fear of a foray by the Marseilles army pervaded the department. Indeed, to avenge an insult to Isoard and another commissioner in August, 1792, a band of 800 Marseillais marched on Manosque and extorted an indemnity of 42,000 livres from the local administrations to pay for the expedition. So-called volunteers from Marseilles also fomented disturbances at Valensole, Puimichel, Etrevennes, and Oraison.[31]

A particularly noteworthy incident took place at Digne, capital of the Basses-Alpes (110 kilometers northeast of Marseilles) in January, 1793. The principal actor in the affair was a soldier of fortune named Hippolyte Peyron. After a lengthy residence in Marseilles, Peyron had moved to Digne in 1792, where, in part because of his membership in the Club, he soon became president of Digne's popular society and a chief of the National Guard. In November, 1792, he quarrelled with the Directory of the department and returned to Marseilles. The Club examined the case, and in a circular to all its affiliates in the Basses-Alpes exonerated him. Armed with a certificate of approval from the Society, Peyron recruited a personal army of 800 men composed of volunteers from Marseilles and from the popular societies of Manosque, Ste.-Tulle, Oraison, Valensole, Pierrevert, Volx, Villeneuve, Lurs, Sigonce, and Niozelles. At one point he actually promised to transfer the departmental seat of the Basses-Alpes to Manosque. On Janu-

[31] See AD, Basses-Alpes, L 851, Popular society of Castellane, sessions of June 24 and 28, 1792; AN, F[7] 3659[3]; C. Cauvin, "Une Incursion des Marseillais à Digne en 1793," p. 247.

ary 10, 1793, this band entered Digne, compelled the "guilty" members of the Directory to resign, and charged an indemnity of 13,000 livres. A week later eight representatives from the popular society at Digne personally begged the Club to permit the departmental seat to remain in their city. When the Dignois pledged to investigate the "unfaithful administrators," the Jacobins of Marseilles agreed to this request.[32]

One of the principal activities of commissioners was the foundation of popular societies. Nowhere was this more true than in the Basses-Alpes. A substantial percentage of the 127 Jacobin clubs in this department owed their existence to a sixty day crusade by Isoard and Tourneau from April to early June, 1792. This mission began, in typical fashion, with appeals for assistance from "oppressed patriots." In early April a letter arrived from Valernes bemoaning the intrigues of counterrevolutionaries and asking commissioners to come to their city to form a patriotic society. On April 6, 1792, the Society resolved "to send Isoard and Tourneau to Valernes and other places, to establish popular societies and to determine the disposition, spirit, and principles of the inhabitants." Five days later they successfully created a club at Valernes. In subsequent weeks, they formed societies at Castellane, Volonne, Senez, and elsewhere—Isoard later claimed a total of sixty.[33]

The creation of the popular society of Riez provides invaluable information on the technical aspects of founding a club. On May 14, Isoard arrived in Riez, accompanied by com-

[32] Cauvin, pp. 247–267; AD, Basses-Alpes, L 856/2, "Dépend de la délibération prise par la société des amis de la liberté et de l'égalité de Marseille" (Marseille, 1792); *JdD*, Jan. 19, 1793, p. 561.

[33] *JdD*, Apr. 24, 1792, p. 89; AM, I₂, carton 1792, To the popular society of Marseilles, Apr. 6, 1792; AD, Basses-Alpes, L 851, L 857, L 861, L 862.

missioners from the societies of Manosque, Pertuis, Rians, and Puimoisson, and convened all the patriots at the former church of the Cordeliers. As a preliminary measure the prospective members inscribed their names on a register. Then all present took an oath to defend the constitution and elected a permanent president and two secretaries. After some discussion an admission fee of one sou was decided upon. Next Isoard pointed out the necessity of buying "instructive newspapers," and the new club chose Carra's *Annales patriotiques* and Monbrion's *Manuel du laboureur*. The regulations of the Club of Marseilles were then read to the assembly, but these rules did not suit the smaller society. Those attending therefore named commissioners to study the different needs of Marseilles and Riez and to draft a new constitution. After these steps the Rieziens dispatched a letter of thanks to Marseilles and an appeal for aid in securing affiliation with Paris. When Isoard and Tourneau returned to Marseilles, the Club sent a certificate of affiliation signed by its principal officers and prefaced with a standard letter from the correspondence committee exhorting the Rieziens "to be prepared to sacrifice everything" to defend the constitution.[34]

The foundation of popular societies was not always so easy. At Sisteron, 110 kilometers from Marseilles, Isoard and Tourneau literally had to besiege and invade the city in order to institute a Jacobin club. Here, some so-called aristocrats dominated municipal offices and through propaganda and economic influence controlled the peasantry. In early 1792, they organized a secret royalist association and twice blocked attempts by Sisteron patriots to form a popular society. At this point Isoard and Tourneau intervened, appealing to neighboring communes to dispatch volunteers. Malijai provided 40

[34] AD, Basses-Alpes, L 856/1, L 856/2.

men, les Mées 150. Oraison, Manosque, Forcalquier, and Valernes also provided troops. Eyewitnesses estimated that the patriotic army that marched into Sisteron on May 19, 1792, amounted to 2,000 armed men. "Our entry was most majestic," wrote Isoard. "All the brave volunteers have been lodged at the homes of the aristocrats. . . . We propose to purge the city tomorrow." The next day the justice of the peace and the mayor resigned, twenty-five priests took the oath to the constitution, and a popular society began to meet. The Directory of the district of Sisteron wrote to the Society in Marseilles on May 20, 1792, praising the zeal of Isoard and Tourneau: "All the good patriots have vowed to defend the constitution." [35]

Vaucluse

The department of the Vaucluse lies north of the Durance and east of the Rhône. Here, as in the Basses-Alpes, the Club wielded enormous power, a minimum of thirty-three societies in this department being affiliated with it. It founded clubs at Pertuis, Monieux, Aurel, and St.-Christol. Others, if not formally created by commissioners began to meet at their instigation. The societies of Apt, Gordes, and probably many others modelled their regulations on those of Marseilles; small societies continually asked for aid or advice. In September, 1792, representatives from Apt and Pertuis sought the Club's ruling on which city had the right to be the seat of their district. A letter from Piolenc, 110 kilometers from Marseilles,

[35] C. Cauvin, "La Formation de la société populaire de Sisteron," *Annales des Basses-Alpes*, nos. 81–82 (1901), 71–79, 139–152; AM, I₂, carton 1792, To Isoard and Tourneau at Volonne, May 17, 1792, and To Isoard and Tourneau at Sisteron, May 21, 1792; AD, B-du-Rh, L 2075, Letter of M. Fabre to Sisteron, May 17, 1792; AD, B-du-Rh, L 3037.

exemplifies the supplicatory correspondence that poured in to Marseilles in 1792: "Generous protectors of the Republic, strengthen us by according us your affiliation. . . . You have saved the departments of the Midi; you are the founders and most zealous defenders of our republic." [36]

In 1792, the southern part of the Vaucluse became part of the Bouches-du-Rhône. Henceforth, the Club's commissioners in this area carried legal powers from the departmental administration. A typical Club-department mission occurred in the winter of 1792–1793 when Isoard and two colleagues visited Ansouis, Cadenet, Goult, Lauris, Villelaure, Apt, Roussillon, Lourmarin, Pertuis, and la Tour-D'Aigues. The Society appointed them and supervised their activities. At its command they interrupted their work at la Tour-D'Aigues on November 10, 1792, to go to Grambois "to defend the patriots of '89 against the hypocritical converts of '92." [37]

Numerous commissioners visited the region of Apt. Monbrion and Jean-François Bousquet [38] began an extended apostolate in March, 1792, which eventually took them from Apt to la Tour-D'Aigues, Pertuis, Cucuron, Villelaure, Saignon, Gordes, Roussillon, St.-Saturnin, Ansouis, Beaumont, Bastidonne, Cadenet, and Lourmarin founding clubs, collecting taxes and patriotic contributions, and spreading the Revolution. At Apt they learned that many babies had not been baptized because of parents' hesitancy to take them before a constitutional priest. Faced with this "fanaticism," they arranged for the baptism of "an infinite number": "Preceded by numerous musicians, who always accompanied our caravan, we

[36] On Apt and Pertuis see *JdD*, Sep. 20, 1792, p. 352; on Piolenc see AD, B-du-Rh, L 2075.

[37] AD, B-du-Rh, L 126.

[38] Bousquet, a wig-maker, was born at Marseilles in 1763.

visited the houses which had been designated to us; then we took the infants and went in pomp . . . to have baptism administered in the churches by the constitutional priest." [39]

A letter dated June 4, 1792, from the Club of Sault (twenty-five kilometers north of Apt) prompted an important expedition to the northern Vaucluse and southern Drôme. The Saltésiens complained of the "black machinations" of the aristocrats of Buis-les-Baronnies (twenty-five kilometers northwest of Sault, in the Drôme), and begged the Marseillais, "saviors of the Midi," to rescue the patriots of Buis. Sault's plan of campaign called for the Club to send commissioners, cannons, and cannoneers and for these to be joined by nearly 1,000 volunteers from local communes.[40]

On June 14, four Marseillais together with thirty-three commissioners from the clubs of Apt, Gordes, St.-Saturnin, Aix, Sault, Manosque, Montbrun, Aurel, Forcalquier, St.-Christol, and Lachau, marched arrogantly into Buis. They presented eleven demands to the Municipality and ceremoniously baptized two children into the constitutional church. Terrified by threats of armed force, the municipal officials promised to disarm suspects, deport non-juring priests, and refund the intruders' expenses. On June 28, 1792, the commissioners returned to Marseilles to report success in bringing peace to Buis. At their solicitation, too the Society granted affiliation to newly-formed societies at St.-Christol, Aurel, Monieux, and Montbrun. "The citizens who compose them," they reported, "speak only of the Marseillais; they regard them as their liberators, and they will always strive to second them in their projects." [41]

[39] *JdD*, Mar. 31, 1792, pp. 45–46.
[40] AD, B-du-Rh, L 2075. To our brothers of Marseilles.
[41] *JdD*, June 30, 1792, p. 210; AD, Drôme, L 774.

Var

The Var, a maritime department to the east of the Bouches-du-Rhône, was one of the regions in which the Marseillais displayed their greatest energy. At least thirty-four popular societies here were affiliated with the Club. The papers of the Society of St.-Zacharie, the most complete record of correspondence of any society in the department, perhaps reveal best the omnipresence of the Marseillais. Monbrion, Bousquet, and a third Marseilles Jacobin named N. de la Porte founded this club on April 14, 1792. Its rules and regulations were founded on the Regulations of the Society of Marseilles, a copy of which still exists in its papers. As one of its first acts it subscribed to the *Journal des départements méridionaux* edited by Ricord. After returning to Marseilles Monbrion and Bousquet regularly corresponded with the St.-Zachariens. On June 28, 1792, for example, Bousquet gave them some fatherly advice on the best choice to make for their new mayor.[42]

The principal affiliate of the Club of Marseilles in the Var was the Society of Friends of the Constitution of Toulon, founded on June 21, 1790. When the Marseillais intervened in the Var, representatives from Toulon often aided them; in October, 1792, for instance, each club sent three commissioners to re-establish order at St. Maximin. The proximity of the two cities, only about sixty kilometers apart, insured a steady exchange of letters and deputations. The tone of the correspondence reveals a much more equal relationship than that of Aix-Marseilles. There can be no doubt, however, that the Club of the Rue Thubaneau stood above its neighbor in the Jacobin hierarchy.[43]

Substantial cooperation between the two clubs dates from

[42] AD, Var, St.-Zacharie.
[43] See Labroue, pp. 1–51; AD, Var. L 1676 (179).

late 1790. Chapter 4 has discussed the joint action of the Friends of the Constitution of Aix, Marseilles, and Toulon against counterrevolutionary decrees of the National Assembly in December, 1790, and January, 1791. In early 1791 Marseilles and Toulon also acted together on behalf of several soldiers unjustly imprisoned and sent to the galleys by their commander. During the crisis of July, 1791, a Feuillantist society began to meet in Toulon. When a "slight melee" involving its members and those of the patriotic society occurred on August 4, the departmental administration of the Var ordered the arrest of a number of the patriots, many of whom fled to Marseilles and spent nearly a year in exile at the Club. There they became officers and militant members as well as spokesmen for their cause. Besides harboring these fugitives, the Marseillais drafted a letter of "profound indignation" to the Directory of the department of the Var that ended with a menacing pledge of "all the assistance and help" that the Toulon Jacobins "had the right to receive." Fearing an invasion, the Directory appealed to the minister of the interior for protection.[44]

The patriotic society of Toulon, in turn, came to the aid of the Marseillais during the Federalist rebellion. On May 3, 1793, a deputation travelled to Marseilles to support the Club against the sections. When the motives of the Federalists became clear, Toulon sent an address urging the people of Marseilles to close the sections and expel "the selfish rich" who dominated them. These appeals went unheeded. Instead, Fed-

[44] On the soldiers sent to the galleys see Aulard, *Jacobins*, II, 350, and Labroue, p. 8. For information on the Feuillantist troubles see AN, F⁷ 3659², The administrators of the Var to M. de Lessart, Aug. 4, 1792; AD, B-du-Rh, L 123, To the minister of the interior, Aug. 25, 1791.

eralists soon rose up in Toulon and purged the society there.[45]

In 1792–1793, few communes of the Var were spared a visit by a commissioner. The existence of two rival clubs at Rians (sixty kilometers from Marseilles) led to several interventions by the Society, and other noteworthy commissions involved Cotignac, St.-Maximin, Méounes, Hyères, and la Cadière.[46] The most significant incident in the Var, however, took place at Salernes, seventy kilometers northeast of Marseilles. It was similar, in many respects, to those of Berre, Auriol, and Salon. At Salernes the Marseillais again sided with the "cultivators" against the "bourgeois." On this occasion, however, they did not have the armed might of the National Guard of Marseilles behind them and had to settle for a face-saving compromise.[47]

The incident began with the arrival of some Salernois at the Club on January 17, 1793, demanding redress, in the name of twenty-eight peasants and their dependents, from the "treacherous bourgeoisie" of the canton. The peasants charged that the bourgeoisie had tricked them in March, 1789, into destroying an aristocratic château and then had betrayed them to the Parlement at Aix. The bourgeoisie also subjected the cultivators, according to the plaintiffs, to the cruelest economic oppression:

The poor always have needs; in the winter they borrow money from the bourgeoisie in order to subsist, but at an enormous rate of interest. The bourgeoisie force these unfortunates to sell their

[45] AD, B-du-Rh, L 2075, L 2076.

[46] AD, Var, L 1676 (179). *Ibid.*, St.-Zacharie. *Ibid.*, L 2012, Méounes. *JdD*, Mar. 12, May 12 and 15, Aug. 21, 23, and 25, 1792, pp. 14, 122–123, 127, 297, 302, 308–310.

[47] On this affair see *JdD*, Jan. 19, 1793, p. 561; AD, Var, 2 L 460, Affair of Salernes; AD, B-du-Rh, L 2072, "Rapport des commissaires de la société populaire de Marseille envoyé à Salernes" (Marseille, 1793).

harvest before it is born, making them yield at the rate of twenty livres what, at harvest time, is worth thirty-five or forty.

Moreover, the "bourgeois" Municipality refused, "even in the hardest times," to lower the price of bread or give credit. If the poor man had no money, "he was allowed to die of hunger."

The Society assigned two commissioners who were already preparing to go to St.-Zacharie to investigate the situation. On January 22, 1793, they presented their credentials to the Municipality of Salernes and announced that they had come to "arbitrate amiably the differences that divided the citizens." After two days of interviews the commissioners completed their plan of settlement. They based their conclusions on the testimony of the "interesting class of workers who were so cruelly oppressed in 1789, yes, also some members of that oppressive class, known under the name of bourgeois." Their report completely vindicated the oppressed cultivators and called for indemnities totalling 9,400 livres from thirty-two citizens, mostly bourgeois and professional people. After recommending these reparations, the Marseillais brazenly urged union and peace in Salernes.

The settlement, of course, had just the opposite results. The Municipality and those taxed sent petitions of protest to Toulon and Draguignan. Rumors spread that the commissioners were mere "brigands" and "incendiaries." Armed supporters of the Marseillais filled their hotel "to protect" them. Bloodshed was only averted when the Marseillais promised to confer with those who had been taxed. On January 26, 1793, a new wave of panic followed a rumor that two individuals had departed for Marseilles to seek national guardsmen "to cut off the heads of those who would not pay." The

Municipality appealed to the departmental administration of the Var for assistance. Finally, a compromise settlement, concluded on January 27 with the help of some deputies from the popular society of Draguignan, reduced the amount of the indemnity by one-half, payable in the form of a donation rather than a forced loan. No evidence exists that it was ever in fact paid.

9
Conclusion

A critic of the Jacobins once charged that to write the history of one club was to write the history of them all. In one sense this statement is correct. The 6,000 or more popular societies had countless characteristics in common. They adopted some standard organizational procedures, took the same oaths, planted trees of liberty, subscribed to patriotic newspapers, influenced elections, scrutinized the conduct of public officials, and combated the intrigues of counterrevolutionaries. Despite these similarities, however, it would be a mistake to assume that no further studies of the clubs are needed. The history of each society offers additional insights into the powerful and important Jacobin movement. Acting collectively under the leadership of the mother society in Paris and individually on the local level, the Jacobin clubs defended revolutionary ideals and dramatically altered the course of French politics. No provincial society played a more significant role in the Revolution or warrants an historical monograph more than the Club of the Rue Thubaneau in Marseilles.

While there has been a great deal of speculation, few hard facts are known about the formation of the clubs. In Marseilles, the immediate origins of the Club of the Rue Thubaneau have been blurred by the passage of time. Initially it was probably an extension of the citizen's militia and the National Guard. The guardsmen had congregated throughout 1789 and early 1790 in such cafés and bars as the Café de François and the Arquier Tavern. In April, 1790, emulating other great French cities, they formed the Patriotic Assembly of Friends of the Constitution of Marseilles. However, the roots of the Society lay more generally in the social world of the 1780's. The Club borrowed and carried on the customs of a number of pre-Revolutionary organizations. Some Jacobins had participated in earlier intellectual societies; others had belonged to religious brotherhoods and masonic lodges. A number of important leaders studied or taught at the College of the Oratory.

The Club of the Rue Thubaneau was one of the largest Jacobin societies in France. Over the period of the Revolution as a whole, its membership probably exceeded 6,000. Most of its members were natives of Provence, middle-aged respectable family men. The typical member of 1790 came from the commercial, professional, and industrial elite of the city. Between 1791 and 1793 a gradual democratization of the personnel took place, but the middle class still predominated on the eve of the Federalist rebellion. Only during the Terror did the petty merchants, artisans, and functionaries come to constitute the greater part of the membership. Similar patterns of change occurred within the leadership of the Club. In 1790 the officers were largely wholesale merchants, bourgeois, and lawyers. By January, 1793, teachers, clerks, and shopkeepers held most of the important positions. In all periods, however, the officers had a higher social status than the rank-and file members.

The sessions and parliamentary procedures of the Society closely resembled those of other patriotic clubs. There were numerous officers and a great many permanent and temporary committees. With its own printing press and newspapers, the Club was the clearinghouse for Jacobin propaganda in the Midi. Women, though not permitted to be members, frequented the assembly and assisted the men in their patriotic activities. In 1790, there were few restrictions on the entry of new members, but by 1792 an elaborate admission procedure had evolved and periodic purges pruned away those members whose patriotism was suspect.

The most distinctive feature of the Club's ideology was an extraordinary regional chauvinism. As elsewhere, Jacobinism in Marseilles assumed many of the characteristics of a militant creed. The Society founded its definition of liberty on the doctrine of popular sovereignty, and from this principle derived political theories similar to those of the Montagnards in Paris. The members were not socialists; but while they always professed respect for private property, they did have great concern for the plight of the poor. As the Revolution progressed, they became more class conscious and denunciations of the rich grew increasingly strident.

Within the Jacobin network independent spheres of influence existed, usually radiating out from the chief city of a region. In southeastern France Marseilles was the acknowledged center of Jacobinism. The Club's propaganda percolated down to the tiniest hamlets of Provence. In turn, the Provençal clubs looked to Marseilles for assistance and instruction. The Society's commissioners were agents of political and social action in the Midi. In the Bouches-du-Rhône, Var, Basses-Alpes, and Vaucluse they founded innumerable dependent societies, performed public works, and intervened repeatedly to settle local disputes.

The Jacobin Society of Marseilles was no obscure local

club. Its political history had national as well as regional impact. Its victorious struggles against the enemies of the Revolution at Aix, Arles, and Avignon made it a standard-bearer
of the democratic cause in France in 1792. The dethronement
of Louis XVI on August 10, 1792, derived in no small measure from the proselytizing republicanism of Marseilles and
the Club's recruitment of the battalion of Provençal federalists. In early 1793, the Society spearheaded a nationwide
drive against the Girondins in Paris. Finally, its conflict with
Fréron, and with Auguis and Serres in the summer of 1794,
reflects an important aspect of the Thermidorian Reaction.

It is beyond the scope of this work to analyze events in
Marseilles after September, 1794. Suffice it to say that the
period between Thermidor and the Consulate was tumultuous
and unstable. The new constitution of the Directory in 1795
forbade all popular societies in France. Marseilles' Jacobin
movement did not die immediately, however; many old Club
members remained politically active, and new radicals appeared on the scene. On the other hand, the violence of the
Terror in Marseilles left festering hatreds and engendered a
powerful counterrevolutionary movement, known as the
White Terror. Emigrés returned from exile and mutilated
trees of liberty and other revolutionary symbols. Reactionary
representatives-on-mission arrested suspected ex-Terrorists
and confined them in the cells of Fort St.-Jean. Relatives of
victims, royalists, deserters, and emigrés formed such gangs
as the famous Companies of Jesus and of the Sun. Armed with
pistols and sabers, they roamed the streets of Marseilles assas-
sinating individuals said to be republicans.

In the turbulent years after 1794 fate did not treat the
former leaders of the Club with an even hand. On June 5,
1795, a group of 127 Jacobin prisoners was massacred in Fort
St.-Jean by a frenzied counterrevolutionary mob. The death

toll would have been higher had not some succeeded in barricading themselves in their cells. Isoard, who had gone into hiding, was tracked down, brought to trial before the Criminal Tribunal of the Bouches-du-Rhône, and executed on September 24, 1795. Beissière, who had been a member of the surveillance committee during the Terror, was murdered by an angry crowd during the later White Terror of June, 1815. By contrast, Pierre Peyre-Ferry escaped the massacre of 1795 and in 1796 founded a Jacobin gazette, *L'Observateur du Midi de la République*. Etienne Chompré was released from Ham, along with Giraud and the brothers Maillet, in 1795 and died in Paris in 1811. Omer Granet survived to become mayor of Marseilles during the Napoleonic Empire; Alexandre Ricord continued to publish minor works and died in obscurity in 1829.

From the vantage point of the 1970's it is difficult to appreciate the true importance of the Society. No echoes of the shouts, martial hymns, and patriotic speeches linger in today's bathhouse on the Rue Thubaneau; no memorials remain of Ricord, Isoard, the brothers Maillet, Chompré and Giraud. Yet these men and their Club possessed enormous political power. A letter written in June, 1793, by the popular society of Nîmes can serve as the Society's obituary:

It was the Club of Marseilles that inflamed Republican spirit in our region. It was the Club of Marseilles that unmasked traitors even at the court, that raised a thundering voice against despotism. It was the Club of Marseilles that prepared France for Republican government, reduced the Chiffonnists to ashes, and unwaveringly defied the corrupt agents of the executive power. It was the Club of Marseilles that provided the impetus for the march of troops on the great day of August 10. Wherever victories were won, the Marseillais were there.

Appendix I

*Professions of the Club Members**

		Number and percentage in Club		
Profession	Representative type	1790–1791	1792–1793	1793–1794
Domestic service	*concierge*	2 0.2%	3 0.3%	27 0.8%
Working class	*artisan, ouvrier*	269 24.9%	306 34.2%	2,243 62.3%
Farming	*cultivateur*	– –	– –	72 2.0%
Shopkeeping	*marchand, maître artisan*	236 21.9%	186 20.7%	747 20.8%
Salaried employees	*commis*	101 9.4%	99 11.1%	215 6.0%
Military	*soldat*	1 0.1%	4 0.4%	54 1.5%
Government officials	*juge*	23 2.1%	31 3.4%	59 1.6%
Artists and professions	*avocat, maître-ez-arts*	103 9.5%	57 6.4%	70 2.0%
Rentiers	*bourgeois, propriétaire*	78 7.0%	39 4.4%	37 1.0%
Businessmen	*négociant*	197 18.2%	124 13.9%	42 1.2%
Ecclesiastical	*prêtre*	49 4.5%	29 3.2%	4 0.1%
Noble	*marquis*	9 0.8%	3 0.3%	–
Miscellaneous		14 1.3%	13 1.4%	25 0.6%

* This classification of personnel is based upon the methodology used by Adeline Daumard in *La Bourgeoisie parisienne de 1815 à 1848* (Paris, 1961).

Appendix II

Names and Professions of the Club Officers[1]

1790 to 1791

Claude Achard (doctor)
Joseph Almaric (oratorian)**
Jean Amy (ship owner)
Jean André (doctor)
Joseph Arnaud (notary)**
Joseph Astier (soap manufacturer)
Antoine Audibert (ship's captain)
Dominique Audibert (wholesale merchant)*
Pierre Baille (property owner)
Charles Barbaroux (lawyer)
Moyse Bayle (bourgeois)
Emmanuel de Beausset (count of St.-Victor)*
Pierre Bernard (bourgeois)*
Bertrand (lawyer)
Mathieu Blanc-Gilly (bourgeois)*
Etienne Bompard (wholesale merchant)

Jacques Borély (wholesale merchant)*
Jean Bosq (calico merchant)
François Boutin (druggist)
Jean Boyer (wholesale merchant)**
Jean Brémond (surgeon)
Antoine Brémond-Jullien (lawyer)
Jacques Brogi (clerk)
Jean Cavalier (priest)
Cayol *fils de Joseph* (wholesale merchant)*
François Cayol-Richaud (ship owner)
Chéry (lawyer)
Etienne Chompré (former teacher, master of fine arts)*
Alexandre Clément (lottery collector)
Coustans (priest)

[1] Only those officers whose professions could be traced are cited in this appendix: (*) denotes presidents; (**) identifies vice-presidents; the remaining officers were treasurers, secretaries, and members of permanent committees.

Joseph Cuzin (wholesale merchant)
Jacques D'Hercules (wholesale merchant)
J. Estienne (wholesale merchant)
Joseph Fabre (oratorian)
Joseph de Falconieri (chevalier)
Le Bailli de Foresta (procurator of the order of Malta)*
Honoré Galici (broker)
Laurent Granet (master cooper)
Charles Guinot (master of fine arts)**
Jacques Guion (bourgeois)
Louis Guirard (wholesale merchant)
Jaubert (priest)
Pierre Langlade (bourgeois)
Pierre Laugier (examiner of commercial records)** ** **
Bernard Laurent (surgeon)
Joseph Lavabre (lawyer)
Louis Long (wholesale merchant)
Augustin Maillet (master of fine arts)*
François Maillet (master of fine arts)
François Malherbe (theater director)
Jean Marçel (bourgeois)
Etienne Martin (wholesale merchant)* * *
Etienne Martin *fils* D'André (wholesale merchant)
Pierre Micoulin (oil merchant)
Jean Millot (wholesale merchant)
Antoine Cabrol de Moncaussou (bourgeois)* **

Elzear de Mongendre (clerk)
Jean Morery (wholesale merchant)*
Thomas Nalis (wholesale merchant)*
Louis Negry (clerk)
François Peyre-Ferry (wholesale merchant)
Georges Pleville-Lepelley (harbor master)
Philippe Rambert (lawyer)**
Noel Richaud (broker)*
Alexandre Ricord (journalist)
Pierre Rivar (bourgeois)*
Louis Rochebrun (printer)
Laurent Sard (notary)
Tassy (former Marquis)
Pierre Trahan (wholesale merchant)
Jean Vence (ship's captain)
Barthélemy Vidal (doctor)

1792 to June, 1793

François Allemand (merchant)
Amy* **
Joseph Arbaud (lawyer)*
Astier**
Antoine Aubanel (master of fine arts)
Beausset*
Mathieu Bec (calico merchant)
Jean Beissière (mirror maker)
Bompard
Clair Bonnet (ship's captain)
François Bontoux (shoemaker)
Joseph Boude (merchant tailor)
Boutin (druggist)*
Jean Boutin (priest)*
Brogi
Chompré*

P.-L. du Couedic (engineer)
Jacques Dupuy (hatmaker)
Charles Ehrmann (wholesale merchant)
Estienne
Fabre
François Fiquet (wine merchant)
François Galibert (master cabinetmaker)**
J. Garoutte (rug merchant)
Jean Gassin (ship's captain)**
Jean Gautier (ship's captain)
Albert Gérin (wholesale merchant)
Joseph Giraud (oratorian)* **
Jean Grasset (merchant)
Guinot*
Guion
Jean Irissac (bookkeeper)
François Isoard (oratorian)**
Henri Larguier (lawyer)**
Laugier*
Lavabre*
Michel Leclerc (lawyer)**
Etienne Lejourdan (lawyer)*
Ambroise Leroi d'Ambleville (lawyer)**
Jean Loys (lawyer)

A. Maillet* **
F. Maillet*
Maurin (lawyer)**
Micoulin
Jacques Monbrion (dry-cleaner)
Mongendre**
Jean Mourraille (bourgeois)
Negry
Jean Peyrache (clerk, soapmaker)
Pierre Peyre-Ferry (wholesale merchant)**
Antoine Piquet (bourgeois)
Pleville-Lepelley
Rambert*
Antoine Réquier (master of fine arts)
Joseph Reynaud (wholesale merchant)
Ricord* **
Jean Romégas (mathematician)
Audibert Rose (wholesale merchant)
Seren (soapmaker)
Etienne Seytres (lawyer)*
Louis Solle (clerk)
Joseph Tourneau (clerk)
Trahan
Jean Vidal (haberdasher)

August, 1793, to 1794

Astier
Beausset
Antoine Bénèche (language professor)
Augustin Berthelot (merchant)
Jean Besson (hatmaker)*
Barthélemy Blain (linen dealer)
Boutin (druggist)
Boutin (priest)*
Dominique Chabre (shoemaker)

Honoré Chastel (shoemaker)
Chompré
Clément
Alexandre Cresp (merchant)
Pierre Cresp (ship's captain)
Jean Deydier (wholesale merchant)
Ehrmann
Henri Ferroul (oil merchant)
Fiquet

Galibert**
Giraud* * **
Granet*
Joseph Guigou (clerk)
Isoard* *
Jean Laliand (proprietary land-
owner)
Nicolas de la Porte (shoemaker)
Leclerc
Loys
A. Maillet* *
F. Maillet**
Mathieu Maurin (departmental
official)*

Micoulin
Libre Morel (former soldier)**
Auguste Mossy (printer)**
Réquier
Ricord
François Rouedy (doctor)
Jean Roumieu (leather manufac-
turer)**
Louis Solle (clerk)
Jacques Thomas (druggist)
Trahan
Jean Trulle (clerk)
Jacques Vernet (apothecary)*
J. Vidal

Selected Bibliography of Sources

Primary Sources

Archives départementales, Bouches-du-Rhône

L 122–130. Correspondence of the Directory of the department.

L 132–142. Correspondence of the central administration of the department.

L 277–278. Minutes and correspondence of the electoral assemblies of the Bouches-du-Rhône.

L 292–300. Troubles. (In diverse communes.)

L 303–314. Indemnities to the victims of the Federalists.

L 1013–1015. Correspondence of the national agent of the district of Marseilles.

L 1021. Electoral assembly of the district of Marseilles.

L 1980. The sections and the popular societies.

L 1982. Census of the population.

L 2025–2070, 2078–2080. Papers of the popular societies. (Aix, Eguilles, les Milles, Peyrigord, Salon, Sault, Martigues.)

L 2071–2076. Society of Friends of Liberty and Equality of Marseilles.

L 3037. Trial of Louis-François-Dominique Isoard.

L 3041–3042. Criminal Tribunal of the Bouches-du-Rhône. Riot of September 26, 1794.

L 3044–3047. Affair of Salon.

L 3104–3106. Papers of the Popular Tribunal.

L 3109–3127. Papers of the Revolutionary Tribunal (especially L 3122.)

IIF, XXIVF, XVIF. Diverse publications.
XXIVF. Fontanier collection. (The penitents of Marseilles.)

Archives départementales, Basses-Alpes

L 849–867. Papers of the popular societies.

Archives départementales, Var

1L 1676 (179). Affair of St.-Maximin.
1L 2012. Popular society of Méounes.
2L 460. Affair of Salernes.
L, supplement. Papers of the popular society of St.-Zacharie.

Archives départementales, Drôme

L 774. Troubles.
L 1085–1105. Papers of the popular societies.
F 207. Society of Friends of the Constitution of Valence.

Archives départementales, Hérault

L 5493–5609. Papers of the popular societies. (See especially L5543, Correspondence sent by Marseilles to Montpellier.)

Archives départementales, Tarn

L 1531. Popular society of Castres.

Archives municipales, Marseille

BB 293–294, 359–360. Letters written and received, 1790.
1D 1–5, 8–13. Deliberations of the Municipality of Marseilles.
4D 1–2, 7–8. Correspondence, 1791–1794.
20D 1, 5–7. Letters received.
2F 6–50. Census of the population, 1793.
G 102–103. Real estate tax register (*Matrice foncière*), 1793.
GG 80. Penitents of Marseilles.
GG 166. List of professors of the Oratory.
10 H 10. Rearmament register, 1794.
I_1, 73–77. Local police. Letters received.
I_2. General police. Uncatalogued letters.

Bibliothèque municipale, Marseille

Recueil des pièces qui ont paru lors de la Révolution de Marseille. 1789. 1790. 1791. 15 vols. 4717. This collection includes innumerable brochures, letters, and posters written or published by the Club.

Recueil des ouvrages concernante la patrouille citoyenne. 5 vols. 4717. This is a supplement to the *Recueil* listed above. Both form part of the 32 volume Collection Michel de Léon.

The Bibliothèque also contains scattered pieces of the same nature too numerous to mention in this bibliography. For partial summaries see Bouillon-Landais, *Catalogue des livres sur la Provence et ouvrages divers* (Marseille: Imprimerie centrale, 1873); E. Barlatier and E. Barthelet, *Bibliothèque de la ville de Marseille: Catalogue des livres de Provence* (Marseille: Imprimerie centrale, 1890).

Bibliotheque Méjanes (Aix)

Recueil de diverses publications faites à Marseille en 1790. 1976–1996.

Ms 873. Society of Friends of the Constitution of Aix.

Bibliothèque municipale, Poitiers

The Bibliothèque of Poitiers contains the archives of the popular society of Poitiers, perhaps the finest collection of papers for any club in France. For correspondence from Marseilles see S 15, S 22, S 26.

Archives de la Chambre de Commerce de Marseille

I 68–70. Political affairs.
B. Diverse deliberations and correspondence.

Archives nationales

AF II 90–91, 185–186. Papers of the Committee of Public Safety.
BB_{16} 86. Justice.
C. Minutes of the national assemblies and attached papers.
D_1 o, 36. The mission of Maignet.
DXXIX bis28. Committee of Inquiries.

DXXIX 54. Committee of Reports.
DXL 18. Committee of Petitions, Dispatches, and Correspondence.
DIII 30. File on Marseilles.
F⁷ 3659¹,²,³. General police. Bouches-du-Rhône.
F⁷ 4603. Correspondence of Blanc-Gilly.
W 86–88. W 329. Revolutionary Tribunal.

Bibliothèque nationale

FM² 282–292. Masonic archives.
The Bibliothèque nationale houses innumerable printed materials and journals which the author utilized. For a partial list see André Martin and Gérard Walter, *Catalogue de l'histoire de la Révolution française: Ecrits de la période révolutionnaire*, 5 vols. (Paris: Bibliothèque nationale, 1943).

Newspapers and Published Collections

Almanach historique de Marseille. By J.-B.-B. Grosson. 21 vols. 1770–1790. BN, Lc³¹ 275.
Annales patriotiques de Marseille. By Antoine Brémond-Jullien and Sarrazin de Montferrier. 10 nos. February 17–April, 1790. BM, Toulon, 19665. BN, Lc¹¹ 635 (93).
Annales patriotiques et littéraires de la France. By L.-S. Mercier and J.-L. Carra. 11 vols. October 3, 1789–Dec. 20, 1794. BN, Lc² 249.
Archives parlementaires. 1st series. 1787 to 1799. Paris, 1868–1902.
Aulard, Alphonse. *La Société des Jacobins: Recueil de documents.* 6 vols. Paris: Librairie Jouaust, 1889–1897.
———. *Recueil des actes du Comité de salut public.* 27 vols. Paris: Imprimerie nationale, 1889–1933.
Buchez, P.-J.-B. et Roux, P.-C. *Histoire parlementaire de la Révolution française.* 40 vols. Paris: Paulin, 1834–1838.
Caron, Pierre. *Rapports des agents du Ministre de l'Intérieur dans les départements, 1793-an II.* 2 vols. Paris: Imprimerie nationale, 1913, 1951.
Courier de Marseille. Anonymous. 6 nos. April 18–May 12, 1790. BN, Lc¹¹ 635 (94).

Journal de Provence (Journal de Marseille). By Ferréol Beaugeard. 1781–1797. BM, 4222, 4223.

Journal des départements méridionaux et des débats des amis de la constitution de Marseille. By Joseph Giraud, Alexandre Ricord, and Pierre Micoulin. 184 nos. March 6, 1792–May 7, 1793. BM, 1716–1717.

Journal républicain de Marseille et des départements méridionaux. By Alexandre Ricord, Sébastien Lacroix, and Pierre Mittié. 62 nos. October 1, 1793–February 8, 1794. BN, Lc[11] 635 (57); AD, B-du-Rh, L 1210 bis.

Manuel du laboureur et de l'artisan, et gazette sentinelle. By Jacques Monbrion. 12 nos. June 6, 1792–August, 1794. AM, Toulon, L 56.

L'Observateur marseillais. By Antoine Brémond-Jullien, Joseph-Alphonse Esménard, and Charles Barbaroux. 51 nos. May 17–August 18, 1790. BN, Lc[11] 635 (95).

Procès-verbaux de l'Assemblée nationale, 1792–1794.

Réimpression de l'ancien Moniteur. 31 vols. Paris: H. Plon, 1858–1863.

Tribune de la Société populaire de Marseille. Anonymous. Extracts in AD, L 2076; one issue in BN, Lc[11] 635 (72).

Secondary Sources

Agulhon, Maurice. *La Sociabilité méridionale, confréries et associations dans la vie collective en Provence orientale à la fin du 18eme siècle*. 2 vols. Aix-en-Provence: Faculté des lettres et sciences humaines, 1966.

Alfred-Chabaud. "Essai sur les classes bourgeoises dirigeants à Marseille en 1789," *Documents relatifs à la vie économique de la Révolution* (Besançon, 1942), 67–166.

Annales du Midi, Vols. 1–78, 1889–1966. This periodical provides a bibliography of books and articles published on Provence.

Aulard, Alphonse. *The French Revolution. A Political History, 1789–1804*. Trans. Bernard Miall. Vol. 1, New York: Scribner, 1910.

Barbaroux, Charles. *Correspondance et mémoires*. Critical edition with unedited letters. Ed. Cl. Perroud with the collaboration of Alfred-Chabaud. Paris: Société de l'histoire de la Révolution française, 1923.

——. *Mémoires de Barbaroux.* Ed. Alfred-Chabaud. Paris: Armand Colin, 1936.

Barras, Paul. *Memoirs of Barras: Member of the Directorate.* Trans. Charles E. Roche. Ed. Georges Duruy. 4 vols. London: Osgood, McIlvaine, 1895.

Barruol, Jean. "Quelques Épisodes de la contre-révolution à Sisteron en 1792," *Annales des Basses-Alpes,* XX (1925–1926), 227–233.

Bergasse, Louis. *Notice historique sur la Chambre de Commerce de Marseille, 1599–1912.* Marseille: Barlatier, 1913.

Bernard, J.-A. "Les Journaux de Marseille pendant la Révolution de 1790 à 1797," *La Révolution française,* XXXVIII (1900), 161–166.

Les Bouches-du-Rhône; Encyclopédie départementale. Vols. III, XI. Marseille: Archives départementales, 1921.

Bourdin, Isabelle. *Les Sociétés populaires à Paris pendant la Révolution.* Paris: Recueil Sirey, 1937.

Brégail, François. "La Société populaire d'Auch," *Bulletin du comité des travaux historiques,* XXX (1911) 143–220.

Brinton, Crane. "Comment on Gay," *American Historical Review,* LXVI (April, 1961), 677–681.

——. *The Jacobins: An Essay in the New History.* New York: Macmillan, 1930.

Busquet, Raoul. *Histoire de Marseille.* Paris: Laffont, 1945.

Cardenal, L. de. *La Province pendant la Révolution: Histoire des clubs jacobins, 1789–1795.* Paris: Payot, 1929.

Carrière, Charles, *et. al. Marseille: Ville morte.* Marseille: Ch. Garçon, 1968.

Cauvin, Charles. "La Formation de la société populaire de Sisteron," *Annales des Basses-Alpes,* Nos. 81–82 (1901), 71–79, 139–152.

——. "Une Incursion des Marseillais à Digne en 1793," Digne: Imprimerie Chaspoul, 1902.

Charpenne, Pierre. *Histoire de la Révolution dans Avignon et le Comtat et de leur réunion définitive de la France.* Paris: Lechevalier, 1892.

Chobaut, H. "Le Nombre des sociétés populaires du Sud-Est," *Annales historiques de la Révolution française*, III (1926), 450–455.

Cochin, Augustin. *Les Sociétés de pensée et la Révolution en Bretagne, 1788–1789*. Paris: Champion, 1925.

Crémieux, Adolphe. "Le Particularisme municipal à Marseille en 1789," *La Révolution française*, LII (1907), 193–215.

D'Arnaud, André Bouyala. *Evocation de vieux Marseille*. Paris: Editions de minuit, 1961.

Darnton, Robert. *Mesmerism and the End of the Enlightenment in France*. Cambridge, Mass.: Harvard University Press, 1968.

Deux Siècles d'histoire académique, 1726–1926: Notice publiée à l'occasion du bi-centenaire de l'Académie. Marseille: Imprimerie centrale, 1926.

Dufraisse, A.M. "La Première Mission de Fréron à Marseille." Unpublished thesis, University of Aix, 1968.

Durand de Maillane. *Histoire de la Convention nationale*. Paris: Baudouin, 1825.

Fabre, Augustin. *Anciennes Rues de Marseille*. Marseille: Barile, 1862.

——. *Histoire de Marseille*. 2 vols. Marseille: Olive, 1829.

——. *Les Rues de Marseille*. 5 vols. Marseille: Camoin, 1867–1869.

Feugère, Anatole. *Un Précurseur de la Révolution: L'abbé Raynal 1713–1796*. Angoulême: Imprimerie ouvrière, 1922.

Fochier, Louis. *Extraits pris sur les registres de la société populaire de Bourgoin*. Vienne: Savigné, 1880.

Fontanier, L. "Les Pénitents noirs de Marseille," *Annales de Provence*, XIX (1922), 34–41.

Fonvielle, Bernard F. *Mémoires historiques de M. le Chevalier de Fonvielle de Toulouse*. 4 vols. Paris: Ponthieu, 1824.

Fournier, J. *Cahiers de doléances de la sénéchaussée de Marseille pour les Etats-généraux de 1789*. Marseille: 1908.

Gaffarel, P. "Marseille sans nom," *La Révolution française*, LX (1911), 193–215.

——. "La Mission de Maignet dans les Bouches-du-Rhône et en Vaucluse," *Annales de la faculté des lettres d'Aix*, VI (1912), 1–100.

——. "La Prise des bastilles marseillaises," *La Révolution française*, LXXII (1919), 314–325.

——. "La Terreur à Marseille," *Annales de Provence*, X (1913), 158–188, 229–262.

Gaston-Martin. *La Franc-maçonnerie française et la préparation de la Révolution*. Paris: Presses Universitaires de France, 1926.

——. *Les Jacobins*. Paris: Presses Universitaires de France, 1945.

Genta, A. "La Vie des sections marseillaises de juin 1791 au 25 août 1793. Unpublished thesis, University of Aix, 1959.

Gérard, René. *Un Journal de province sous la Révolution: Le "Journal de Marseille" de Ferréol Beaugeard (1781–1797)*. Paris: Société des Etudes Robespierrists, 1964.

Guibal, Georges. *Mirabeau et la Provence*. 2 vols. Paris: Fontemoing, 1901.

——. *Le Mouvement fédéraliste en Provence en 1793*. Paris: Plon-Nourrit, 1908.

Ingold, A.M.P. *L'Oratoire et la Révolution*. Paris: Poussielgue, 1883.

Labroue, Henri. "Le Club Jacobin de Toulon, 1790–1796," *Annales de la Société d'études provençales*, IV (1907), 1–51.

——. *La Société populaire de Bergerac*. Paris: Société de l'histoire de la Révolution, 1915.

Lameth, Théodore de. *Mémoires*. Published with an introduction by Eugène Welvert. Paris: Fontemoing, 1913.

Lautard, J.-B. *Histoire de l'académie de Marseille: Depuis sa fondation en 1726, jusqu'en 1826*. Vol. I, Marseille: Achard, 1826.

Lautard, Laurent. *Esquisses historiques: Marseille depuis 1789 jusqu'en 1815*. 2 vols. Marseille: Achard, 1844.

Le Bihan, Alain. *Loges et chapitres de la grande loge et du grand orient de France (2e moitié du XVIIIe siècle)*. Paris: Bibliothèque nationale, 1967.

Lefebvre, Georges. *The French Revolution*. Trans. Elizabeth Moss Evanson. 2 vols. New York: Columbia University Press, 1962–1964.

Libois, H. *Délibérations de la société populaire de Lons-le-Saunier*. Lons-le-Saunier: Declume, 1897.

Louche, Jules. "Marseille et ses habitants à la veille de la Révolution," *Revue de Marseille*, XXXVIII (1891), 233–261, 324–334, XXXIX (1892), 94–114, 192–217, 221–238, 314–332.

Lourde, C. *Histoire de la Révolution à Marseille et en Provence depuis 1789 jusqu'au Consulat*. 3 vols. Marseille: Senès 1838–1839.

Martinet, Guy. "Les Débuts de la réaction thermidorienne à Marseille: L'Emeute du 5 vendémiaire an III (26 septembre 1794)," *Actes XC^e Congrès national des sociétés savantes*, II (Nice, 1965), 149–166.

Masson, Paul. *Marseille depuis 1789: Etudes historiques*. 2 vols. Vol. I: *Le Commerce de Marseille de 1789 à 1814*. Paris: Hachette, 1919.

——. *La Provence au XVIII siècle*. 3 vols. Aix: Annales de la faculté des lettres, 1936.

Mathieu, Joseph. *Célébration du 21 janvier depuis 1793 jusqu'à nos jours*. Marseille: Lebon, 1865.

Mathiez, Albert. *After Robespierre*. Trans. Catherine Alison Phillips. New York: Knopf, 1931.

Pollio, Joseph and Adrien Marcel. *Le Bataillon du 10 août. Recherches pour servir à l'histoire de la Révolution française*. Paris: Charpentier, 1881.

Ponteil, Félix. "La Société populaire des antipolitiques et le sentiment patriotique à Aix-en-Provence en 1792–1795," *Revue historique de la Révolution française*, X (1916), 202–218, XIII (1918), 30–47, 266–290, 454–474, 577–589, XIV (1919), 40–55.

Portal, Félix. *Le Bataillon marseillais du 21 janvier*. Marseille: Ruat, 1900.

Poupé, E. "Une Brochure de propagande révolutionnaire en 1792," *La Révolution française*, VIIIL (1905), 328–332.

——. *Lettres de Barras et de Fréron*. Draguignan: Latil, 1910.

——. "Les Papiers de la société populaire de St.-Zacharie," *Bulletin de la Société d'études scientifiques et archaéologiques de Draguignan*, XXV (1905), 59–74.

——. "La Société populaire de Villecroze, 1792-an III," *La Révolution française*, XL (1901), 132–152.

Radiquet, Dominique. "Foules et journées révolutionnaires à

Marseille: Août 1789–25 août, 1793." 2 vols. Unpublished thesis, University of Aix, 1968.

Robert, P.-Albert. *La Justice des sections marseillaises: Le Tribunal populaire, 1792–1793.* Paris: Rousseau, 1913.

Rouvière, François. *Histoire de la Révolution française dans le département du Gard: La Constituante, 1788–1791.* Vol. I. Nîmes: Catélan, 1887.

Segond-Cresp. "Le Temple de la vénérable mère-loge écossaise de France à l'orient de Marseille," *Répertoire des travaux de la Société de statistique de Marseille.* Marseille: Cayer, 1871.

Sergent, L.-G. *Les Tribunaux révolutionnaires dans les Bouches-du Rhône.* Aix: Faculté des lettres, 1874.

Soboul, Albert. *Les Sans-culottes parisiens en l'an II.* Paris: Librairie Clavreuil, 1958.

Sydenham, M. J. *The Girondins.* London: Athlone Press, 1961.

Taine, Hippolyte. *The Origins of Contemporary France.* Vols. II and III. Trans. John Durand. New York: Henry Holt, 1876–1894.

Tavernier, Félix-L. "Marseille sous la Convention," *Marseille,* No. 51 (1963), 37–46.

Thompson, J. M. *Robespierre.* Vol. 1. New York: Appleton-Century, 1936.

Vaillandet, Pierre. "Les Massacres de la Glacière et l'opinion publique," *Mémoires de l'Académie de Vaucluse,* XXXII (1932), 27–47.

Verrier, René. *Le Mère Loge écossaise de France à l'orient de Marseille, 1751–1814.* Paris: Editions de centenaire, 1950.

Vialla, S. *Marseille révolutionnaire, l'armée nation (1789–1793).* Paris: Chapelot, 1910.

Viguier, Jules. *Les Débuts de la Révolution en Provence.* Paris: Lenoir, 1895.

——. "Episodes inédits de l'histoire de la Terreur à Marseille," *La Révolution française,* XXVIII (1895), 40–65.

——. "Marseille et ses représentants à la Constituante," *La Révolution française,* XL (1901), 193–201.

Vovelle, M. "Essai d'analyse idéologique des sections marseillaises," *Bulletin. Institut historique de Provence*, No. 2 (1963), 138–140.

——. "Prêtres abdicataires et déchristanization en Provence," *Actes du quatre-vingt-neuvième congrès national des sociétés savantes*, I (Lyons, 1964), 63–95.

Young, Arthur. *Travels in France during the Years 1787, 1788, and 1789*. Ed. Constantia Maxwell. Cambridge: The University Press, 1929.

Index

The Jacobin Club
of Marseilles, 1790–1794

Designed by R. E. Rosenbaum.
Composed by Vail-Ballou Press, Inc.,
in 11 point linotype Janson, 3 points leaded,
with display lines in monotype Janson.
Printed letterpress from type by Vail-Ballou Press
on Warren's 1854 text, 60 pound basis,
with the Cornell University Press watermark.
Bound by Vail-Ballou Press
in Columbia book cloth
and stamped in All Purpose foil.

Library of Congress Cataloging in Publication Data (prepared by the CIP
Project for library cataloging purposes only)

Kennedy, Michael L.
 The Jacobin Club of Marseilles, 1790–1794.

 Bibliography: p.
 1. Société des amis de la constitution de Marseille. 2. Marseille—History.
3. France—History—Revolutions, 1790–1794. I. Title.
DC178.K46 1973   944.04   73-8410
ISBN 0-8014-0794-X